D1154422

DEAD LAST

PHILLIP G. PAYNE

DEAD

LAST

The Public Memory of Warren G. Harding's Scandalous Legacy

Ohio University Press

Athens

Ohio University Press, Athens, Ohio 45701
www.ohioswallow.com
© 2009 by Ohio University Press
All rights reserved

To obtain permission to quote, reprint, or otherwise reproduce or distribute material from
Ohio University Press publications, please contact our rights and permissions department at
(740) 593-1154 or (740) 593-4536 (fax).

Printed in the United States of America
Ohio University Press books are printed on acid-free paper ⊗ ™

16 15 14 13 12 11 10 09   5 4 3 2 1

Library of Congress Cataloging-in-Publication Data

Payne, Phillip G.
  Dead last : the public memory of Warren G. Harding's scandalous legacy / Phillip G.
Payne.—1st ed.
       p. cm.
  Includes bibliographical references and index.
  ISBN 978-0-8214-1818-5 (cloth : alk. paper)—ISBN 978-0-8214-1819-2 (pbk. : alk.
paper)
  1. Harding, Warren G. (Warren Gamaliel), 1865–1923. 2. Harding, Warren G. (Warren
Gamaliel), 1865–1923—Ethics. 3. Harding, Warren G. (Warren Gamaliel), 1865–1923—
Historiography. 4. United States—Politics and government—1921–1923. 5. Presidents—
United States—Biography. 6. Political corruption—United States—History—20th century.
I. Title.
  E786.P39 2008
  973.91'4092—dc22
     [B]

                                                                        2008043916

CONTENTS

ACKNOWLEDGMENTS

Two themes often emerge when authors discuss writing a book. The first is the image of the lonely historian researching and writing. The second theme is that of community, where the author thanks those folks who helped influence the thinking and research and thus made the book possible. In my experience, both themes ring true. I spent a lot of hours sitting in front of computers and microfilm readers and working with piles of documents. Of course, other people also helped make it possible for me to do all this sitting around researching and writing by offering support and help while I was writing this book.

Several people read and commented on all or portions of the draft. My wife, Penny Messinger, read several versions of the manuscript and offered by far the most substantial comments. Others who helped shape my thinking about Warren Harding and his legacy and who commented on drafts include Robert Ferrell, Richard Frederick, Mark Huddle, John A. Morello, A. S. Sibley, and Victoria Wolcott. Even though this is not the book he envisioned years ago, I want to thank my graduate advisor, Warren Van Tine, for training me to be a historian.

I thank the librarians, archivists, and others who helped my research along the way. I was assisted by archivists at the University of California at Los Angeles, the University of Massachusetts at Amherst, and the College of Wooster. I am particularly thankful for the help from professionals at the Ohio Historical Society, where most of my materials came from. More fundamentally, it was at the society that I first discovered Harding at an early point in my career. Melinda Gilpin, the current manager of the Harding Home, has been very helpful. Shannon Morris, who proved an excellent amateur historian and top-notch summer tour guide, really helped me understand Harding and his relationship to the town of Marion. Joan Milner's enthusiasm for the Harding Home and Marion was always welcome.

Charlie Evers had a contagious enthusiasm for Marion. As can sometimes be the case with intellectuals and academics (especially since I am not from Marion), I sometimes did not fully appreciate the value that can come with boosting, but Shannon, Charlie, and others in Marion showed me that a love of town did not have to mean avoiding historical inquiry or facts.

At St. Bonaventure University, faculty research grants funded research trips. A sabbatical allowed me time to revise this manuscript. Deans Jim White and Steve Stahl provided funding for me to present papers on Harding while this project was in development. Likewise, Dave DiMatio, dean of Clare College, proved helpful in overseeing the research grants. St. Bonaventure is a small teaching school where we are fortunate in having a first-rate library. Its director, Paul Spaeth, is always ready to help with projects. Theresa Shaffer works miracles with interlibrary loans. I have also been fortunate in working with colleagues who value scholarship and publish. I am lucky to be in such a department. My patient students, who had no idea that Warren G. Harding played such a large role in American history, deserve recognition.

I also thank the editors and reviewers who commented on my articles at *Timeline, Prospects: An Annual of American Cultural Studies, Mid-America: An Historical Review,* and *The Historian.* I wrote these articles while I was working on this book, and the book is much better because of their insights; I also appreciate their willingness to allow me to use that material in this book. Likewise, I am thankful for those who commented on my papers at various conferences over the years. While they didn't always agree with me, the discussion at these conferences confirmed for me that this is a good profession.

Rick Huard and the people from Ohio University Press greatly improved this book. They did an excellent job in shepherding my manuscript into a book, helping me avoid embarrassing mistakes along the way. Any remaining mistakes are mine.

I am sure I have forgotten some individuals. Hopefully they will forgive me and know that I appreciated their help.

Finally, I thank my family. My children, Laurel and Russell, put up with my working a lot at home and being gone to do research. I know it was not always clear why I got up so early and drank so much coffee. Hopefully, when they hold a copy of this book it will become clearer. I hope we didn't miss too many soccer games. My wife, Penny, not only put up with my years of Harding obsession but also read drafts, making suggestions that helped immeasurably. I want my family to know that despite the time I spent on the book, it was never the most important thing in my life.

Questions Asked

Democracy has no monuments. It strikes no
medals. It bears the head of no man on a coin.

—John Quincy Adams

To enter into any serious historical criticism of
these stories [regarding George Washington's
childhood] would be to break a butterfly.

—Henry Cabot Lodge

Harding and the Log Cabin Myth

Warren G. Harding's story is an American myth gone wrong.
As our twenty-ninth president, Harding occupied the office that
stands at the symbolic center of American national identity.[1]
Harding's biography should have easily slipped into American
history and mythology when he died in office, on August 2,
1923. Having been born to a humble midwestern farm family,
what better ending could there be to his story than death in
the service of his nation? What stronger image could stand as a
lasting tribute than grieving citizens lining the railroad tracks,
as they had for Lincoln, Garfield, and McKinley, to view Harding's body? The public grief that accompanied the passing of
Harding's burial train would seem to have foreshadowed a
positive place in the national memory. Warren and Florence
Harding were laid to rest in a classically designed marble mausoleum in their hometown of Marion, Ohio, a mausoleum that
was the last great memorial in the older style popular before
the rise of presidential libraries. However, the near perfection

of his political biography and his contemporary popularity did not follow him into history. Today Harding is one of our least respected historical figures and is considered the worst president in American history.

Harding's legacy derives from the contradiction between the symbolic role of the presidency and the scandals that define his life and presidency. The core of the role of the presidency in America's national civic religion is the character of the individuals who occupy the office. Further complicating any discussion of presidential legacy is that the office is both lofty and of the common people. Long before Americans had rags-to-riches Horatio Alger stories, they embraced the idea that boys born of humble origins could grow up to become presidents. So powerful was this belief that influential men living in plantations and mansions fabricated humble origins and fictive log cabins to further their political ambitions. Evan Cornog has written that "humble origins proved a valuable resource even to politicians without them."[2]

Warren G. Harding did not have to make up his humble origins. Harding was a midwestern farm boy who became president; he was living proof of this potent American myth of democracy and opportunity. So well does his life fit the expectations of the presidency that historian Edward Pessen uses Harding to begin his study of the log cabin myth and the social origins of the presidents: "In one respect, certainly, Phoebe Elizabeth Dickerson Harding of Blooming Grove, Ohio, seemed like mothers everywhere in the United States. Her great dream was that one day her son would grow up to become the president of the United States. In this enduring American legend, the rise to the presidency of so ordinary a boy as Warren Gamaliel Harding is yet one more proof that the greatest office in this nation is accessible to, and has in fact been occupied by, men born to modest circumstances."[3]

Scholars have long given Harding a poor rank among U.S. presidents, one that is matched by his poor reputation with the public. This provides us with an opportunity to study the role of myth and scandal in the making of memory and history. What does Warren Harding's reputation mean for the American civic religion and our understanding of the role of the presidency in it? This question has been asked of presidents we consider great, but what of a president considered a failure? Harding's image, and his later legacy, spanned the full range of patriotic iconography, from his electoral triumph in 1920 to his death, his disgrace, and his role as an icon of presidential failure. Harding was not considered a failure, or a poor president, until after his death. Given his poor reputation, it is ironic that Harding's contemporary supporters and partisans were pioneers in the art of crafting political images.[4] Beginning with the 1920 election and continuing after his death, those associated with Harding and the Republican Party paid careful attention to how the public perceived Harding. The story of the creation and use of Harding's image illustrates the role of reputational entrepreneurs in shaping the national civic religion.

Harding did not enter the national consciousness until he became a presidential candidate in 1920. In death his reputation underwent such an enormous and rapid degradation that much of the complexity and nuance of Harding's life evaporated. This simplifying of his story—first to fit the log cabin myth that permeated the 1920 campaign and then to condemn—is one of the components separating public memory from history. While academic history tends to offer complex, multicausal explanations, public memory is often a narrative that teaches a lesson while flattening out the complexities of the past. In contrast to his earlier image, Harding's legacy, by virtue of the scandals associated with him, became that of empty Babbittry or personal tragedy.

Despite the popular tendency to discuss history as a force of nature or to personify it (as in *history's judgment*), various individuals and constituencies have constructed Harding's image and reputation. Harding himself started this process by consciously cultivating an image of a newspaper publisher and booster. Harding's early success came from his ability to promote his town. On the national stage, the Republican Party carefully crafted Harding's image during the election of 1920. Because of the use of the log cabin myth during his front porch campaign for the presidency, Harding's hometown of Marion, Ohio, plays a prominent role in the story of Harding's rise and the subsequent fall of his reputation. In 1920, Marion looked like an all-American town, characterized by nice homes, pleasant streets, and tidy schools. Today, as with many towns, Marion has tourist attractions and a place in history that helps define its identity. As a presidential hometown, Marion's stake in our national history is more substantial than that of most other small towns. The Harding name and image are common throughout the town. Each year thousands of people visit the Harding Home and the Harding Memorial. However, the Harding Memorial commemorates a man many Americans consider unworthy of commemoration or celebration. Those visiting Marion's most famous memorial might find irony in Alexander Hamilton's words that the American people "build lasting monuments of their gratitude." They might well ask, if Harding was so bad, how did he end up with such a grand monument?

Judging Failure

The ranking of presidents and their legacies can be reduced to a parlor game that has little bearing on either politics or scholarship.[5] However, at its best it can be an important exercise in evaluating policies and politics. Legacy debates are not only about the past but also about the present and the future, as well.[6] The process of ranking presidents is a subjective one, and while scholars debate the qualities necessary for greatness there is no similar set of criteria for failure. Part of the process of defining failure and success is the selective use of public memory and the success of commemoration. Presidents who followed Harding would not be held to the standard of his successes but rather measured against the excesses of his scandals.

The story of Harding's image demonstrates that the strands of history and memory intertwine. To understand public memory, we also need to understand how academic historians rank presidents. Arthur M. Schlesinger Sr. conducted the first poll of experts, mostly historians, in 1948 and presented the findings in *Life* magazine. He repeated this poll in 1962, and the results appeared in the *New York Times Magazine*. In both polls, the top-rated presidents were Abraham Lincoln, George Washington, Franklin Roosevelt, Woodrow Wilson, and Thomas Jefferson. Ulysses S. Grant and Warren G. Harding vied for worst president. Critics charged that the rankings were elitist, relying heavily on professors with ties to research and to Ivy League universities. Similarly, critics pointed out that a preponderance of the experts had ties to the Northeast and did not represent the nation as a whole. Given that the topic was the presidency, partisanship entered into the debate, and critics noted that the experts were overwhelmingly liberal Democrats. Despite these charges, the ranking of presidents was popular and was repeated periodically. Although the polls varied somewhat in the categories, questions, and experts consulted, later polls showed little variation from Schlesinger's initial findings.[7] Harding is in a special category in these polls; as Tim Blessing writes, "The Republican Dynasty of the 1920's has its own dynamic." He continues, "Harding's ranking is at the very bottom of all presidential rankings (37), Coolidge's is only marginally improved (31) and Hoover's (21), through quite a bit better than Coolidge's, still mires the entire Republican Dynasty among the bottom half of the presidents."[8]

Throughout this book you will find references to these polls and to the historical debate among academics regarding Harding and the presidency, especially as that debate bleeds into the public image and political uses of Harding's memory and image. These rankings appeared in popular news magazines and as such could be considered a form of popular history. However, my primary focus is on the public memory of Harding and so encompasses much more than a handful of academic rankings. The totality of Harding's image comes through the use of his legacy in partisan debate, popular culture, literature (both good and bad), and, of course, acts of commemoration.

Another place where we find academic judgments regarding Harding as part of a public discourse is in textbooks. In a typical treatment, historian Alan Brinkley describes Harding as an "undistinguished senator from Ohio" who as president "recognized his own unfitness."[9] The distinguished historian Eric Foner summarizes the Harding administration:

> Warren G. Harding took office as president in 1921 promising a return to "normalcy" after an era of Progressive reform and world war. Reflecting the prevailing get-rich-quick ethos, his administration quickly became one of the most corrupt in American history. A likeable, somewhat ineffectual individual— he called himself "a man of limited talents from a small town"— Harding seemed to have little regard for either governmental issues or the dignity of the presidency. Prohibition did not cause him to curb his appetite for liquor. He continued a previous illicit affair with a young Ohio woman, Nan Britton. The relationship did not become known until 1927, when Britton published *The President's Daughter*, about her child to whom Harding had left nothing in his will.
>
> Although his cabinet included men of integrity and talent, like Secretary of State Charles Evans Hughes and Secretary of Commerce Herbert Hoover, Harding also surrounded himself with cronies who used their offices for private gain. Attorney General Harry Daugherty accepted payments not to prosecute accused criminals. The head of the Veterans' Bureau, Charles Forbes, received kickbacks from the sale of government supplies. The most notorious scandal involved Secretary of the Interior Albert Fall, who accepted nearly $500,000 from private businessmen to whom he leased government oil reserves at Teapot Dome, Wyoming. Fall became the first cabinet member in history to be convicted of a felony.[10]

Foner emphasizes the corruption within the Harding administration, shows Harding's small-town background to be a liability, and catalogues the failures of Harding's weak but likeable character. Foner's characterization of Harding is well within the mainstream of both academic and popular history. Rather than becoming the subject of an inspirational story told on President's Day, Harding is best known for both a scandalous life and a failed administration.

In testimony to Harding's poor reputation, John Dean's popular biography of Harding begins, "Warren G. Harding is best known as America's worst president." Dean is not the first biographer, nor will he be the last, to write such a statement about Harding. Although Dean argues later in his book that Harding's poor reputation might not be justified, nevertheless this is the first thing he writes about our twenty-ninth president.[11] On the surface it might seem appropriate for a man famous for his involvement in the Watergate scandal to write about Harding. However, Dean claims that it was not a shared experience in scandal that inspired his curiosity but rather it was "while living in Harding's hometown of Marion, Ohio, that Harding first came to my attention." In Marion the young Dean was fascinated by the "old gossip that was still being whispered decades after the fact, picked up by young ears from adults and passed from generation to generation" (1–2). Dean went on to write a traditional biography, albeit a more positive one than is generally the case with Harding.

In September 1999, C-Span visited Marion as part of its series *American Presidents: Life Portraits,* which included visits to presidential sites throughout the country.[12] The programs featured tours of homes, gravesites, and memorials. In doing so, C-Span offered viewers public history that combined public reputations, academic analysis, and commemoration. In addition, curators and historians answered questions from both the host and the viewers. The C-Span visit to Marion points to the difficulties of commemorating Harding and to the role that his legacy plays in the national memory.

As the program begins, viewers see black-and-white silent-film footage of Harding with a narrator explaining that Harding was "Mr. Nice Guy," a man fond of people and dogs. However, the narrator continues, "some might say he liked people too much" because his "good-natured trust" was exploited by friends to scandalous ends. Next, viewers learn that Harding was a "reputed womanizer" who had at least two extramarital affairs, "one of which may have resulted in the birth of a daughter." Harding "poked fun" at his own image, once publicly repeating the words of his father: "Warren, it's a good thing you wasn't born a gal, because you would be in the family way all the time. You can't say no." As a first impression, the program's opening minute conveys a definitive, but negative, image of Harding.

The harsh indictment of Harding's character is followed by a description of Harding's life in Ohio, complete with a picture of his modest childhood home, his early career as a newspaper publisher, and his marriage to divorcée Florence Kling. Harding entered politics when "his good looks and easy manner captured the attention" of Harry M. Daugherty, a well-connected political operative. Daugherty would oversee Harding's election to the U.S. Senate and the presidency. Once in the presidency, Harding admitted his limitations: "I don't know what to do or where to turn. Somewhere there must be a book that tells all about it. My God! But this is a hell of a place for a man like me to be in."

However, the narration goes on to explain that the public loved Harding and forgave his shortcomings. Florence and Warren Harding enjoyed greeting the public. Harding played golf and hosted twice-weekly poker games with a group dubbed the poker cabinet. The narration does not dwell on the love of the people but transitions to a different type of love. Harding liked stepping out with other women. Nan Britton "scandalized the nation" with her tell-all book in which she said Harding had fathered her child (notice that this is the second mention of the child). Awkwardly, the narration transitions to explain that Harding was not all bad, as we learn that he brought "a measure of honor" to the office, speaking on civil rights in Alabama, creating the Bureau of the Budget, and hosting an international arms talk. However, these accomplishments were "overshadowed by graft and fraud" as scandals emerged after his death at age fifty-seven, the most famous being Teapot Dome.

Following this less-than-flattering prologue the host introduces guests Robert Ferrell and Eugene Trani, both respected historians who have published books about Harding.[13] Their job this day would be to answer questions about the life and times of the twenty-ninth president, providing an intersection between Harding's academic and public reputations. Theirs was not an easy job. Many of the questions demonstrate that Harding's reputation involves both innuendo and fact. The first caller, from Pensacola, Florida, asks if Harding was murdered because of his philandering. The second caller asks the historians about the mysteries of Harding's death. The host then enters with questions about the Harding Home and the election of 1920. Later callers mention a manuscript by Gaston Means (who alleged that Florence murdered Warren Harding) and ask about Harding being a Negro. Another asks if Harding could be compared to President Bill Clinton (this in the wake of the Monica Lewinsky scandal) and if it is possible that Clinton will replace Harding as the worst president in the ranking polls. Another viewer asks about Harding's African American ancestry. As Ferrell and Trani debate the validity of the presidential polls and Harding's poor ranking and the callers ask questions ranging from the substantial to the trivial, the substance of Harding's place in our national memory emerges.

There is no significant difference between Harding's popular reputation and his reputation in academia. Warren G. Harding's legacy has been dominated by scandals but there has been little explanation as to why Harding is regularly considered the worst president, other than an assumption that the scandals alone are proof enough. Francis Russell's *Shadow of Blooming Grove* (1968) is the reigning interpretation of Harding. Russell points out that the subject of his major biography was "neither a fool nor a tool, but an astute and able Ohio politician (not the highest breed of that animal) who knew how to get what he wanted." Even so, Russell explains, by "a twist or two of fate Harding has come to be regarded right, left, and center as the worst President this country has ever had." Russell proceeds with some familiar questions regarding Harding's private life, questions that drive his biography: "Was Harding a mulatto? Did he have a child by his mistress? Was he murdered? What were the papers his wife so hastily burned after his death?" Significantly, Russell does not ask about Teapot Dome, the Veterans' Bureau, or the Justice Department. Russell is defensive about having written a biography of Harding, arguing that he was the "most neglected" of presidents, but that even so he "deserves a biography, not so much for himself—though in many ways his life was more interesting than those of more notable Presidents—but because he came at a dividing point in history."[14]

Like so many students of Harding, Russell leaves it to the reader to implicitly understand what he will not explicitly write. Russell, like others, emphasizes the parochial nature of Harding's small-town background. Note, for instance, Russell's disputing of Harding as a fool and a tool. Rather than saying Harding was his own man, he delivers the backhanded compliment that Harding was an Ohio politician. Harding was not an incompetent, but he was an Ohio politician. This is a common theme in the various pronouncements on Harding and reflects the declining respect held for civic boosters and midwestern small towns. Historians of the Midwest point to the Progressive Era as the height of national respect for midwestern culture. After World War I, however, the Midwest's reputation began to decline.[15] Harding was a spokesperson for the small-town heartland. To understand Harding's politics, we need to return to Marion. His was the ideology of a civic booster. The economic philosophy of civic boosters such as Harding tended to be more Hamiltonian than Jeffersonian. Although conservative, Harding was not a laissez-faire conservative. Harding's ideology has often been dismissed as inconsistent or incomprehensible, but his was the booster's impulse to foster cooperation between businesses and government for the greater good. Harding the booster saw a role for government in supporting business and promoting cooperation between factions, even as he praised the virtues of limited government.

One of the few academic defenses of Harding is Robert Ferrell's *Strange Deaths of President Harding*. Ferrell writes that Harding's "fate does not seem fair," noting that in every presidential ranking "Harding has been in the failure category, and not only there but at the bottom." To Ferrell, such a judgment is wrong: "Should he not stand at least above the three or four other holders of the presidency whom even the slightest student of the presidents can name as failures?"[16] Ferrell argues that Harding's poor reputation is undeserved because most of the Harding scandals do not stand up to close scrutiny. Ferrell claims that Harding's reputation was destroyed by attacks from people more interested in cash than in accuracy. Yet Ferrell's question is pertinent to this study. How did Harding beat out Franklin Pierce, James Buchanan, or U. S. Grant for the dubious honor of worst president? The answer is, generally speaking, the combination of the political scandals, such as Teapot Dome, that damaged the reputation of the administration and the personal scandals that damaged the reputation of Harding's character. As many have noted, Harding was hardly alone as a president who sinned or had political scandals. Russell notes in his introduction that Franklin Roosevelt died with his mistress and Harry Truman also had his scandals.[17]

While Ferrell works to debunk many of the falsehoods that permeate Harding's biography, sociologist Gary Alan Fine, in *Difficult Reputations*, examines Harding's place in our collective memory. Although starting from a different place, Fine also points to the work of "reputational entrepreneurs" who destroyed Harding's reputation because they disagreed with his politics or because they were interested in turning a profit. Their work was made easier because it coincided with the decision of the Republican Party to abandon Harding. Furthermore, Fine offers alternative, positive, interpretations of Harding's presidency, including Harding as the first black president and Harding as a politician who ushered in an age of conservative rule. Still, his treatment is brief: one chapter on Harding in a broader treatment of individuals with bad reputations. Overall, Fine's analysis suffers from the same lack of research in primary documents that has plagued so much of the scholarship on Harding.[18]

President Warren G. Harding, with all the discussion of his failures and his horrible reputation, resonates with those who wish to understand the American experience. As we have seen, Harding tops the list of those presidents considered failures. Harding's reputation rests not only on the troubles in his administration and his life but also on the work of those who have used or attacked Harding's reputation. What is the significance of Harding's reputation? First, we must realize that Harding's legacy is directly related to his image and reputation during the presidential election of 1920. Second, Harding's legacy and reputation are linked to his hometown. Third, Harding has a continued significance in our national public memory as an icon of failure.

Civic Religion

The questions that help form Warren Harding's legacy come back to a central issue. Harding lived the log cabin myth, so his life should have neatly fit into our national narrative of progress, democracy, and opportunity. Contradictorily, Harding is significant not only because he lived the American dream but also because he failed to achieve the amorphous goal of presidential greatness.[19] The examination of this tension is central to this study.

Harding's reputation as our worst president makes him an ideal candidate to study public memory as it relates to community and to national identity. What has Harding's legacy meant in our national memory? The commemoration of Harding speaks to the American civil religion. As David Blight defines it, public memory consists of the "ways in which groups, peoples, or nations remember, how they construct versions of the past and employ them for self-understanding and to win power and place in an ever-changing present."[20] Blight's observation that memory "is often treated as a sacred set of potentially absolute meanings and stories, possessed as the heritage or identity of a community" is applicable to the commemoration of the presidency and Harding. Memory, he continues, "often coalesces in objects, sacred sites, and monuments; history seeks to understand contexts and the complexity of cause and effect" (2). Building on the work of sociologists, Benjamin Hufbauer identifies four elements to the American civil religion, elements similar to Blight's definition of public memory: saints, sacred places, sacred objects, and ritual practices. The present study examines the efforts to turn the relics and places important to Harding into something sacred to our national civic religion.

Harding's initial commemoration, following his death in 1923, came at a time of transformation in the way in which presidents were remembered. The dedication of the Lincoln Memorial in 1922 by President Harding marks the beginnings of that transition: the "presidential monuments of the past—the obelisks and classical temples built by and for posterity—have largely been replaced by presidential libraries built outside Washington, D.C."[21] Harding was the last president for whom a classical temple was built in his hometown. Memory and myth are not just about the dead. The nature of politics and usefulness of the civic religion to politicians gives it vibrancy for the living.

The Vernacular Presidency

The log cabin myth, by its very nature, emphasizes place. The log cabin, of course, denotes a humble birth, but it also symbolizes social origins, being from a place that is more fundamentally American because it is neither urban, sophisticated, nor a seat of power. With its origins in the nineteenth century, the log cabin myth is decidedly Jacksonian in its emphasis on the common and humble. People built log cabins on frontiers and farms. As we saw with Eric Foner and C-Span, most commentators disparage Harding's small-town background; they certainly do not grant Marion, Ohio, the status of a sacred place or repository of relics important to our nation.[22] This was not always the case. In his 1923 hagiography of Harding, Willis Fletcher Johnson, a professor at New York University, emphasizes community and the log cabin myth: "Neighbor, I want to be helpful [was the] keynote of President Harding's life, and when the news of his sudden death in San Francisco was flashed across the country on the night of August 2, 1923, the people felt that they had not only lost a President but a great-hearted neighbor." All Americans, he writes, paid tribute to "one of the most loveable figures in American history."[23] Johnson's account of this man born on a "typical farm homestead" invokes the log cabin myth. "Deep rooted in American soil and fast fixed in the pioneer traditions of the new world was the family whose name Warren G. Harding brought to the highest eminence when it came to adorn the door-plate of the White House" (15–17). As a boy and a young man, Warren Harding worked in the fields and on the railroads. As is typical of presidential biographers, Johnson sees in Harding's labors both a common experience and a potential for greatness: Harding "learned to fell trees and to split rails, even as Abraham Lincoln had learned before him and thousands of other American lads" (22).[24] In 1923, before the scandalous headlines Johnson's commemorative account struck familiar, even clichéd, notes.

Harding's reputation as a national figure always connected him to Marion. This is common enough, as birthplaces and homes of presidents are routinely celebrated for their historic significance. However, we rarely speak of the inverse, where they are not celebrated but denigrated. Marion's reputation rose and fell with Harding's reputation, especially because he was viewed as a representative of small-town America. Because public memory lacks chronological context but is often rich in local and regional context, place became increasingly important as Harding's legacy developed. Although Harding and those who shaped his memory could not have been clearer or more explicit in connecting Harding to his hometown, scholars have tended to dismiss Marion and Harding's identification with it without significant analysis. In doing so, scholars have missed the importance of the booster ideology in understanding Harding.

As a newspaper publisher, Harding was beyond all else a civic booster, a role that infused his political philosophy, and during the election of 1920, Harding ran as a civic booster. At the heart of the booster ethos was the belief in the virtue of a harmonious community, the importance of prosperity and progress, and the leadership of solid and moral businessmen. In 1920 Harding pointed to what was attractive, even romantic, about small towns as idealized villages; following his death the scandals confirmed the belief of those who thought of small towns as backward and parochial. In this sense Harding was a Babbitt. Intellectuals and journalists rejected Harding as being as empty as the Sinclair Lewis character. However, there is no reason to believe that the average American shared the intellectuals' contempt for the small-town booster. Similarly, Americans embraced Calvin Coolidge, the New England puritan complete with a farm, as their new icon of simplicity, one who offered a contrast to the moral ambiguity of modernity. Further, the negative attitude toward such boosters helps explain why Harding gets little credit for his political victory.

Harding's booster ethos stood in contrast to the sophisticated internationalism and intellectualism of Harding's predecessor, Woodrow Wilson. Progressive writers who favored the policies of Woodrow Wilson have had a great influence on the way we remember Harding. Given Harding's defeat of James Cox (who carried the banner of Wilson and the League of

Nations) in 1920 and his subsequent popularity, Wilson's supporters con-
soled themselves by attacking Harding. Those who attacked Harding also
had to attack the results of the election of 1920 and so their attacks assumed
an undemocratic flavor.[25] While this is significant, scholars have overempha-
sized the Progressive attack. We should ask how the partisan attack on Harding's legacy differed radically from any other president. Surely it is to be
expected that partisan opponents will attack the reputation of an opposition leader. To note that Wilsonian Progressives disliked Harding is not
particularly insightful. Like that of any other president, Harding's legacy
became a part of partisan politics. This is readily apparent in the role of intellectuals and politicians in shaping Harding's legacy. But that is not all
there is to the story. Memory is not shaped exclusively by intellectuals.

While many question the appropriateness of honoring Harding as
a president, Marion and the Harding Memorial are places where the local
speaks to the national historical narrative.[26] With Harding there was a
contest, rather lopsided, between the local and the national, between the
need to celebrate a fallen president and the need to condemn corruption.
The debate was, almost literally, over whether Marion should become sacred ground in our national secular civic religion, one of the mystic chords
of memory that bind us together, to paraphrase Lincoln. As the scandals
emerged, most prominent Republicans distanced themselves from Harding's reputation and the official memory became that of tragic failure. The
vernacular memory also shifted. At first, Harding's popularity helped push
the national leaders toward honoring Harding, but as Harding became an
embarrassment, it was in Marion that the vernacular asserted Harding's
greatness against the prevailing national memory. In the end, not only did
Marion contribute to the log cabin myth, but some of the most controversial and embarrassing aspects of Harding's reputation were linked to the
local memory.

Whispers

The whispers about Harding that John Dean described hearing as a young
man growing up in Marion can still be heard there. Most of these rumors
have made their way unquestioned into the national discourse. However,
Harding's reputation was contested within his hometown. At one point
during the C-Span visit, the host asks Melinda Gilpin, director and curator
of the Harding Home, how the people of Marion felt about Harding. Gilpin
says that Harding was a great civic leader and that the people of Marion

tried to strike a balance.[27] In Marion one might expect a certain amount of over-the-top boosteristic pride. However, Marion residents held a variety of opinions. One could envision a resident insisting, "Don't believe those stories, Harding was a great man!" Alternately, one could imagine tired, embarrassed Marionites pleading with journalists to just move on and forget about the scandal-plagued Harding and his mistresses and cronies. A third alternative (to put these into simple categories) would be the community leader interested in Harding as part of that holy grail of town revitalization, historic tourism. Finally, there would be those who just do not care. Variations of all these categories coexist in Marion. As we saw with the questions C-Span viewers asked, the questions the public asks about Harding reveal the ongoing fascination with his private life and the extent to which the Harding scandals were part fact and part myth. Harding might not have been a great president, but he was interesting.

Harding in Context

Given Harding's prominence and the firm judgment of history as to his failure, it is amazing how much ambiguity exists about his life. As can be seen on C-Span, it is hard to give definitive answers to many of the questions about Harding's life. This is because of a lack of historical documentation. Ironically, many of the extant documents that are easily available are of dubious value. Did Harding have an affair with Nan Britton? Maybe, but she left no direct proof. Did Harding have an affair with Carrie Phillips? Yes, but their letters are sealed. Why did First Lady Florence Harding destroy a large portion of the presidential papers? We are not certain, but she said it was to protect Warren's memory. Did Florence murder her husband? No, but this is widely believed, and Harding's death did leave some mysteries. Was Harding black? Probably not, but he would not deny it.

We are on firmer ground when it comes to the political scandals. There can be no doubt of the corruption in the Harding administration. Albert Fall and Charles Forbes did go to prison for their activities at the Department of the Interior and the Veterans' Bureau, respectively. Attorney General Harry Daugherty was indicted and stood trial for corruption. The Harding scandals set the benchmark for corruption until surpassed by Watergate a half century later.

What sets the Harding scandals apart from other scandals? Why is it, as Francis Russell asks in his influential account that the scandals of other administrations have faded into history while Harding's persist?[28] Russell is correct in his supposition that the Harding scandals have outlived other scandals, but he leaves his question unexplored except for emphasizing those personal scandals of character that now seem iconic and timeless. The Harding scandals have transcended academic debates to become part of our national memory. Indeed, context is one of the crucial differences between memory and history. Public memory loses context as it becomes commemoration and mythology, while history is all about context. Harding's scandals reflected the tensions and the contradictions of the 1920s, but in our public memory of Harding that context often remains incomplete. The personal scandals can live on as gossip and so Harding's reputation has been remarkably resistant to change. Indeed, Russell demonstrates a proclivity to speculate about Harding's private life, from the state of his marriage to his race.

I hope to restore a historical context to Harding and in so doing explore the meaning of the scandals. In writing about leaders, especially great men, historians are moving toward a more complete understanding of political ages and their leaders. No longer do historians see the relationship between leader and context as a one-way street, where a great man shaped an entire age; instead they see it as a two-way street where the age shaped the man and vice versa. There is emerging a blending of cultural, social, and political history through the study of image and public memory.[29] While Harding was the first Republican elected during the Republican Era, the 1920s were not the Age of Harding in the sense that he was not the dominating political figure. However, the decade was the Age of Harding in the sense that Americans saw in Harding something familiar and understood Harding's life as part and parcel of the times. Indeed, according to one scholar of the presidency, the "most significant variable that influences a president's ranking is date of service, in that the period in which a president serves is most likely to shape retrospective evaluations of the presidency."[30] Harding's failures are often used as examples of the perceived shortcomings of the period.

According to political scientist Stephen Skowronek, presidents such as John Adams, John Quincy Adams, Franklin Pierce, James Buchanan, Herbert Hoover, and Jimmy Carter have been "singled out as political incompetents" in part because they came to symbolize the nation's ailments and "systemic political failures." Yet despite Harding's consistently poor ratings, Skowronek does not mention Harding.[31] If the 1920s was the decade of paradox, then Harding was our president of paradox. Harding's private life presents a metaphor for the collapse of Victorian morality. Harding's political career was a celebration of small-town America even as small-town America was overshadowed by the growth and dominance of large cities. Harding won the presidency the same year that the census announced that the United States was an urban nation. As Americans moved past their longing for a mythical simplicity, Harding's midwestern small-town image became a liability to his legacy.

As president, Harding served alcohol in the White House while enforcing Prohibition, a near perfect reflection of America's ambivalence toward the Prohibition experiment. He split the difference in what would later be called the urban-rural conflict by proudly being a small-town booster. He was a writer who had a reputation for garbled grammar and unclear sentences, although he was a newspaperman and a publisher who became a celebrity politician in part because he got along so well with the press. His political career merged politics and show business and he helped blur the lines between news, politics, and entertainment. Warren G. Harding enjoyed the emerging sexual revolution of the 1920s but took no notice of its social and political ramifications. For him, the Victorian double standard evolved into the sexual revolution with little reflection. The two women rumored to be Harding's extramarital sexual partners were Carrie Phillips, a dissatisfied small-town wife who longed for a more sophisticated life, and Nan Britton, a flapper. Both were from Marion. Britton achieved celebrity status with her claim to have been the president's mistress despite her inability to produce tangible evidence; the revelations of Harding's affair with Carrie Phillips brought her belated fame during the sexual revolution of the 1960s.

Contrary to the public's general impression of his failure, Harding did accomplish some worthwhile goals. One of the difficulties with remembering them, however, is that they run counter to the narrative of Harding as a failure. Public memory often takes the form of stories lacking in complexity and context. Furthermore, Harding's accomplishments do not neatly fit into contemporary notions of what is liberal and what is conservative. Herbert Hoover wrote that Harding was a "kind of a dual personality"; he had a "real quality in geniality, in good will and in ability for pleasing address." Although Harding lacked the intellect or experience to be president, Hoover wrote, he "was neither a 'reactionary' nor a 'radical.'" Harding, according to Hoover, pursued solid policies for the good of the people.[32] Following Hoover's line of reasoning, Harding seems more progressive on women's issues than other presidents of the age with his refusal to fire women from government positions when they married and his signing of the Sheppard-Towner Maternity and Infancy Act, which provided funding to states to subsidize prenatal and child health clinics and medical care for pregnant women and new mothers. Again, such policies seem confusing from a president who is commonly depicted as a henpecked husband and womanizer. Harding also appointed prominent Progressive and internationalist Republicans to the cabinet, including Hoover and Charles Evans Hughes. More predictably, given his conservative reputation, Harding moved with the nativist climate of the times, signing the Emergency Quota Act of 1921 (restricting immigration for any nationality to 3 percent of its number living in the United States in 1910). He also supported the Budget and Accounting Act of 1921 (creating the Bureau of the Budget), which brought businesslike efficiency to the federal government. He satisfied conservatives by appointing William Howard Taft as chief justice of the Supreme Court.

Harding's private scandals have lived on in part because they are easier to understand than are the scandals of his administration. The private scandals exhibit no complexities of leases, contracts, and national security. We know that Harding liked to eat, drink, smoke, and indulge himself. While we may argue about the specifics, these broad parameters are hard to dispute and, in the arena of public memory, perception can be as important as reality.

Harding as Icon

Much of this book deals with these efforts to create, control, and use Harding's reputation and the scandals that define his place in our national memory. As an American icon, Harding stands for what it means to fail as a president. Is this a fair assessment of Harding? No, it is not. Harding was not a good president and this book does not attempt to revise his reputation so that his place in the presidential pecking order will rise to the top ranks. Neither is it an attempt to discount the importance of the scandals at the Interior Department, Justice Department, and Veterans' Bureau. These scandals, however, are not the dominant part of Harding's narrative as a failure. Harding was not the worst president to ever occupy the White House. His was a short administration with successes and failures. Harding is our worst president not because of Teapot Dome but because he was judged as an example of what happens when a man falls short of the American myth of governance by the virtuous common man. Harding is seen as a failure because he personified the worst aspects of a place and a time.[33]

As Blessing writes, presidential success as partisan leaders rarely figures into presidential rankings to the extent that it is an "important function of the presidency." He also argues that through "partisanship presidents create the paradigms—the myths—by which our political psychology is organized."[34]

The various aspects of the public's memory of Harding do not necessarily add up to a cohesive picture of the man. As with so many other presidential myths, from Washington's cherry tree chopping to Lincoln's rail splitting, the Harding scandals are grounded in reality but also should be taken with a grain of salt. A central point of my argument is that historical accuracy has not always been important to our assessment of Harding. As Cornog has written, in the "world of narrative, the boundaries of fact and fiction are permeable, and in politics the intermingling of fact and fiction is a common process."[35] The shaping of Harding's memory was often done out of political expediency, opportunism, or sloppiness. Ironically, Harding's friends often inflicted the most damage to his reputation. Harding's story also raises questions about sources and evidence, such as, how is history created in the absence of documentation? What if the remaining evidence has been heavily censored? The lack of information regarding Harding left room for the exploitation of the historical Harding. Depending on which source you consult, you could conclude either that Harding was our first black president or that he was the president who joined the Ku Klux Klan in a White House ceremony. To top things off, it was rumored that Florence was secretly Jewish. These are some of the Harding scandals that include a bizarre mixture of fact and fiction.

The literature on Harding is guided by the answers to unwritten questions. Much of the debate over Harding revolves around the issue of guilt. Was Harding an essentially naive and trusting man who was duped by his friends? Did Harding participate in the corruption of his political associates? These questions cannot be fully answered. Given the absence of evidence, most scholars and journalists have assumed that Harding played the patsy in a ring of corruption.

Most scholars and journalists have questioned Harding's intelligence and ability, maligning him as a commoner whose story provides proof that in America we should not let just anybody grow up to be president. Harding's commonness and popularity became proof of his lack of greatness. Rather than being a great man with a common touch, in death Harding has been condemned as a fluke of history, a man of the masses who was mistakenly elevated to prominence by the work of others. Every president seems to have at least one figure who is reputed to be a kingmaker. These are familiar presidential tropes. As we shall see in a later chapter, biographers, novelists, pundits, and scandalmongers have not hesitated to twist these tropes for self-interest or to make a point about the nature of America. Harry Daugherty, in his memoir, claimed the title of kingmaker. His story of having discovered Harding is often repeated as part of the inverted logic of the log cabin myth as it applies to Harding. Nan Britton's story is disputed among scholars but is an iconic scandal for the presidency, ranking with Marilyn Monroe's rendition of "Happy Birthday" to John Kennedy as an eyebrow-raising moment in American history.

As we begin the twenty-first century, Warren Harding continues to rank as our worst president. This is a subjective standard. When I tell people I am writing on Harding, I have to explain a little about him. Invariably, someone will say that Harding will not be considered the worst president after the current president leaves office (as we saw with the C-Span caller's question about Clinton).[36] This reflects the partisan inclination of the person and a fair amount of cynicism, but it is equally clear that this is not going to happen. Reactions to my work on Harding are similar to the reactions that Annette Gordon-Reed describes in response to her significant book on Thomas Jefferson and Sally Hemings: "Not one of them launched into a discussion of the Kentucky Resolutions or the Louisiana Purchase. Almost instantly each of my friends asked, 'What's the story with Sally Hemings?' or 'Wasn't there something about him and a slave woman?' or 'Didn't he have mistress named Sally Hemings?'" While Harding's stature is nowhere near that of Jefferson, there is the same danger that "the American obsession with the personal lives of great figures will exceed their awareness of the contributions of those figures."[37] People, scholars and nonscholars alike, obsess about Harding's private life and, unlike Thomas Jefferson, the questions about his private life have come to dominate his legacy. People do not launch into a discussion of the Washington conference on naval disarmament, Prohibition, the Bureau of the Budget, or taxes when the topic of Harding as president comes up. It is now a custom, part of our collective historical experience, that Warren Harding is our worst president.

The President's Hometown

This wonderful land of ours is but the aggregate of communities, the sum total of cities, villages and farms, and the mutual interest and the necessary harmony of purpose, if we are to go on, must lie in conference, in council, in the concords of many minds, in the vision of plural leadership, in the never-failing righteousness of intelligent public opinion, not in the glory of the super-human.

— *Warren G. Harding, accepting the Republican nomination*

This is America—a town of a few thousand, in a region of wheat and corn and dairies and little groves. . . . Main Street is the climax of civilization.

— *Sinclair Lewis, introduction to* Main Street, *1920*

On November 2, 1920, Warren Harding won the largest land-slide in American history to that point in time, garnering over 60 percent of the popular vote. Election day took place on Harding's fifty-fifth birthday, but more important, the election of 1920 was a watershed that marked the ascendancy of conservative Republicanism and the end of progressive reforms as a new decade dawned. In 1920 Democrats offered Americans membership in an international community of nations while Republicans emphasized the symbolic community of small-town America. On the national stage, Harding's small-town image stood in stark contrast to Wilson's internationalism and intellectualism. The real power of Harding's invocation of normalcy was that it promised much but left the details to the future at a moment when much of the political debate was focused on the recent past: the Great War, as well as Teddy Roosevelt and Woodrow Wilson, men who would never be president again. Harding and the Republicans won the debate over which American past to celebrate and so won the debate over what the future should be. Harding's front porch campaign used the ideology of civic boosterism to present an idealized past to in order to convince voters that this was the future they wanted.

Harding's close association with the small Ohio town of Marion only helped the Republican cause. Americans had long celebrated small towns as prototypically American and the Republicans continued that emphasis in 1920. During the election, Harding's slogan Return to Normalcy could be seen on the streets of Marion. As typically interpreted, normalcy was shorthand for a conservative rejection of the reforms of the Progressive Era.[1] However, normalcy also intertwined place and past in a way that provided Americans with a sense of belonging that was not necessarily a rejection of progress, especially when understood as an outgrowth of civic boosterism.[2] In his role as civic booster, Harding presented the nostalgic and comfortable image of a harmonious and prosperous community.

Although his life fit the log cabin myth and his election ushered in a political era featuring market-based conservatism, Harding was not a rugged individualist but rather a man who had found success through community and service. Harding's front porch campaign brought the well-worn slogans of boosterism to the Republican Party by offering a narrative of a glorious past (marked by the Founding Fathers, town founders, and the frontier) followed by a period of aberrant decline (during the Wilson years) with the promise of restoring progress through the return to traditional ideals and business leadership. This narrative would have been familiar to any American who had lived through booster campaigns for civic improvements. Boosterism, as championed by Harding and countless other local leaders, had at its heart two interrelated principles: the importance of community harmony and the importance of economic growth as a means to that harmony.[3] Under the booster ideal, harmony and growth were to be achieved through the leadership of local businesspeople who, rhetorically and ideally, engaged in business from motives of civic responsibility and leadership rather than purely for profit. Of course, it was not always possible to reconcile profit with community, and the booster ethos decidedly favored business.

Although many scholars have commented on Harding's small-town credentials, they have not recognized that Harding, as a spokesman for Main Street, did represent an ideology other than the conservative rejection of reform. Harding offered a classic booster worldview that encapsulated elements of boosterism that, as described by historian Sally Foreman Griffith, were "assembled from such disparate sources as Puritan theology, classical republican ideology, Hamiltonian political economy, and Emersonian idealism." "Boosters," she notes, "raised practicality to the level of an ideal."[4] Boosterism was driven by the practicalities of economic growth, but its emphasis on community and harmony represented a form of idealism. Historian Douglas Flamming points out that for boosters "this fusion of self-interest and social uplift was no mere rationalization." Boosters, he writes, "believed that manufacturing enterprises and the growth they create would mitigate the unrest associated with economic stagnation and unemployment."[5] In the aftermath of the First World War, voters were looking to end unrest and economic hard times.

As a form of boosterism, normalcy took on a different meaning in the context of postwar America. Harding promised Americans—in deeds and in appearance, if not in clear words—a "root paradigm," a "reference for interpreting the current situation." Normalcy promised Americans an end to reform and to war, with small-town simplicity as the alternative. The evocation of nostalgia and tradition served to create a welcome social cohesion.[6] Harding captured the national mood when he said what the nation needed was "not heroism but healing, not nostrums but normalcy, not revolution but restoration, not agitation but adjustment, not surgery but serenity, not the dramatic but the dispassionate, not experiment but equipoise, not submergence in internationality but sustainment in triumphant nationality."[7] The vagueness and vernacular nature of the promise were what made it so evocative in 1920. While normalcy has not stood the test of time, few bother to go beyond pointing out the grammatical awkwardness (or innovation) of Harding's language or interpreting the speech as a call for an end to progressive reform. While Harding's rhetoric rarely received intellectual approval, he did sound like a small-town newspaper publisher with his sweeping generalizations, alliteration, and purple prose. The term *normalcy* was Harding, the editor and booster, speaking for the people's desire for harmony and prosperity.

For Americans of the late nineteenth and early twentieth centuries the civic booster was a familiar sight. Every town, every city had its boosters and they tended to sound remarkably the same. Main Street, or perhaps more accurately, Mount Vernon Avenue, on which Harding lived, went hand in hand with normalcy. Harding's contemporaries recognized the close association between Harding and small-town America. Harding's fellow small-town newspaper editor, William Allen White wrote that Harding was "Main Street in perfect flower."[8] Journalist Samuel Hopkins Adams reluctantly recognized the appeal of the small town, even as he was repulsed by the election: "there was no enthusiasm anywhere in the country except the pleasant and personal warmth of the front porch; merely a mental and moral torpor, the dull smolder of resentment over the aftermath of a war which had left behind its ashes of glory."[9] Adams's repulsion aside, a majority of Americans embraced Harding as a small-town spokesman with the credo Boost, Don't Knock. One journalist noted at the time, "the intimacies of a small town made life worth living" for Harding.[10] H. G. Wells wrote, "If Harding is a product of 'Main Street,' what the world needs is more 'Main Streets.'"[11] Harding's front porch campaign, with its familiar set of events such as parades, fireworks, baseball games, and speeches, represented a form of what John Bodnar has called "uncontested patriotism."[12] Here, patriotism was not simply national but based in the community and under the control of local boosters.

The patriotism emanating from Marion was softer, more comforting, than the harsh jingoism of wartime. By campaigning from his front porch, Harding was inviting the electorate into his home—almost. Harding's home was, as one Harding partisan described it, "the simple, modest, but comfortable home of a substantial American."[13] In addition to evoking the nineteenth-century style of campaigning, front porches were places where people visited. Voters were invited to visit with the Hardings in the semiprivate world of the porch, a shelter from the national storm that had been blowing.

This campaign image projected from the front porch of Harding's home was crafted consciously by the national Republican leadership, with substantial assistance from Harding's fellow Marion boosters. Using the campaign as a catalyst, civic leaders attempted to transform their city to meet the expectations of being the hometown of a president. Indeed, a central tenet of boosterism was the establishment of expectations, communicated through the bully pulpit occupied by a community leader who harangued the community to meet those expectations. Boosterism was aimed inward to promote change just as often as it was aimed outward. Marionites, by their very example, would personify an American myth even as it was playing out on the national stage. The election of 1920 gave civic leaders the opportunity to put past troubles behind them, and Marion, as we shall see, had had its share of problems. In the booster spirit, Marionites combined idealism with crass self-promotion.

Marion, the Home of Harding

On a Saturday night in June the news flashed from the *Marion Star*'s office: Harding had won the nomination. A spontaneous celebration spread throughout the town. Locomotive and factory whistles, car horns, and fire-works signaled spreading festivities that lasted well into the night. Before long, the mayor and other civic leaders appeared at the courthouse to address a crowd. Harding's longtime friend D. R. Crissinger told the crowd, "Warren G. Harding represents all that is good in Americanism." He continued, "I want to congratulate you on the great privilege you have in being a neighbor of Senator Harding."[14] Crissinger, who had twice run for Congress as a Democrat, would play a large part in organizing Marion for the upcoming campaign and would go on to be part of the Harding administration. Community harmony immediately became the theme of Marion's campaign, a message expressed by Crissinger: "whatever your political faith, it is going to be your privilege to extend the right hand of fellowship to the Republican nominee for the president, your fellow townsman, Warren G. Harding." The mayor declared that from "now on we are not Republicans, we are not Democrats, we are not socialists, but we are citizens of Marion for the purpose of electing Warren G. Harding president of the United States."[15]

Marion's leaders evoked the log cabin myth, foreshadowing themes emphasized in the campaign, as the celebration was as much about place as it was about national politics. The political rally merged with a booster rally to organize the town for an economic transformation led by those who shared Warren Harding's vision for Marion.[16] The crowd paraded to places important to Harding and now to national politics. George T. Harding was introduced as the "father of the next president." At Trinity Baptist Church, where Harding was a member, Dr. T. H. McAfee struck a classic theme that would be repeated over the next few months: Harding's nomination proved that a poor boy could grow up to achieve the greatest office in the land.[17] One observer, of many who would soon be visiting the nominee's hometown, noted that on the next day there were "still evidences of a great celebration" as every "electric light post on East Center Street was adorned with a cluster of flags. Crude half-tones and gift photographs of Harding were hastily posted in the windows of homes and stores."[18] Harding's nomination brought to Marion a renewed sense of community and a connection to important American myths.

Town boosters, friends of Harding, saw in the nomination a golden opportunity to "put Marion on the map," as they liked to say. Public pronouncements and editorials expressed concern for Marion's reputation and the ways in which the town's enhanced reputation would create business opportunities and a place in history. However, there were practical matters that needed attention. Marionites had two ceremonies immediately facing them: Harding's homecoming and the formal notification of his nomination.

Crissinger, Dr. Charles Sawyer, and other leading citizens approached the election in classic booster fashion, emphasizing the attractiveness of the town to outsiders while shaming those who they believed did not do their part.[19] Fully immersed in the contradiction of boosterism, they argued that Marion had an opportunity for profit and progress by selling itself as a community that had not advanced beyond village status. Before Marion could welcome its leading citizen home, town leaders announced a "general cleanup of the city." Officials from the Hocking Valley Railroad Company enlarged Union Station to accommodate the expected crowds. An oversize picture of Harding with the caption Marion, the Home of Harding was visible from the windows of passing trains.

Most dramatic, Mayor T. E. Andrews successfully pushed to replace the old city hall, which had been "a blemish on the business section of the city" and "an eyesore to our citizenship," with a modern building. Even before the pile of rubble was cleared away, nostalgia appeared. For years the city hall had been a "huge joke" that had been from "time to time" declared unsafe, a "menace to human life." People had expected the building to fall before a stiff breeze, but when time came to level the building, the "condemned walls proved strong." The central school building was next to be replaced, but it "would not be surprising, were it permitted to escape the hand of the wrecker, should it remain standing after some of our school structures erected four or five decades since had crumbled away." The booster began to see value in some of the older structures in town. Perhaps new did not equal better. The old buildings became a metaphor for the transformation Marionites foresaw. The old building had not blown away before a stiff breeze but rather required work to destroy. Still the old building, like the old village, had surprising resilience and value for a town that was now marketed as part of a mythical history.[20]

Erecting new buildings, signs, and parking lots were only part of the task facing Marion's leaders. Additionally, there was the matter of organizing the citizenry behind Harding. This was the other side of boosterism. Crissinger became the chairman of a group of leading citizens who spearheaded the effort to prepare Marion for the national spotlight. In addition, the group included Hoke Donithen and Sawyer, both of whom were close friends of Harding. George Christian Jr.'s house, which neighbored Harding's Mount Vernon Avenue home, became the publicity headquarters for the committee. In the end, thousands of citizens would be involved.

One citizen aptly summarized the feeling in the town: "Marion will never go back to the place she occupied before his nomination."[21]

While Marion, located in Marion County, was Harding's hometown, it was not his birthplace. Harding was born on a farm near the small farming community of Blooming Grove, twenty-four miles northeast of Marion, in neighboring Morrow County. Presidential birthplaces hold a special place in the log cabin myth and commemorative practices. The *Morrow County Sentinel* asked, "A president from Morrow County? Why not?" Millions would read about Harding and his birthplace. This was the proudest moment in Morrow County's history. The paper's editor, in a fit of boosterism, asked, "Who among us is not proud even to stand in the light of reflected greatness?" The proper presidential qualities were ascribed to Harding, as reflected in his physical appearance: the "nose is strong as is the brow, shaggy, gray and black. But the jaw is stronger." Harding's face was described as giving the "impression that the man is a little tired, even a little melancholy." Harding's ultimate qualification, however, was his background as "plain folk."[22] Clearly, boosters in Marion and in Morrow County understood the importance attached to a presidential birthplace and hometown in the mythology that surrounds candidates, and they began to situate their localities rhetorically within Harding's campaign biography. Morrow County faded from view during the campaign as the connection between Harding and his birthplace was eclipsed by the candidate's active association with his adopted hometown. Today the birthplace is distinguished only by a historical marker.

The announcement of the Republican Party's decision to conduct a front porch campaign guaranteed that the transformed Marion would be on center stage throughout the 1920 contest. One by one, major Republican leaders endorsed Marion as the setting for the campaign, noting that a front porch campaign added dignity to the election. An Associated Press story described the "senator's home at Marion" as "adapted admirably" for a front porch campaign, especially since it had "a large front porch on a wide street. The porch would serve for a speaker's stand" and the street was wide enough "for hundreds of enthusiastic Republicans who would journey to Marion."[23]

The Harding campaign resembled a civic celebration with its parades and events. As historian David Glassberg reminds us, "civic celebrations first and foremost are forms of communication, arenas for the expression of ideas and emotions." The front porch campaign would be a one-way discussion, and as such conforms to civic celebrations as a collective history.[24]

The front porch campaign in and of itself was generally evocative of the nineteenth century and specifically evocative of the 1896 election. Marion, with its tree-lined streets and shaded parks, complimented that image. Historian Robert Murray writes that Harding on his front porch "was the picture of American respectability, greeting delegations in his white trousers, blue coat, and sawtooth straw hat. His friendly house, painted dark green with white trim, its front porch handsomely tiled, appeared solid and inviting to many in the various delegations who had left similar small-town homes to make the journey to Marion."[25] Friends of Harding contrasted the wholesomeness of a front porch campaign with the impropriety of Harding's opponent, Cox, barnstorming the country, telling Harding that "'one night stands' are not in keeping with the dignity of a candidate for the highest office in the land."[26]

Amid all the excitement a clear theme began to emerge: the election would restore Americanism. The term Americanism, of course, was hardly original and, again, had the virtue of being as vague as normalcy. In 1920, Americanism was already a well-worn word. Woodrow Wilson had also used the term in his own campaign. During the 1916 election he praised his administration for its "100 percent Americanism" and attacked his opponents as "disloyal Americans."[27] Robert Ferrell, in his classic biography of Wilson, writes that the failure to protect civil liberties during the war grew from patriotism that "welled up in a demonstration of loyalty to the United States and to ideals known as Americanism, sometimes as 100 percent Americanism, which easily became conformity, and the other side of the coin of conformity is intolerance."[28]

The application of Americanism to the image of Marion stood in contrast to Wilson's use of the word. This contrast was made in editorials that proclaimed that Marion was the site of Harding's "humble origins" and the source of his "foursquare American" virtues. Americans, so editorial writers noted, were tired of Wilson and had a deep desire for "sound conservatism" and an "emphatically American point of view, for a commonsense consideration of American problems." Harding would "protect their welfare during these days of doubt, change, and disintegration."[29] Harding "exemplified the best type of American who has started at the foot of the ladder and climbed, hand over hand, unaided, to the topmost rung. Senator Harding hails from the small town of Marion, Ohio, where his life activities in journalism, ownership journalism, for he is the owner of his newspaper" made him "a true Ohioan of the best type."[30] Harding's background, with a few modifications, fit the old clichés of presidents born in so-called log cabins, and Marion was a fitting source of Harding's character.[31]

A Purely Civic Organization

How did the partisanship of a national presidential election square with the nonpartisan marshaling of community resources? In the same way that businessmen reconciled individual profit with the good of the community. Leaders of the Marion Civic Association downplayed the obvious themes of partisanship by emphasizing the historic importance of the election and the economic opportunities that the election presented. Seemingly oblivious to the contradiction of a nonpartisan organization working to elect a Republican candidate, the Civic Association declared that as a "purely civic organization," it did not require "any man to resign from his party to serve on committees" because it was "strictly a non-partisan affair, an organization of boosters of Marion."[32]

In its activities, the Civic Association followed the lead of the national Republican leadership, particularly in evoking William McKinley and the election of 1896. To underscore Harding's role as the new McKinley, the Republican Party placed the flagpole from McKinley's Canton, Ohio, yard in Harding's yard, cementing the bond between local and national, past and present. Local boosters noted the great crowds that had traveled to Canton for McKinley's front porch campaign. They expected that the notification ceremony alone would bring thousands of people to see Marion and participate in the making of history. Crissinger and the Civic Association would ensure that nothing was overlooked in the safe and efficient handling of the "vast crowds" that were anticipated to be twenty-five thousand.[33]

The Civic Association showed a decidedly heavy hand during the celebration. Crissinger appointed citizens to committees without consulting them, declaring that "none will wish to withdraw." Still, tension existed between individual and community opportunities, a point Crissinger noted with a stern warning: "I heard of a case where a man was charged five dollars for a place to sleep last night. If you want to ruin your city that is the quickest way to do it." This was only the first of many warnings the association would issue against profiteering as boosters like Crissinger, who clearly hoped to gain politically from the election, attempted to channel the material ambitions of their fellow townspeople into a single community vision.[34]

Like the expressions of the Civic Association, the apparent nonpartisanship of the *Star* is best understood as the traditional role of a newspaper in boosterism. Predictably, the front and editorial pages were dominated by local and national stories concerning Harding, with editorials expressing a strident booster spirit. The *Star,* like booster newspapers described by Griffith, promoted harmony, downplayed strife, and fostered a "sense of reciprocal obligation between commerce and the larger community: businessmen must improve the town and townspeople must in turn buy at home."[35]

The *Marion Star* exhibited little evidence of its close connection with Harding. Presumably, everyone knew that Harding owned the *Star.* His "ownership journalism" was mentioned frequently in the nationally released stories, and local spokespeople were not above repeating the obvious. *Star* employees, from retired newsboys to current typesetters, were regularly featured as evidence of Harding's role as a civic-minded employer. Rather than emphasizing this connection with Harding, much like the boosters who ran the association, the editors emphasized the newspaper's role as a community institution. The *Star*'s editors took great pains to make sure that readers understood that the campaign was more than a passing opportunity. Now, they wrote, "opportunity knocks" and Marion "may begin to acquire publicity in a degree far beyond the ordinary on her own merit and merit of her people." To take advantage of the opportunity, they urged the town's citizens to "act as one to send visitors away with the most pleasant impression of Marion and Marionites." Every visitor would become a "booster, a walking advertisement, and the good name of Marion" would be "carried to all parts of our land."[36] The editors emphasized community boosterism over partisan politics, leaving unstated boosterism's role in electing the newspaper's owner.

Plans for the notification ceremony proceeded rapidly after the arrival of Harry Daugherty, Harding's campaign manager at the Chicago convention and a member of the Republican National Committee. Although Daugherty was in Marion as the official representative of the Republican Party, the *Star,* of course, noted that he hailed from another Ohio small town, Washington Court House. Daugherty stressed the need for local organization to manage the size of the crowds that were expected. Clearly pleased with the planning, Daugherty assured Marionites that the notification ceremony was "a purely local affair." In keeping with the Civic Association's tone, which sounded odd coming from the highly partisan Daugherty, he stressed that the "arrangements and informal program" would be "entirely in the hands of a nonpartisan organization." He was "pleased to learn" that Marionites agreed that there would be "no profiteering, as the committee on arrangements has taken the necessary precaution to this end."[37]

As a civic celebration, the notification ceremony would be an unquestionably patriotic event that demonstrated community unity behind the candidate. A band would escort Harding and a parade of citizens to Harding's home, where Crissinger would give the welcoming address. Organizers incorporated into the ceremony the county fair and a belated Independence Day celebration that included fireworks and airplane races. If there were any Marionites who wished to find a community event unrelated to Harding, they were simply out of luck. Anticipation built, and the importance of the event was highlighted, as the national press followed Harding's trip from Washington to Marion. The boosters noted, with some satisfaction, that "the influx of newspaper and press association men, so noticeable immediately following the nomination of Senator Harding by the Republican national convention in Chicago, has again started and by Sunday a large number of them is expected to arrive here." With the increased presence of the national press, boosters wanted to ensure that all members of the community worked toward the common goal.[38]

Even with the emphasis on community, Marion's bifurcation along economic, gender, and racial lines was apparent. Glassberg's observation that "the particular dilemma of those planning civic celebrations—like those planning political campaigns at this time—was eliciting mass participation to give the illusion of an outpouring of public sentiment while maintaining control of the prevailing imagery and institutions" is applicable to the local efforts of Marion's leaders.[39] A Woman's Harding-for-President Club was formed and over one hundred of its members combed the city with a "fine-tooth comb" to find spare rooms that could be used for guests. Many homeowners, in "excellent spirit," offered the best room in the house to the cause, according to the *Star.* Successful canvassing swelled the ranks of the woman's club, which soon reached nearly two thousand members.[40] The Civic Association reached out to black members of the community, announcing an "enthusiastic meeting" of the Colored Harding-for-President Club. Crissinger was concerned that the business community do its share. He admonished the owners of hotels and restaurants that "the business people of the city are asleep and do not realize what will be necessary to take care of these visitors," whom he predicted could number one hundred thousand. Sawyer, Harding's physician and friend, was blunter, noting that the reputation of Marion now rested with those who would feed and care for the people: "What we do in the inception of this campaign will mark us all the way through." Using the historical analogy, Sawyer joined other boosters in evoking Canton's experience. That city had "made its reputation" in the McKinley campaigns, Sawyer maintained, "because the people took care of the visitors." Even the town of Delaware, forty minutes away by interurban, was preparing to house those who could not find lodging in Marion, including members of the National Woman's Party who planned to picket Harding's house until he gave his full support to woman suffrage.[41] Thus we can see social tensions played out within the effort to foster unity, or at least the appearance of unity, around the building of the town's reputation and the downplaying of individual profit.

The Eyes of the Nation

On the day of Harding's homecoming, Marionites began arriving at his front yard hours before the 6 P.M. starting time. Marion's Typographical Union no. 675 led a parade of citizens along Mount Vernon Avenue. Standing on the front porch with Florence Harding, Harry Daugherty, and George Christian Jr., before guests, reporters, and motion picture cameras, Crissinger introduced his "boy hood chum and life long friend," Warren Harding. Crissinger's speech stressed community and diligence. The election, he said, would be the "supreme hour in our civic life," but he noted that Marion stood ready for its moment in history because "the citizenship gathered here is not cosmopolitan but rather a neighborhood assembly." Crissinger emphasized that the community was built on friendship, with citizens representing every vocation, creed, and political faith bound together to boost Marion and Harding. Harding's homecoming marked a "new epoch for Marion and its citizens." Crissinger now turned to America's civic religion and Marion's new place in it. The town, he proclaimed, would become the "Mecca for many pilgrimages." In Marion, Americans could see the community and friends from which Harding derived his qualifications for the presidency. Crissinger described Harding's character, evoking a romantic and not completely flattering description of small-town America. Harding was "calm minded and evenly balanced and unspectacular," Crissinger said. He described Harding as "generous and forgiving to a fault, with a trusting and helpful disposition, he brings to himself friend and foe alike. He harmonizes conflicting elements by intelligent, yet unselfish, understanding."[42] Later, after Harding's death, and after the emergence of the scandals that had dragged down Harding's reputation, these same characteristics would be frequently given as the reason for

Harding's downfall, but in 1920 they stood at the center of his civic identity. Harding would lead the way from war and uncertainty to a community based on small-town locality, friendship, and harmony.

Harding responded to Crissinger's speech with humility, evoking the commonness of the place he came from. He said that for "thirty-eight years we have been friends and neighbors," and noted that only a few miles "away are the treasured scenes of birth and boyhood." Injecting a sense of irony but also serving to further emphasize his commonplace origins, Harding said that the stories of his boyhood had "been recalled and recorded, very recently, with touches of imagination I fear, because the real story is a very ordinary one, which might be related concerning any of us, but that doesn't mar the understanding among home folks."[43] Harding bridged the gap between the national campaign and the small town and between community and self-interest: "You and I, all of us Marionites, have been boosting this Marion of ours together for considerably more than thirty years, and have shared in varying degrees the achievements attending its development." Having dealt with his own and his town's history by explaining how they had been motivated by the future, Harding declared that the "thought of development and progress, a desire to find our place on the map of Ohio inspired us, and there was common interest in spite of the seeming selfishness attending rewards. We were all boosters together, because it is an engaging pursuit."[44]

The themes of Harding's homecoming played well not just with the local audience but nationwide. Soon after his nomination, journalist Henry Stoddard described a visit to Harding's home: "in one of those modest village homes that are the greatest asset of American life we found the candidate." Harding, in his Victorian home, exhibited "physically a splendid type of manhood."[45] The tone of the 1920 Republican campaign had been established.

Harding implicitly criticized Wilson's vision of Americanism for its lack of community-based decision making. His numerous calls for party rule featured the theme of community. The Republican Party, led by Harding, would restore the American values of representative government, as opposed to the autocratic and detached government of Woodrow Wilson. The political party system was at the heart of community decision making, according to Harding. However, there was little evidence of dissent or substantial debate in Marion during the election. Marion became a one-party town during the summer and fall of 1920. The sometimes thinly veiled and heavyhanded warnings that boosters such as Sawyer and Crissinger issued to those who might not cooperate hints at the possibility of dissent, but if dissent existed, the dissenters left little evidence behind. Of course, during the 1920s many writers and intellectuals found the Main Street values of Harding and Crissinger oppressive. However, we must keep in mind what Marion's boosters were asking in 1920. Sawyer and Crissinger were not asking citizens to surrender their civil liberties in the name of patriotism but rather to contribute to a cause that, hopefully, would enrich the community. It might have been easier for those Marionites who were not pleased with the Civic Association to hold their tongues long enough for the election to pass and perhaps make a few dollars in the interim.

In the wake of Harding's return, other dignitaries appeared in Marion.[46] Harding's campaign manager, Will Hays, and other prominent Republicans arrived in the second week of July to work closely with Harding on his acceptance speech and other similar concerns. Highlighting the need for unity, significant attention was paid to former Progressive Party leaders who had returned to the Republican fold.[47] Other dignitaries visited Harding's home as well, including the governors of various states and Gen. Leonard Wood, who had lost the nomination to Harding in Chicago. The list of dignitaries only served to further underscore the importance of the nomination, especially when it was announced that Henry Cabot Lodge would make the official presentation.[48]

Marion's boosters were not the only ones to recognize both the opportunities and pitfalls of being in the national spotlight. The *Ohio State Journal* noted that while front porch campaigns "bring new duties and lay heavy obligations," Marionites were going about the task in a "business way" with "energy and enthusiasm." The commentary continued that Marionites had wisely turned to people of Canton to learn the lessons of the 1896 campaign. The conclusion assuredly pleased boosters: "It's a great day for Marion, [it] will be the greatest summer in its history, and the people there intend to meet the demands. Marion is a live place, has many enthusiastic citizens, plenty of generous people, is enthusiastic over the distinction that has been brought to the city and will master the situation."[49] Marion boosters did indeed hope to master the unfolding of history.

In preparation for the notification ceremony, which would require even more of the community's resources than had Harding's homecoming, the Marion Civic Association announced that it would build a bandstand and facilities on school property to serve as the staging grounds. Almost as an afterthought, the association assured citizens that the campaign would not interfere with school. The concern with profiteering did not go away. Local businesses began to sell recordings of Harding's speeches, with one store using Harding's position on the League of Nations to promote men's clothing.[50] There was, as Harding noted, a fine line between self-interest and community.

While pleasing to community leaders, the publicity and praise that national leaders granted their efforts did not make the job of preparing for the campaign any easier. Although the Civic Association took the lead in preparing Marion for its responsibility, it had no formal authority. After Sawyer and Crissinger had pressed and cajoled citizens to participate, the association found itself in the awkward situation of having a great deal of responsibility without having resources. The Republican Party paid for most of the expenses related to the nomination events, leaving, as Crissinger described it, the "relatively small expense" of $20,000 unpaid. In a call for financial support from the community, Crissinger assured citizens that the expenses are "not only purely local, but also strictly non-partisan." The executive committee was confident that the citizens, recognizing the value of the town's enhanced reputation, would make donations "without solicitation," again avoiding the obvious point that the announcement was a solicitation, just as the election was partisan. Crissinger again stressed community over party, arguing that "regardless of political affiliation and any political ties whatsoever, it is felt that the people of the city, with their characteristic broad-mindedness and liberality, will respond to this civic call."[51] The question of how to spend community resources troubled the association's claim to speak for the entire community.

A flurry of activity ensued as the notification ceremony approached, much of it stressing community. Crissinger and Sawyer emphasized the role that women would play in hosting the town's guests, organizing a meeting for women at the high school to explain their expectations. Crissinger wanted a thousand Marion women on the streets, each wearing a reception badge and boosting Marion. Sawyer was not so reassuring. He feared that the women of Marion did not realize their great responsibility. He asked, "do you realize that the citizens of Marion are to be hosts and hostesses to the nation Thursday and that among the guests are to be leading and representative people of every state in the United States?" Sawyer followed his reprimand with instructions: "You women should be particularly courteous to all who come here and your business is to introduce yourself to every stranger you come in contact with and show these strangers hospitality."[52] Women had the role of community hostesses, which, for the most part, included providing accommodations. Arrangements were made for a women's parade through the town, in which all the women were asked to wear white.[53]

Despite the emphasis on traditional women's roles, party leaders were keenly aware of women's expanding citizenship, if not sure exactly how best to react to it. The Woman's Harding-for-President Club and the Marion League of Women Voters took the lead in organizing the women.[54] However, while suffrage promised to change politics, boosters saw women's organizations as being within women's traditional roles in political parties. While Sawyer and Crissinger saw the women as essentially fulfilling the roles of substitute mothers and wives for the guests, it is entirely possible (although difficult to tell, given the lack of records) that the women saw their role in a different and more proactive light.[55]

Although the Nineteenth Amendment created uncharted waters for boosters and Republicans, it did not interfere with planning for an old-fashioned campaign. Marion's Garfield Park, with its gazebo and stately trees, was the site of the notification ceremony. On a practical level, the special trains that would carry the crowds to Marion were of great importance. The Civic Association posted train and event schedules and asked every resident to memorize them so that they might be prepared to assist visitors.[56] The Civic Association had placed twenty-five hundred seats in the park but long before 2 P.M., the time for the beginning of the ceremony, there was standing room only. Harding, Henry Cabot Lodge, and other leading Republicans ate breakfast at Charles Sawyer's White Oaks Sanatorium before traveling to Harding's home. At 7 A.M., Harding raised the flag up the McKinley flagpole, an activity followed by a short speech by Theodore Roosevelt's son.[57] After these tributes to the party's past, the next part of the ceremony pointed to the future. Alice Paul and a delegation of over one hundred women from the National Woman's Party visited Harding at his home at 10 A.M. to urge him to pressure the Tennessee legislature to ratify the suffrage amendment.[58] The Harding Marching Club, dressed in blue jackets, white trousers, and straw hats, assembled on the school grounds and led a parade from Union Depot to Harding's home and then to Garfield Park. The Ohio Harding Woman Club, while making no demands regarding suffrage, had a prominent place in the parade. The entire route was decorated, but the "court of honor," from Main to Center streets, was lined with columns and streamers of oak leaves.[59]

At the park Henry Cabot Lodge praised Harding's character. Harding's reply seemed almost anticlimactic. Harding told his fellow citizens that he believed in "party government as distinguished from personal government, individual, dictatorial, autocratic or what not." Harding spent much of his speech addressing foreign relations, promising the people of Marion to uphold a constitutional government, to preserve the independence of the United States, to avoid a world "super-government" and wars.[60] Pronouncements of efficiency in government paled beside the banners and the hoopla. The *Star* declared that the ceremony was the "most notable exercise of its kind in history and drew more people than any similar ceremony within memory."[61] Indeed, the entire ceremony connected national and local and spoke to the unfolding of history from the past to the future.

The size of the crowd, the patriotic small-town pageantry, and the prominence of the guests surpassed the expectations of boosters. The estimates of the crowd's size ranged from forty to eighty-five thousand, with the *New York Times* (as the *Star* happily reported) putting it at sixty thousand.[62] The "eyes of the nation" had turned to Marion, the *Star* editorialized, and the citizens of Marion could be "forgiven a feeling of civic pride" for having successfully entertained "the greatest notification gathering in the history of our land." The town's ceremony eclipsed even the national convention. Fully recognizing the role Marion was playing in defining the Republican Party, the editorialist argued that while the platform had been written in Chicago, it had been interpreted in Marion and thus the ceremonies took on "added significance." Marion had brought into focus the meaning of the campaign. No longer did boosters worry that Marion would be left behind in the race to modernity; now they embraced the idea of Marion as a successful small town, for the "handling of such a gathering as this which comes to Marion is something of a proposition to a city of our size."[63] The *Star* said it was "just a bit amazed over the great success of her undertaking—in itself the best tribute possible to the thoroughness of the work of her Civic Association."[64]

The notification ceremony was, however, just the first stage in a campaign stretching into November. The front porch campaign began on July 31 and promised vast crowds, parades, and national attention throughout the fall. Again, for Marionites the campaign brought with it the same tensions between individual gain and community needs. The various dignitaries continued to visit and the campaign followed a pattern established by the Civic Association. Various constituencies would visit Marion to be greeted in a festive atmosphere. There would be a parade through town, usually ending at Harding's front porch. Then Harding would emerge, sometimes with the appropriate guest, and address the crowd. His campaign speeches were notoriously vague and full of the booster spirit. In many ways, however, it was not the content of the speech that was important; it was the event and the composition of the gathering. Each event was a reaching out to some particular constituency, a reassurance that they and their concerns would not be forgotten in a Harding administration. Harding's front porch campaign was a county fair, an example of hospitality in an inhospitable world. It was also an example of old-fashioned political public theater. Harding showed his appreciation of the constituents with an opportunity for just plain folk to march in parades and have their pictures taken.

Neighbors All

During the campaign Harding brought the guests into their own version of the log cabin myth. With the opening of the campaign, fellow Ohioans, greeted as neighbors, were the first to arrive for the festivities. As part of his standard speech Harding would recount bits of the history of the delegation's community, always emphasizing pioneer days and the progress that followed. For example, Harding told the delegation from Wayne County that they "must be confidently and fearlessly American to measure to the renowned name of Wayne. The story of Wayne County is that of the great beginning of the Northwest Territory, whose sturdy citizenship was strengthened by the hardship of the forest pioneer." What had been the result of the work of these sturdy pioneers? They contributed to "the conquering westward march of civilization." How did they accomplish this? "They didn't indulge many finely-spun theories, there were not many 'isms' then. They faced stubborn facts, and dwelt in grim determination. They were not asking what the Republic could do for them, they were seeking to do for themselves and thereby add to the glory of the Republic." Thus Harding told the crowds that America was not a place of ideologies but of action, the booster elevation of pragmatism. America was a place where people sacrificed for the common good. Finishing with the sturdy pioneers Harding went on to evoke the Founding Fathers Hamilton and Washington, who "knew what was safe, and preached security," which, Harding implied, meant that the founders wanted America to avoid the problems of the Old World. Having finished with the lessons of history, Harding went full circle to explain that a "community of homes" was "the ideal community."[65] Many of Harding's speeches invoked America's pioneer heritage and the importance of community. For example, Harding told the delegation from Wyandotte County that women had earned the right to vote through their "sturdy patriotism" during frontier days and thus their contribution to the community had earned them the right to participate in the national political process.[66]

In his speech to the delegation from Richland County, Harding held up Richland and Marion counties as representative of the spirit of American institutions, for in both places "hundreds of your neighbors and mine came from lands across the sea. They came to become citizens and accept the obligations as well as the advantages of American citizenship." These ancestors, he said, "walked with us in the fraternity and mutuality of citizenship, and are of the empire builders and the Republic's defenders." As a true booster, Harding saw the development of the Erie Railroad from a regional railroad to a national institution as the culmination of this historic progress. As progress demanded, businessmen introduced new technologies. Harding asked, was "there not an application in the advancing way of America?" His conclusion was that Americans "must cling to the sure route of splendid development and meet the new demands by so building as to eliminate the grades by which our activities are impeded."[67] Mythological local histories that stressed unity and community as the way to progress (defined as peace and prosperity) were mainstays of Harding's campaign speeches.

Much was made at the time, and afterward, of Harding's decision to not mention his opponent by name in his campaign speeches. Harding seemingly paid little attention to either his opponent Cox or Cox's fellow Democrat and the incumbent, Wilson. But notice the themes of his speeches praising Ohio communities. He praised these American communities as places of progress and practical endeavors that rejected ideologies and isms. In doing so, Harding placed himself and his party on the side of patriotic Americans, while leaving those who advocated Wilsonian internationalism or European communism outside the mainstream of community values.

Given the national turmoil of 1919, Marion's Labor Day celebration, because of its origins in the working class, held the possibility of disrupting Harding's idealized American community. However, the campaign turned Labor Day into a celebration of community spirit and emphasized the booster ethos when explaining the history of the holiday. Members of the eighteen unions that composed Marion's Central Labor Union were joined by members of the National Education Association, the American Federation of Teachers, and the Illinois State Teachers' Association in a parade through Marion. During the campaign Labor Day was not so much about labor as it was about entertainment and harmony. For Labor Day the Harding campaign brought in the Chicago Cubs to play against a local baseball club, with the revenues going to improve playgrounds. Harding himself briefly took the field.[68] Baseball gave Harding the opportunity to once again affirm what it meant to be American: "I like the game, just like every other real American."[69] Of course, Harding enjoyed watching the "rooters," who showed real zeal for the home team. Harding drew on the popularity of baseball, telling the Cubs that "team play in government, as well as in baseball, is what wins victories." He continued, "This harmony of endeavor, where every man plays his part, no matter who is starring, is what wins in baseball and will win victories for these United States."[70]

The stressing of baseball's all-American qualities served another purpose: emphasizing Harding's credentials as a representative of the common man. Albert Lasker, who did much to control Harding's image as the primary advertising man for the campaign, arranged for the Chicago Cubs to visit Marion to counter negative public reaction to newsreel footage of Harding playing golf. Harding loved to play golf, but it was considered an elite, country-club sport and did not mesh with his everyman campaign.[71]

During the campaign Harding wove a romantic and antiquarian vision of farm and factory that emphasized cooperation between labor and capital.[72] His vision stood in stark contrast to the economic realities of 1920. Inflation and labor-management strife had dominated the economic news in 1919. The economy fell into a postwar depression that lingered into the 1920s; in 1921 unemployment among nonfarm workers hit 20 percent. Harding's vision, however, was consistent with his booster background and his campaign's historical mythology of America. Without mentioning the nation's troubles, Harding argued that Labor Day was not so much about labor as it was about the opportunity for those born in the laboring class to advance into the business class. He told the Harding and Coolidge Club from Richland County that here, "in the Middle West, where farming is free from tenantry and holds to the normal way, and manufacturing is mainly confined to the plants of that moderate size," life was good.[73] During another speech, Harding rather confusingly proclaimed, "Life is labor, or labor is life, whichever is preferred." He then went on to recount, without giving names, the stories of business leaders he knew who had begun working as humble laborers but had succeeded, by "industry, thrift, love of work, interest in their tasks, ambition to get on."[74]

While's Harding's vision of labor harked back to the nineteenth century, the *Star* pointed to the history of Labor Day in explaining Marion's pride in the holiday. Harding's role in Marion's Labor Day celebrations became part of the campaign narrative that demonstrated a consistency with Harding's positions on labor. Warren Harding had been one of the town's leaders who supported the first local Labor Day celebration held in Marion, in 1903. He was also the featured speaker. In a 1903 *Star* editorial that he wrote about the event, he de-emphasized labor and claimed that Labor Day is "wholly and completely labor's day, or more broadly stated, the people's day." Although the holiday was "inspired and conducted by union laborers, the event was enjoyed and appreciated and bided [*sic*] mental Godspeed by thousands not identified with any labor organization." In a manner that foreshadowed the themes of the 1920 campaign, Harding's 1903 comments concluded with a return to the theme of community. A community, Harding asserted, could not be built by capital or labor alone but by both working in harmony.[75]

Following the Labor Day celebration, Harding's 1920 campaign continued to emphasize the importance of community and harmony for American values. When he campaigned through the Midwest, he told an Illinois crowd that he preferred speaking in small towns: "I grew up in a village of six hundred, and I know something of democracy." He continued, "I do not believe that anywhere in the world there is so perfect a democracy as in the village." Harding argued that the village had no "social strata." It was a place where every son had the "same opportunities of this America of ours." Harding again returned to the theme of opportunity for all. Of his childhood friends, the least bright had become a local banker while the brightest of the lads had become a janitor. The janitor was, according to Harding, the happiest. Harding explained that his childhood friend was happy because there "is more happiness in the American village than any other place on the face of the earth."[76] After his swing through the Midwest, Harding returned to Marion to continue his front porch speeches. Now, local politicians joined him to speak out on national issues. Judge Grant Mouser denounced the League of Nations as a violation of the United States Constitution. While few outside Marion knew of Judge Mouser, not only did his speech highlight a campaign issue but in doing so he implicitly compared the unconstitutional international community with Harding's celebration of small towns as real Americanism.

As Harding welcomed veterans, African Americans, women, laborers, and businessmen to Marion and to his home, he also greeted the constituencies he saw as necessary to build a community—and win an election. Each was incorporated into the historical narratives that were central to his

speeches. Perhaps because of the nation's deep racial divide, special attention was given to a delegation of African Americans. Harding had received
many requests for audiences from black organizations, and the campaign
consolidated their requests into one event. A large contingent of African
Americans arrived in Marion representing the African Methodist Episco-
pal Church, the National Race Congress of America, the Harding and
Coolidge Negro Women's Club of Philadelphia, and the National Negro
Baptists. William H. Lewis, formerly an assistant attorney general in the
Taft administration, spoke for the Baptist delegation. He declared that the
black vote was crucial for the Republican Party in New York, New Jersey,
Connecticut, Ohio, Indiana, and Illinois. Lewis and other black voters, like
their white counterparts, wanted a sound economy and efficient government. Lewis, however, went further, saying that black citizens had been
"the victims of the present administration far more than any other class of
citizens—eliminated from the participation in the government, segregated
in the civil service and denied the equal protection of the law."[77] Harding
urged them all to join a party, to vote, and to participate in the republic. In
September 1920, in the wake of the ratification of the Nineteenth Amendment, in August, he particularly urged women not to be independents: "I
do not mean that I would fail to urge those whose conscience separates
them from the allegiances to remain silent or passive, but I mean that the
fashion of parading independence is to be deplored."[78] Women active in
political reform efforts had debated the merits of partisanship for some
time and now Harding weighed in, urging partisanship.[79]

Social Justice

By October the campaign had found its voice and Marion fulfilled its un-
official function as the nation's hometown. It seemed a natural evolution
that in the final month of the campaign Harding would stress social justice.
Emphasizing social justice allowed Harding and the Republicans to evoke
community and inclusiveness, themes that were aimed at the new women
voters in particular and that allowed Harding to reach out to former Progressives, who had aggressively courted women in 1912 by taking a stand
for suffrage.[80] As a campaign event, Marion's Social Justice Day presented
a simple alternative to Wilson's League, with, as Harding and the Republicans argued, its loss of control and danger of entanglement in the wars
of other nations. Social Justice Day also represented the flexibility of the
booster ethos. Boosters, like Harding, embraced change as long as it brought

progress, which they defined as economic improvement led by the business element. William Allen White used the booster ethos in his support of progressive reforms, in which he envisioned the "small town as a progressive ideal in which shared 'social sympathy' provided the cohesion necessary for true democracy."[81]

On October 1, 1920, which the campaign dubbed Social Justice Day, Harding announced that if elected, his administration would create a federal department of public welfare. Harding deftly picked up some progressive themes and wedded them to traditional conservative concerns. Speaking to Mrs. Raymond Robins, a local Republican leader, and a group of women, Harding declared, "There can be no more efficient way of advancing a humanitarian program than by adapting the machinery of our federal government to the purposes we desire to attain." The new department would be part of a general reorganization of governmental bureaucracies designed to increase efficiency and end bickering among the agencies already charged with bettering the human condition. Thus Harding left the issue of expanding the federal government and its responsibilities vague even as he promised new constituents more government action.

Returning to the private sector, Harding spoke in the vein of the booster ethos. He said that social justice was an obligation, not paternalism. In a direct appeal to women, he called for employers to protect maternity and to "break down the distinctions of sex and establish equal pay for equal work." Seemingly oblivious to the controversial nature of these pledges, he promised to hire qualified women for state and federal boards. Harding noted the need for industrial peace, stating his "full belief in labor unionism and in the practice of collective bargaining." Harding, of course, did not leave business out of the picture he was painting. To achieve this new age of peace and justice, "humanitarian brotherhood" needed to permeate America's businesses.[82]

Significantly, it was before the crowd of women assembled for Social Justice Day that Harding made it as clear as he ever would that he did not support the League of Nations, and it was here that the difference between Wilson's and Harding's communities stood in stark contrast. Marion, as the stage for the appeal, had received high praise for its hospitality. In particular, the women of Marion had worked hard to make Social Justice Day a success. Indeed, the *Star* praised women, both locals and visitors, for the nature of their "big nonpartisan parade." This oddly nonpartisan event (which, of course, had all the trappings of an election rally) was not confined to women from Ohio towns and cities but had a strong representation of national Republican women, again symbolically connecting the local and the national. L. C. Fleming, general director of the Republican Colored Women, led "quite a number of colored women." Flush with the praise from journalists and with the "great crowd of women visitors" gone home, the citizens of Marion held a Back to Normal day.[83] On Back to Normal day the citizens cleaned up their town, but one has to wonder to wonder if the Civic Association and Marion citizens were symbolically restoring the "normal" social relationships of the community as well.

Because Harding needed to attract women voters in the wake of the Nineteenth Amendment's ratification, he took progressive stands during the election, partly because old-line politicians were not sure how women would vote. In the context of 1920, Harding's pledge to support equal pay for equal work was within the context of the booster ethos, couched as it was in terms of progress attained through efficiency, harmony, and business leadership. Harding's social agency was, in fact, a proposal to bring together various Progressive Era efforts to protect women and children under one agency in the name of efficiency.

While courting the vote of women and laborers, Harding also cultivated the support of the press. Indeed, as a former editor and reporter and as a current publisher, Harding was one of the boys when it came to the press. On Social Justice Day, the press corps covering the campaign celebrated Harding's forthcoming success. Various journalists gave testimony to Harding's good character and his potential to make a fine president. One journalist toasted the honored guest: "If you don't make a great president, our judgment is no good and we are in the wrong trade."[84] Following the success of Social Justice Day, Harding took his show on the road in the final month before the election. He spoke at a historic marker honoring fallen soldiers in Fremont, Ohio, on the ninety-eighth anniversary of President Rutherford B. Hayes's birth. Harding then traveled to Louisville and Indianapolis to speak. After attending rallies in Chattanooga and St. Louis, Harding returned to Marion before leaving for Rochester and Buffalo.[85] Social Justice Day and Harding's two trips concluded his campaign. Now it was time to wait for election day.

Marion also had to plan for election day, another event that local boosters wanted to ensure was a success. Employers announced that they would close their plants early to give workers time to vote.[86] The *Star* reminded citizens of their civic duties, which included the obligations that

"knit us together into a nation of ideals; they include right living in our relations to ourselves, to our families and to our homes, to the communities
in which we live and to our national welfare." The writer marked the
change in the national mood, arguing that patriotic duty "includes not only
our duty in time of war when patriotism is aflame, but also in times of peace
when patriotism calls all the more for our service because some other man
or woman may be forgetting the duty to serve."[87] Women were given particular attention in the discourse on citizenship. Since shops and factories
were closing early so that men could vote in the afternoon, the election
board urged women, being unemployed for the most part it was assumed,
to vote in the morning.[88] Unlike typical calls to patriotism, and in stark contrast to the recent war, the editorial writer summed up the patriotic tone
of the front porch campaign.

The assumption that women were both middle-class housewives and
voters reveals one of the underlying messages of the front porch campaign.
While the public rhetoric surrounding the campaign emphasized the connection to McKinley in the creation of a past usable for the election, the
symbolism was also about hearth and home. During the election, Florence
Harding was constantly in the background as her image shifted from that
of modern businesswoman to homemaker. It was significant that Harding
campaigned from home and, in particular, from the front porch, where
the Hardings, like many other midwesterners, greeted their "neighbors."
The front porch served as a transition between the public and the private
arenas and as a symbolic link between the male world of politics and the
female world of the home. Just as women were emerging into full citizenship, having gained the vote in 1920, Harding welcomed them into his
home as neighbors and supporters.

In the final weeks of the campaign, Marionites rejoiced in the large
crowds that filled local restaurants. Here was some of the payoff that the
Civic Association had promised. Students from Ohio Wesleyan College, and
thirty-five other colleges, rallied before the front porch. Akron and Cleveland held large rallies for Harding, complete with women marching through
Cleveland in a traditional political torchlight parade. The only unpleasant
note in the late stages of the campaign was the necessity for Harding to
declare that he was "unbossed" to counter charges that a Senate cabal had
selected him.[89] When election day arrived Republican journalist Joe Chap-
pel's description reflected the image that the Harding campaign and the
Civic Association had worked hard to create: "Through it all there was no
formality, but the hospitality of home life."[90]

Victory

November 2, 1920, was, in the increasingly inflated rhetoric of Marion's boosters, the greatest day in the history of the community. Cameras clicked as Warren and Florence Harding cast their votes. They then left for the state capital, Columbus, where Warren played golf. Upon his return to Marion, employees from the *Star* presented him with a solid-gold printer's rule as a birthday present; it was, after all, not only election day but Harding's fifty-fifth birthday. That night Harding learned that he had won in a landslide and the next morning he awoke to the simple but powerful headline Harding Wins. Harding declared that the overwhelming Republican victory was not a personal victory.[91] Still, Marion did turn out for Harding, who carried the normally Democratic county, and other local Republicans rode his coattails. In fact, no Democrats were elected to county office. The *Star* editorialized that this was "not only the choice of the men voters as in past years, but the women played their part well. The honor falling to Marion was to have the opportunity of lending assistance to the election of Warren G. Harding, Marion's own son, to the presidency."[92] The Marion Civic Association announced a parade for 7:30 P.M. on November 3 so that citizens could "break forth in one big jubilee of victory."[93]

Amid all the celebration, the editor of the *Star* confessed, "the *Star*, as all its readers know, is a newspaper and not a political or personal organ." The editor had given more than usual coverage to politics but felt that that was justifiable. He stated that he had always tried to maintain a "decent restraint" and to approach the news with "absolute fairness." Now came the acknowledgment of what everyone in the town already knew, that because the *Star*'s "founder and head was the candidate of his party for the highest office in the country," the editor's "support of his candidacy was naturally appealing." In addition to his personal relationship with Harding, he wrote that "the community served by the *Star* gave such an illustration of friendship and neighborly affection as has seldom been known in a heated political campaign. Party lines were obliterated, party and personal interests and ambitions were sacrificed, and the whole county came loyally to the support of the local candidate."[94] Marion was "wild with enthusiasm" and "mad with joy," according to the *Star* editor, as the town celebrated the campaign that had brought together "the great majority of the people, Democrats loyal to their fellow citizens as well as to the Republicans."[95]

With the election over, Marion would indeed become the president's hometown. Dignitaries vying for patronage and for the ear of the new president visited the town.[96] Marion had entered into American history and its local history was now and forever woven into the national narrative. Harding would return to Marion only once more before his death, on July 4, 1922, for the centennial celebration of Marion's founding. In addressing his hometown, Harding proclaimed his desire to "come simply as a Marionite and speak as one, because it is easily possible for me to feel a peculiar intimacy toward such an occasion." He made no great claims for himself or for his office, but rather emphasized his newspaper work, when he did "a lot of cheering, which is no less essential to the forward movement in a community than it is in football or baseball." However, Harding could no longer act just as the booster of his hometown. He pointed out that a speech discussing nothing but Marion's history would seem "rather trivial to the larger community which is habituated to expect some form of broadcasting to every presidential utterance," although he lamented that "it would be good to talk about Marion, just among ourselves." Harding continued to see citizenship and community as tied together: "I know nothing more interesting to any man than his community. If he is not interested, he is a not a good citizen." Harding wove together the national narrative, local history, and his own biography by recalling his visit to Plymouth to commemorate the three-hundredth anniversary of the landing of the Pilgrims, where he was constantly reminded that New England had "preceded us two centuries in the making of America." Harding, however, said that making America was not a function of centuries. He "became a citizen of Marion 40 years ago, almost to the day" and had been "a resident of the county just about 50 years. And it all has the seeming of being but a little while. Yet I could almost qualify as a pioneer." In that short period, the "little while view," Harding and Marion had participated in the transition from the pioneer days to a modern progressive town marked by industry and growth. Progress rather than centuries made American identity. When he first arrived in Marion in 1882, Harding had not realized how "countrified" he and Marion had been because he lacked the vision. Soon, industrialization and progress would remake both him and his town. He concluded, "You see, I came from the farm and village, and the county greater," and so returned to his theme of nostalgia.[97]

Harding's address at the Marion centennial eschewed a discussion of his presidency, but he did place Marion within a narrative that was part myth and part history, just as he had done with so many other small towns during the election. Marion was part of America's national story of opportunity and progress even as he, without saying so, was an example of the same. This narrative had served Harding, Republican leaders, and Marion boosters exceptionally well during the election of 1920. Harding reaffirmed in his conclusion his place in the narrative of opportunity rising from commonness. After Harding's death and the collapse of his reputation, Marion would remain the one place where people would consistently evoke Harding's positive role in this historical myth of democracy and progress. As we will see, Marion's own history did not always live up to the expectations of a president's hometown, and many would come to see the association between Harding and Marion in a less than flattering light. Ironically, the idealized version of America's hometown that the Republicans highlighted during the 1920 election was blamed both for limiting the political vision of Harding and for his shortcomings.

Commemorating the Tragedy of Warren Harding

I know my limitations. I know how far removed
from greatness I am. Be that as it may, I intend
to approach every problem with good will in my
heart instead of hatred. Most questions which are
settled by armed force are never permanently
settled. . . . People may think of me as they please,
but I shall continue to be just what I am, Warren G.
Harding as he is and as God fashioned him—a man who is trying the best he
knows how to throw into the discard age-old, discordant ways of doing things,
ways which never have succeeded in bringing happiness into the world.

—*Warren G. Harding, speech, Marion, Ohio, July 2, 1920*

The election of 1920 brought Marion fame as the president's
hometown. Republicans, journalists, and boosters celebrated
Marion's all-American qualities. However, the citizens of Marion
faced a crisis during the summer of 1923, brought on by Harding's death in San Francisco on August 2. A great outpouring of grief swept the country as huge crowds turned out to
watch the train carry Harding's body from San Francisco to
Washington, D.C., and then to Marion. As the nation grieved,
the popular view was that Harding had fulfilled his promise
to return the nation to what he called normalcy. He was hailed
for successfully calming the nation after World War I, restoring effective government, and promoting international peace.
Harding's popularity would seem to have ensured that he would
be fondly remembered. Over the next decade, however, the
American people would see Harding's memory significantly
disparaged. The shift in Harding's image was not a passive evolution but resulted from the work of constituencies who had
a stake in Harding's reputation. Although boosters and com-
memorators demonstrate an "impulse to remember what is

attractive or flattering and to ignore all the rest" when developing the heritage industry, in Harding's case the emergence of scandal overwhelmed the impulse to remember the positive, giving way to a narrative of failure and tragedy. The narrative of tragedy was necessary to prevent a disruption in nostalgia, a "beguiling sense of serenity about the well-being of history,"[1] that permeates civic memory.

The campaign to commemorate Harding was the last presidential commemorative campaign in the nineteenth-century style, which was marked by the construction of large mausoleums, built outside the nation's capital by private funding campaigns. Fittingly, given the themes of the front porch campaign, Harding's commemoration more closely resembled those of Lincoln, Grant, Garfield, and McKinley. Neither Coolidge nor Hoover was commemorated in this style. Coolidge has no national memorial beyond the preservation of his home and birthplace as the Plymouth Notch Historic District in Vermont. President Hoover has been given a more modern commemoration, with the Herbert Hoover National Historic Site, which contains the Hoover Presidential Library. However, the Hoover Presidential Library and Museum was not dedicated until 1962. The institutions associated with Harding's commemoration would limit the debate. As we will see, the state of Harding's papers precluded the building of a presidential library or archives. It was for Harding that the last national commemorative campaign to build a grand, classic memorial was conducted.

The Harding Memorial Association

Republican leaders, taking note of Harding's popularity and the public grief expressed at his death, incorporated the Harding Memorial Association (HMA) on October 8, 1923, under Ohio law. The association's mission was to honor the late president by raising funds to build a memorial that would serve as a mausoleum and to turn his house into a museum. The association accomplished these two tasks, but not without difficulty. The contrast between Harding's popularity at the time of his death and his low reputation today is not apparent in the memorial the association built. Warren G. Harding has a magnificent memorial, fitting for a national leader. Many consider it the most attractive presidential memorial outside Washington, D.C. While it is difficult to prove such statements, it does seem plausible. One travel writer has noted that it "is a pleasing, inspiring and peaceful place."[2] The Harding Memorial represents the high esteem in which Harding was held at the time of his death. Kirk Savage has written that "public monuments exercise a curious power to erase their own political origins and become sacrosanct."[3] However, time did not stand still around the memorial and thus it did not become sacred ground. Even before its completion, the memorial had been reduced to an important piece of local, not national, architecture.[4]

Throughout the first decade of the association's existence, tensions arose between Washington members, who had their eyes on national politics, and Marion members, who were focused on boosting Marion. During the association's first meetings the national membership proved dominant, with President Calvin Coolidge attending "practically all" the early meetings.[5] As long as Harding remained popular, both groups found common cause in embracing the log cabin myth. However, the public enthusiasm of Coolidge and other national members cooled as scandals emerged. Before Harding's death, the public had paid little attention to Charles Forbes's resignation from the Veterans' Bureau, in January 1923, or Albert Fall's resignation as secretary of the interior, in March 1923. Nor had the congressional investigations into Fall's leasing of the naval oil reserves at Teapot Dome and Elk Hills attracted much attention. This too would change. And the political scandals were followed by even more damaging scandals regarding Harding's private life.

Harding had accomplishments that supporters could have used to offset the scandals, but they did not do so. Because the effort to commemorate Harding coincided with the ongoing revelations of scandal, the association never explained to the public why Harding deserved to be memorialized. Those active in the association who sought to shape and use Harding's legacy borrowed themes from the 1920 presidential election and the period of public grieving but made little reference to Harding's presidency.[6] By contrast, those seeking to discredit Harding or to place blame for the scandals produced an extended degradation of his reputation that focused on his character and presidency. Much of the resulting debate focused on revealing Harding's "true character."[7] While Harding's death prompted some to place the problem institutionally within the office of the presidency, a consensus eventually emerged that Harding had lacked the character to be president; thus the scandals could be blamed on him and not on the office of the presidency or the Republican Party. Only at the local level did Harding's memory escape this degradation.

How was Warren G. Harding's legacy created after his death? There is more to the standard interpretation of Harding as a naive man with poor judgment who oversaw the most corrupt administration in American history.

John Bodnar has written that "the shaping of a past worthy of public commemoration in the present is contested and involves a struggle for supremacy" between political factions. According to Bodnar, public memory represents the "intersection of official and vernacular expressions"; proponents of official culture are elites who promote "interpretations of past and present reality that reduce the power of competing interests that threaten the attainment of their goals."[8] Under such an understanding of public memory, Harding's legacy would have served the purpose of electing President Coolidge in 1924 and furthering the political gains of the Republican Party. Therefore, it stands to reason that Coolidge and his fellow Republicans would embrace Harding when his death evoked public sympathy but use Harding as a scapegoat when the scandals broke. This is, without doubt, part of the story. However, Coolidge and his associates did not attack Harding's reputation but rather simply ignored him, letting his reputation sink under the weight of the scandals and the resulting media attention. Eventually, Republicans would define Harding's legacy as a tragedy.

Some scholars point to various individuals or groups with motivation to ruin Harding's reputation. These include progressive intellectuals, Democrats, and profiteers. Among intellectuals Harding's election and subsequent disgrace stood as a black mark against the people who voted for him.[9] While many intellectuals certainly disliked Harding, this was not the whole story. Common sense would suggest that Democrats and progressives would be less favorably inclined toward Harding. Also, it should come as no surprise that some would exploit Harding's legacy for financial reward and that controversy would ensue as to who fell in this category.

To focus on Harding's legacy as only the outgrowth of the election of 1924 would be to neglect his image before his death but also to place the power to create memory solely within the hands of a few nationally powerful individuals. It would ignore the conflict that took place between national and local interpretations of Harding and the vagaries created by shifting political conditions. In examining the association it is apparent that clear distinctions between local and national were difficult to maintain and that motives were not readily revealed. Harding came to the presidency by emphasizing his humble origins and, as president, brought his fellow Marionites into the national government; the local and the national were thus intertwined. Once the log cabin myth no longer seemed attractive or viable, the local and national themes had difficulty coexisting.

Missing from the debate over Harding's legacy is the ritualized role that his death held in fulfilling a cultural need. That Harding died while president, with the subsequent national mourning, made his death particularly significant. That it evoked the death of past presidents only added to the weight of the moment. Fittingly, Harding had died on a Voyage of Understanding, a tour undertaken with his wife in the summer of 1923 to prepare for the 1924 election. As we have seen, Harding had the ability to please a crowd and to look the part of a president. Harding's ability to harmonize, as he dubbed it, was a key political asset. Harding's Voyage of Understanding was harmonizing on a grand scale, as he and key members of the administration crossed the continent. Joe Chapple, who was traveling with the president when he died, wrote that Harding was "called upon when the tumult and shouting was over to reconcile antagonisms and offer practical solutions of pressing problems."[10] During the trip Harding spoke to large and enthusiastic crowds. The presidential party was returning from Alaska when Harding died. In death, Harding provided one more moment of harmony and community. Herbert Hoover recalled that as the train carrying Harding's casket crossed the country, "crowds came silently at every crossroads and filled every station day and night. There was real and touching grief everywhere." "The affection of the people for Mr. Harding was complete," he concluded. "Had it not been for the continuous exposure of terrible corruption by his playmates, he would have passed into memory with the same aura of affection and respect that attaches to Garfield and McKinley."[11]

The affection that Hoover described was not the result of a personal connection with Harding but rather the symbolic mourning of a fallen leader. Sociologist Barry Schwartz points to the unifying nature of national grieving at the time of Lincoln's death: "every citizen knew, as he gave expression to his personal sorrow that he was acting in concert with others."[12] The same would have been true of those lining the train tracks for Harding. Harding's image had been linked with McKinley's during the 1920 front porch campaign. The comparison of the two Ohio Republicans now went beyond campaign biographies. Harding, like McKinley before him, had died in office. Following McKinley's assassination there was no discussion of his policies and accomplishments. He was described as "beloved," "trusted," and "cheerful."[13] The initial rhetoric commemorating Harding followed a similar pattern, praising Harding's personality but saying little of his administration. As Hoover noted, McKinley did not have enduring scandals. Harding did.[14] Nevertheless, the nation would mourn Harding in 1923 as it had mourned McKinley in 1901. Harding's death offered Americans an opportunity to come together.

True Sentiments?

Despite the eventual fate of his reputation, Harding came close to fulfilling his ambition to be the best-loved president.[15] In 1923 many saw his short administration as a success. Harding received international praise as a man of peace, which was high praise in the wake of the Great War. Journalists called Harding "the greatest commoner since Lincoln," and many referred to him as a martyr. Although no assassin's bullet had killed him, some wondered if the presidency itself was not the weapon. Wilson had been broken and now Harding was dead. The robust Theodore Roosevelt had died only a few years earlier, at the comparatively young age of sixty. Given the examples of Roosevelt, Wilson, and Harding, some wondered if the office had become too much for one man. Chapple, in his commemorative biography, wrote that Harding "realized his work was a man-killing job, but the tasks and long hours of labor were never shirked. His handclasp with the people never relaxed."[16] Hoover explained that Harding "faced unprecedented problems of domestic rehabilitation" at a "time when war-stirred emotions had created bitter prejudices and conflict in thought." Harding's character and leadership had guided the nation. Hoover struck a familiar chord when he described Harding as "kindly and genial, but inflexible in his devotion to duty, he was strong in his determination to restore confidence and secure progress. All this he accomplished through patient conciliation and friendly good will for he felt deeply that hard driving might open unhealable breaches among our people." Hoover was not alone in his praise. Coolidge and nearly every high-ranking member of the government sang of Harding's virtues. When Secretary of State Hughes delivered the formal eulogy before Congress on February 27, 1924, he also spoke of the importance of Harding's calmness, courage, and friendliness in guiding the nation out of the postwar chaos. Hughes predicted that Harding's accomplishments would long be remembered.[17] Hughes was correct in his prediction that Harding would be long remembered, but he could not have been more wrong in his assessment of how he would be remembered.

Leaders of the Harding Memorial Campaign, as the association was called at first, had national stature and began creating an official commemorative history. As was typical of these efforts, an impressive list of national leaders joined the association, including President Calvin Coolidge, his cabinet, and every member of Congress. New Jersey senator Joseph S. Frelinghuysen, who had been a friend of Harding, served as the association's president. George Christian Jr., D. R. Crissinger, Hoke Donithen, and

Charles Sawyer represented Marion on the executive committee. All the Marionites, except for Donithen, had been brought to Washington by Harding and remained in the Coolidge administration. The association opened an office in Washington, allowing it to work closely with the Coolidge administration. In grand fashion, the association announced that it would raise $3 million to fund a tribute to the president, an effort of the "greatest national importance."[18]

Charles Sawyer became the first chairman of the campaign, and as the most aggressive of Harding's boosters he was on the national stage, but he was also an important advocate for Marion. As we have already seen, Sawyer rallied Marion to take part in the campaign of 1920. Sawyer rose to national prominence on Harding's coattails, following him to the White House, where he worked as the president's physician and picked up the honorary title of brigadier general. It was Sawyer who combined the local and the national in the official interpretation of Harding's life, a mixture similar to the one that had worked well in 1920.

Sawyer's message contained themes familiar to anyone who had followed Harding's rise to the presidency. In a representative address to Rotary International, Sawyer discussed Harding's place in history. He could not have picked a better audience; Harding had been a Rotary member and exemplified the spirit of business and community boosterism that Rotary represented. Sawyer revisited the state of the country following the Great War and dwelled on Harding's relationship with his hometown. As the nation emerged from World War I, the president's character had guided the nation: "Every act, every thought, every deed originating with Mr. Harding was based upon honesty of purpose, generosity of disposition and the hope of honorable accomplishment," Sawyer said. Drawing on his background in homeopathy, Sawyer explained that Harding's charisma grew from "what we doctors call an astral body, which emanated in spirit of sympathy, of generosity, of honesty, of earnestness, of conscientiousness, all attributes which go to make one good, great, and useful." Sawyer defensively dismissed those who claimed to be Harding's friends, saying that "no one is submitted to greater misrepresentation as to his friendly relationship than is the man in the White House." Unfortunately, as Sawyer explained, these false friends were responsible for the "conditions" in Washington (that is, the scandals) but he "was sure that were the whole truth known of conditions as they actually existed under the leadership of this great American, that nothing but applause could possibly result from anything which he genuinely sanctioned." Sawyer argued that Harding's character had guided the nation and stood as the primary reason to commemorate him.[19]

While the use of character to argue for presidential greatness is common enough, Sawyer was already defensive about scandals, including his role in Harding's death. When Harding had died in San Francisco, foul play had been suspected, and Sawyer was at the center of those suspicions. As we saw with the questions C-Span viewers asked, and shall revisit in the following chapters, Harding's death became a scandal in its own right, the subject of speculation and rumor.[20] Despite his outwardly robust appearance, Harding had long suffered from various health problems. While Warren's health problems were not fully revealed to the public, Florence's ill health had been well documented. Florence believed that only Sawyer, who had dubious medical credentials, could treat her kidney ailment. When Harding became ill on the Voyage of Understanding, Sawyer proclaimed him to be a victim of food poisoning. As Harding lay on his deathbed in the Palace Hotel, Sawyer rejected aid from physicians more qualified than he, out of a desire to maintain his position as the president's physician. While it is difficult to be conclusive, it is likely that Sawyer's treatment of Harding hastened the president's death.[21] At a minimum, Sawyer certainly misdiagnosed Harding's heart problems. Furthermore, as we will see, more than a few people saw Sawyer as a sycophant who exploited his friendship with the Hardings. Thus, when Sawyer accused others of being false friends, he might have been deflecting criticism of his own behavior.

Having rejected the corruption and the false friends of the capital, Sawyer turned to the story of Harding's rise in Marion. Marion was the true reflection of Harding's character, Sawyer maintained. This was a familiar booster theme from the front porch campaign. Harding had made Marion "a home city, a really American community, filled with home-lovers, living in the glory and satisfaction of their dwellings." Harding taught the people of Marion that lawns, gardens, and bees "were all essential to the betterment of American citizenship." By rejecting Washington and emphasizing Marion, Sawyer had put in place the narrative that would help Marion remain nationally prominent, but he had also opened the door for diminishing the prestige of Harding's legacy. Harding's role as president was now subordinate to his role as town booster. Remembering Harding for teaching Marionites to love their homes and gardens would not build a legacy of statesmanship. Sawyer tried to move beyond his parochial appeal by arguing that Harding's many accomplishments in Marion had prepared him to step onto the national stage, where his "God-like influence" served the republic, but he offered no examples of Harding's service to his nation.[22] As Sawyer painted the picture, the unnamed scandals were an outgrowth of Washington politics and did not touch Harding's character or intentions. However, he failed to adequately explain how Harding's character had touched the nation.

The commemorative campaign to raise funds was similar to the 1920 campaign, when Republican leaders and advertising agencies had sold Harding to the public.[23] The initial members of the association formed six committees: Publicity, Special Gifts, Speakers, Cooperation with Existing Organizations and Associations, Organization, and Ways and Means. To create a nationwide organization, the association appointed governors as honorary state chairmen. The governors, in turn, appointed active state chairmen. The campaign culminated in Harding Memorial Week, planned for December 9 to 16, 1923. Acknowledging the difficulty of completing their work in a week, the members declared that the campaign would be a success if they organized 75 percent of the country and raised 50 percent of the $3 million. Such success would spur a "few large gifts." Thus, the association planned a nationwide effort that copied the 1920 campaign's innovative strategy of "decentralized gifts." In 1920 the Republicans had asked local parties to conduct fund-raising campaigns similar to those waged by the Red Cross. The emphasis would be on many smaller contributions rather than having a few large donors finance the campaign.[24] In retrospect it only makes sense that the leaders of the association adopted the organization and style of a political campaign. After all, most, if not all, of the leadership were veteran politicians, and the Republican Party was fresh from its enormous victory in 1920.

The campaign also fit another pattern. During the nineteenth century—especially at the height of efforts to commemorate the Civil War—it was common for the leaders who organized and promoted a memorial to conduct a campaign to generate public support. Thus the memorial, they could argue, was an outgrowth of the will of the people. If the people showed no interest in the campaign, then the memorial would become an empty vessel and not a believable historic interpretation.[25] This helps explain why a presidential cabinet (all of whom served on the association) that boasted some of the richest men in America conducted a campaign to raise money from average citizens a few dollars at a time.

Along with its national organization, the association adopted the theme of national grieving. Publicity chairman John Weeks and the association hoped to recreate the spontaneous reaction to Harding's sudden death. Weeks wrote to newspapers throughout the country requesting copies of editorials regarding Harding's death, stories that, as Weeks saw it, reflected the true sentiments of the American people. Publicist Frank L. Murphy worked with companies, chambers of commerce, neighborhood associations, and other organizations to recreate the spontaneous demonstrations of grief, including public gatherings. The nationwide appeal for funds would be delivered at carefully planned events featuring President Coolidge, members of the cabinet, the Harding family, the armed forces, and other prominent Americans.[26] And just as Sawyer had emphasized Harding's character and his Marion roots rather than presidential accomplishments, national leaders emphasized symbolic grieving rather than Harding's achievements.

Leaders hoped membership would soar during Harding Memorial Week, raising money to build a "conservative, but fitting" tomb. Following Coolidge's radio address on December 10, association members appeared on local radio programs across the country. There was vague talk of an endowed Warren G. Harding Chair of Diplomacy and Functions of Government at "some central university." Discussion of the endowed chair pointed to Harding's accomplishments (disarmament and government efficiency), but financial problems and a lack of enthusiasm on the part of universities brought an end to such talk. The association prepared certificates for distribution to every adult who had contributed one dollar and to every school at which all the students contributed, regardless of the size of their contributions. The association's public relations people wanted to place three words describing Harding on the certificates. Among the words that had been suggested by HMA members were *humanitarian, philosopher,* and *statesman.* Sawyer objected to the words *neighbor and citizen,* arguing that if a person was a good neighbor he was also a good citizen.[27] Publicist Frank L. Murphy's proposed text for the membership certificates emphasized the association's theme of Harding as a neighbor:

> Human Being Always
> The Loyal Neighbor
> He Loved to Serve
> Rebuilder of America
> Martyr to Duty
> Man of Open Heart
> Courageous but Humble
> Our Cherished Leader

President and Neighbor
Sympathetic to All[28]

Frank Murphy, in various suggestions, depicted Harding as a humanitarian and a good person, but made only vague references to Harding's accomplishments. The closest he came was to point out that Harding had rebuilt America after the Great War. Although this could have been an argument for presidential success, it was not pursued.

During Harding Memorial Week, the association returned to the theme of children, this time addressing the nation's children on behalf of the childless president, tying Harding's commemoration to the log cabin myth and the need to create a national shrine. Harding, the association announced, "had great love for the children of America." He had not had "boys or girls of his own, so he adopted the millions of young people like you for his family." The association explained to these "adopted children" that Harding had not grown up expecting to be president but that as president he had worked hard for peace for the sake of the nation's children. The association intended to "erect a mausoleum in which his body will be placed, at Marion, Ohio, where he lived so long," and would "make his home at Marion into a shrine where people may come and see the things that belonged to him, and understand how simply and beautifully he lived." The announcement closed with an appeal for the children to donate their pennies.[29] Giving certificates to school children might seem insignificant. However, they would become an important part of the lore surrounding the memorial—Harding's memorial was built with pennies donated by children.[30]

Except for the use of the title *president*, the association made little mention of Harding's administration in its public pronouncements. By omitting a discussion of Harding's administration, the Washington Naval Conference, the creation of the Bureau of the Budget, William Howard Taft's appointment to the Supreme Court, tax cuts, or in fact of any accomplishments, Harding was left with the roles of small-town booster and corrupt politician. Eventually, the two images would merge as Harding's friends came to be blamed for the scandals. Through its strategy the association helped create an interpretation of Harding that offered the public little reason to honor him. As Schwartz has written, people "cannot participate in venerational ceremonies unless they see a reason for doing so."[31] The association asked the people to repeat their prior ritual without considering motivation or context.

The Harding Memorial Association had waged a national campaign similar to the successful 1920 presidential campaign. The results, however, were very different. Harding, in effect, lost this early campaign for a good reputation. Harding Memorial Week did generate publicity for the association. Newspaper clippings poured in from around the country as the nation observed the memorial week. However, Americans were not as generous as the association had anticipated: contributions totaled less than $1 million. Unfortunately for the association, the planning for the memorial week had overlapped Charles Forbes's testimony before the Senate, and Harding Memorial Week coincided with Albert Fall's testimony before Congress.[32] The mixed results of Harding Memorial Week proved to be the high point of the fund-raising campaign. Furthermore, the results suggested that the period of public mourning had run its course. Harding's death was old news; Teapot Dome was not. Americans might have remembered Harding with sympathy, but the vivid reminders of his shortcomings conflicted with the campaign of commemoration.

As the political scandals began to dominate the political landscape, cabinet members who once praised Harding now found it necessary to proclaim their innocence. Making the situation worse for those who would champion Harding's reputation, the scandal at the Veterans' Bureau clearly could be placed at Harding's feet, for it grew from Harding's disastrous mistake in appointing Charles Forbes to direct the agency. The federal government had created the Veterans' Bureau in 1921 to facilitate the care of wounded veterans. A great deal of money passed through the bureau. Forbes was part of Harding's circle of friends and was positioned to do well in the Harding administration. In 1916 then senator-elect Harding had met Forbes on a congressional junket to Hawaii, where Forbes was in charge of the building of the naval base at Pearl Harbor. Harding was immediately charmed by him.[33] When in charge of the Veterans' Bureau, Forbes campaigned to have all that agency's money channeled through his office, even enlisting the aid of the American Legion.

Charles Sawyer became suspicious of Forbes but was vilified by the legion and the media for opposing aid to wounded veterans. Once in control of the bureau's finances, Forbes established, as one historian called it, an "opportunistic patchwork of individual bribery and greed." When Harding learned of Forbes's corruption, he reportedly cornered him in the Red Room of the White House. A visitor to the White House describes finding the president pinning Forbes to the wall, yelling, "You yellow rat! You double-crossing bastard!"[34] Although Harding confronted Forbes, he did not turn him over to authorities; instead Harding allowed Forbes to resign and flee to Europe. Congress began investigating activities at the Veterans' Bureau on October 22, 1923, some two months after Harding's death, and by the close of the year the corruption of Charles Forbes and his associates was evident. Eventually, Forbes was found guilty of conspiracy to defraud the government.[35] Although it is possible, as Robert Ferrell has done, to argue that Harding acted correctly in dealing with Forbes, Forbes's corruption contributed to the demise of Harding's reputation.[36]

Although Harding Memorial Week was the peak of the commemorative effort, it did not end the effort to eulogize Harding. The association had not decided where to build its memorial. Charles Sawyer now became an important player in deciding Harding's place in history. Sawyer was determined to bring the memorial to Marion and honor Harding as a leading member of the community. As Sawyer saw it, there were two important local projects: "one the enlargement of the Harding residence, and the other the building of a mausoleum on property yet to be selected." Sawyer envisioned the home as a successful national attraction, estimating that a quarter million people had visited the home during the presidential campaign and thirty thousand since Harding's death. Just as during the election, Sawyer was upset by what he saw as opportunism on the part of local landowners who wanted the association to pay an "unreasonable" price for land. Sawyer worried in a letter to Marion attorney Charles H. Conley that "unless there is a great change in this attitude, this memorial will not go to Marion at all." Consistent with his earlier statement regarding Harding's legacy, Sawyer concluded that "it is very important that Marion avail herself of the opportunity now presented her to do what is right in the burial of our beloved fellow citizen." Sawyer did not mean national citizenship but membership in the community of Marion. Following long-winded negotiations the association bought farmland just outside town.

While it is perfectly understandable why Sawyer, as a booster and resident of Marion, would want to follow the pattern of building the mausoleum and memorial in the presidential hometown, the unintended results of his approach contributed to the diminishing of Harding's legacy. The placement of the Harding Memorial in Marion, which made so much sense given the tradition of presidential commemoration, also placed the memorial in limbo. It would not fit into the emerging pattern of commemoration in Washington, D.C., a plan advocated by some stakeholders, and it would

Commemorating the Tragedy of Warren Harding

also lack the museum and archival components of future presidential sites. Of course, Sawyer could not have foreseen these consequences, in his concerted focus on the commercial and civic possibilities associated with building a presidential memorial in Marion.

In July 1924, Sawyer left his position as White House physician under pressure from Coolidge and moved the association's office to Marion. For Coolidge, Sawyer's association with Harding (as well as his medical training) had become a liability. Sawyer took the office and the leadership of the association with him without objections from his fellow board members.[37] Marion played an increasingly prominent part in the association as the national momentum waned.

The goals of national Republican leaders and of Marionites differed because their political agendas differed. As historian Patricia West has demonstrated, historic homes were often founded to meet political needs.[38] Although national Republicans desired publicity and worked to build a memorial, they showed no interest in commemoration beyond completing the memorial and purchasing Harding's home. The Republican Party no longer had a need for Harding's front porch. For local boosters, however, the front porch was a reminder of Marion's moment in the national spotlight and held the promise of becoming a tourist attraction. Sawyer did not need to organize 75 percent of the country, as had been the goal during Harding Memorial Week; thirty thousand visitors to Marion would do nicely. For decades, Sawyer had worked with Harding to boost Marion. The high point of Sawyer's career as a booster was in helping to organize Marion for the front porch campaign. National and local members looked back to 1920, but they remembered that year differently. Here was the dual nature of Harding's legacy. Republicans at the national level had little motivation to continue their high-profile association with Harding's legacy. By contrast, local boosters could ensure that Marion would remain the president's hometown.

Despite the efforts of Sawyer, Crissinger, and other Marion boosters, the reality, and subsequently the image, had changed from the summer of 1920 to the summer of 1923. For Marion residents, the election had been about Harding as a neighbor and patron; they had found common cause with the leadership of the national party in this approach. On the national level, having been a friend of President Harding was quickly losing its appeal. The difficulty was that it was Harding's friends, including Sawyer, who were getting into trouble.

61

Designing Harding's Reputation

In September 1924 the Harding Memorial Association trustees announced a nationwide competition to select a design for the memorial. At the same time, the board issued a report. Their report made no mention of the continuing bad news for former Harding associates. When Charles Sawyer died, on September 23, 1924, Marion lost its chief advocate as the memorial project moved into a critical phase. With Sawyer's death, Marionite Alfred "Hoke" Donithen became the executive director. Donithen had been Harding's lawyer and was committed to the Marion memorial, but he lacked Sawyer's connections. Donithen was appointed while Florence Harding was critically ill; she would die on November 21, 1924. Florence bequeathed the Hardings' home and what remained of their papers to the association. With the deaths of Florence Harding and Charles Sawyer, Marionites lost local voices that could be heard nationally.[39] The final design competition took place in New York City on July 20, 1925; Henry Hornbostel and Eric Fischer Wood won with a classical design featuring Greek Ionic columns and made of white marble.[40] Plans were made for a $100,000 endowment for the continued upkeep of the planned memorial. However, the HMA had little money and donations had all but stopped. In the wake of the design selection, Donithen closed the association's Marion office.[41] Whatever design the association chose, it would be hard for news about the memorial's design to compete with news regarding the scandals.

The emerging scandals were coming closer and closer to home. Since his election, Ohio stood at the center of Harding's image. Unfortunately for Harding's partisans, Ohio was now being linked to scandal. Rumors of corruption had circulated before Harding's death, starting with the 1923 suicide of Jess Smith, a longtime associate of Harding's longtime political ally Harry Daugherty and Daugherty's right-hand man in politics. Smith had committed suicide shortly before the Voyage of Understanding began, but the real questions about his death followed the investigation of Attorney General Daugherty, which began with a February 19, 1924, resolution by Democratic senator Burton K. Wheeler. Under Daugherty, the Justice Department was reported to be home to widespread corruption, most of it related to violations of Prohibition, property that had been seized by the government during the war, and presidential pardons. Daugherty had few friends in Washington and, as one historian has written, Republicans "quailed at the thought of having to defend him." The Senate adopted

Wheeler's resolution by a vote of sixty-six to one, and the Sixty-eighth Congress was consumed by "investigation mania."[42] Harding's closest political ally from Ohio was now immersed in scandal.

While Teapot Dome represented the corruption of oil money, Daugherty's scandals more closely touched on Harding's character. The group of people associated with the corruption in the Justice Department became known as the Ohio Gang. Harding had appointed Daugherty to the post of attorney general over the protests of some Republicans, and now Senators began demanding that Coolidge fire him.

The extent of Harding's knowledge of Daugherty's corrupt dealings is unclear. In his memoirs, written several years after he left office, Secretary of Commerce Herbert Hoover recalled a distraught and nervous Harding inviting him to the presidential cabin as they steamed for Alaska, where he asked, "If you knew of a great scandal in our administration, would you for the good of the country and the party expose it publicly or would you bury it?" Hoover told the president, "Publish it, and at least get credit for integrity on your side." What scandal were they talking about? That remains unclear; Hoover attempted to press the issue, but Harding would not discuss Daugherty's possible involvement in the scandals with Hoover.[43] Before departing on the Voyage of Understanding, Harding had confronted Jess Smith regarding his activities at the Justice Department. Shortly thereafter, Smith burned his papers and committed suicide. There is also the infamous moment when Harding pinned Forbes to a White House wall. Hoover's account presents a calm Harding who realized the importance of the scandals but was torn between duty and friendship.

Wheeler's investigation offered sensational testimony, especially that of Roxie Stinson. Stinson could not have better fit the role of star witness if she had been cast by Hollywood. She was stylish and, as one historian understated, "interested in a good time." She hailed from the small Ohio town of Washington Court House, which was also the hometown of Harry Daugherty. She was divorced from Jess Smith but still maintained a relationship with him, although few knew its exact nature. Smith was not only Harry Daugherty's political associate but also, it was rumored, his lover.[44] Stinson testified that the center of corruption associated with the Justice Department was the infamous "little green house on K Street," where "big deals" involving oil, stocks, liquor, and large sums of cash were arranged. A string of witnesses followed Stinson, all of them placing Jess Smith and Daugherty at the center of the corruption.[45]

The Ohio Memorial

With the scandals making national news and linking the corruption to Harding's Ohio roots, the association scaled back its agenda by the mid-1920s. Donithen, like Sawyer before him, avoided discussing the scandals and made no effort to justify honoring Harding. Instead, he focused on the construction of the memorial, perhaps even more than he focused on the memory of Harding. Donithen was consumed with arguing with Edward Mellon, the advisory architect and the nephew of Harding treasury secretary Andrew Mellon, as well as with architects Hornbostel and Wood, about the details of the memorial. Donithen's fears were driven by financial realities. A 1925 audit revealed there was less than $15,000 available for an endowment to care for the memorial, not the $100,000 that had been envisioned earlier.[46] Those members of the Coolidge cabinet still involved with the association met in October 1925 in Secretary of War John Weeks's office, where they decided to leave the details of construction to the architects. With the fund-raising campaign behind them, Harding's reputation in decline, and the architects in charge of the memorial, there remained little to connect national members to the activities of the local component of the association.[47]

Here we see the split between the vernacular and the national images, but the two remained connected by the marble structure that was being built in Marion. Another reminder of the cause of the financial troubles came on March 21, 1926, when Charles Forbes entered the U.S. penitentiary at Leavenworth. In April the association broke ground for the base of the memorial. On May 30, 1926, Vice President Charles Gates Dawes laid the cornerstone. This would be the last Harding ceremony attended by a national figure from the Republican Party until the dedication ceremony in 1931. The memorial would rise in Marion with little support from Harding's party.[48]

Until 1926, Hoke Donithen was able to avoid the unpleasant reality of Harding's plummeting reputation, but as the memorial neared completion, that became increasingly difficult. The memorial, which would serve as a tomb for both the president and the First Lady, needed to be dedicated, and such a dedication required a president. This became less likely as the scandals took a new turn, with many of the revelations now concerning Harding directly. Former attorney general Daugherty was tried for corruption. The jury deadlocked and Daugherty was acquitted, but Daugherty's refusal to testify, according to Harding biographer Murray, encouraged rumors of his guilt throughout 1926 and 1927. Because of his close relationship with the president, his silence severely damaged Harding's reputation.

The association's lack of political influence was evident on December 16, 1927, when the ceremony moving the bodies of Warren and Florence Harding into the memorial took place with no national representatives in attendance. Even Edward Mellon and Frelinghuysen were absent. The transferring of the bodies was a local event that reinforced the bond between the Hardings, the memorial, and Marion. For the nation, President Harding had already been laid to rest in Marion.[49] The Marion members of the memorial association decided that the memorial would have no inscriptions except for the Hardings' names and the dates of their births and deaths. What was not said spoke volumes. The Marion members made no attempt to engrave in marble for all time any sentiments regarding Harding. For all its grandeur, the memorial stood less as a mark of Harding's place in national history and increasingly as a local architectural triumph.[50]

The chances of a presidential dedication became dimmer as the election of 1928 neared. The year 1927 did not bring a dedication; instead, Marion returned to the national spotlight as scene of the most personal of the scandals. Nan Britton's book *The President's Daughter* appeared in the summer of 1927 and sold nearly seventy-five thousand copies. The Britton book proved to be a devastating blow to the reputations of Harding and his hometown. As Britton told it, she and Warren Harding had had an affair culminating in the birth of Elizabeth Ann, for whom the book was titled. With the Britton story making national news and Democrats attacking Republicans as belonging to the party of corruption, Coolidge informed Mellon that the memorial should be dedicated during the summer of 1929, after he had left office. By denying Harding a presidential dedication, Coolidge had also denied the value of Harding's national service. With President Coolidge's refusal to dedicate the memorial, the task fell to Herbert Hoover, who also postponed dedication. Only in 1931 did Hoover, then in the third year of his term, agree to speak at the Harding Memorial.[51]

Dedication

The Harding Memorial Association never succeeded in arranging a presidential dedication and had given up in its efforts. It was Indiana senator Harry New who began the process that culminated in Hoover's trip to

Marion. New wrote to Donithen, as "a loyal, devoted friend of Warren Harding" and an original member of the association, that he had raised the issue with Dr. Joel Boone, the White House physician. Boone reported that Hoover was reluctant to go to Marion because he felt unwelcome. Hoover's feelings were justified, as stories circulated in local newspapers that Donithen did not want Hoover to attend a dedication. Perhaps Donithen felt resentment over the way Coolidge and Hoover had abandoned Harding's friends. Boone, who had also served as a physician in the White House in the Harding and Coolidge administrations, revisited the issue with Hoover. Reports appeared that Hoover would travel to Marion. New wrote the HMA of his fervent hope that the matter might "be put into such shape that further failure is impossible." As to the prospects of Coolidge attending the ceremony, New commented, he "never did want to go and now he has the additional reason of not wanting to be found playing second fiddle to the President of the United States." It was only after the announcement that the trustees, now an almost exclusively Marion body, passed a resolution inviting Hoover and Coolidge.[52] The dedication meant that local and national legacies would once again cross.

With a dedication in the planning, Americans resumed discussion of Harding's legacy. By 1931 the political climate had changed. Hoover was an unpopular president and Harding's scandals did not look so bad when compared to the Great Depression. Now Harding emerged as a victim of the heartless politics played out in Washington. As the public began to reflect on the Harding years, letters, often containing newspaper clippings, began to arrive at the nearly moribund Harding Memorial Association. Some in Ohio took offense at Coolidge's and Hoover's treatment of their favorite son. For example, the *Akron Beacon Journal* declared that Ohio had no reason to be ashamed of Harding's public service and maintained that Coolidge and Hoover had brought disgrace to the presidency by delaying the dedication. Average citizens also made their opinions known. Ohioan Ann Cohen pronounced Coolidge's and Hoover's actions disgraceful and said, "they bask in the glory of work begun by President Harding." She added, "We, the great army of unemployed, fail to see any improvement in the Hoover regime." She passed along a California editorial that praised Hoover's decision to dedicate the memorial but that added, "Alas, poor Harding. This celebration and Mr. Hoover's acceptance remind you of a western funeral at which no one rose to say a good word for the deceased, until after 10 minutes waiting, one tall man got up and was asked, 'Are you a friend of the deceased?' He replied, 'Not exactly, for I never heard of him. But I'm a friend of any man who has as few friends as he seems to have here.'" One correspondent, Richard Harvey, had trouble believing that the idea of a dedication was "still a live one." Harvey, like others, assumed the memorial would never be dedicated.[53] Most correspondents condemned Coolidge and Hoover for failing to properly perform the rituals of the presidency. They now ascribed to them a lack of empathy and loyalty, characteristics that were now commonly acknowledged as Harding's weak suits.

A letter from Peter Gouled reflected on the difficulty of Harding's legacy. Gouled understood Harding's importance to Marion and acknowledged the damage that had been done to the reputation of Harding's character. Gouled wrote that in 1923 he had found the official funeral in Washington empty. Rejecting the official ceremony, he traveled to Marion to find satisfactory closure. Shocked by the scandals, he had "defended the President as the man whose congenial, splendid soul was grossly abused by the selfish, unscrupulous politicians that like parasites were thriving on the President's political body." He found Gaston Means's *Strange Death of President Harding* particularly offensive. In an influential but fraudulent account, Means, who will be discussed extensively later, began the rumor that Florence Harding murdered her husband. Gouled wrote that he had asked Chief Justice Charles Hughes, who had been Harding's secretary of state, to "remedy the unpardonable evil that is perpetrated by the free circulation of that infamous publication." Hughes had delivered Harding's eulogy before Congress, but he chose to not reply to Gouled, who then turned to the Harding Memorial Association, "as the custodian of the lasting value [Harding] left to his fellowmen," in the hopes that it "might display interest in the defense of the President's memory." Gouled had made the same journey to Marion as the association had. The association, however, lacked the vigor to promote Harding's "lasting value." Ignoring the chance to defend Harding to a partisan, Donithen responded that he wanted "to make enough out of the dedication to pay for the mortgage on the [George] Christian property, if it is possible."[54] Donithen's low expectations demonstrated how demoralized and parochial the association had become. Those who did defend Harding found no assistance from the association.

Nearly a decade after his death, Harding had developed a reputation not only for corruption and incompetence, but also as a victim. In death, presidents become national symbols. They become icons that summarize the point in history during which they served. Harding had become a symbol of parochialism and corruption. All that was left of the historical Harding was a puppet that had been used, usually for the worse, by others. Harding, the commoner from Marion, had become the victim of his friends, then of his alleged mistress, and finally of Coolidge's and Hoover's politics as they distanced themselves from Harding.

When President Hoover spoke on the steps of the Harding Memorial on June 16, 1931, he had little good to say about Harding's character. Since Coolidge was content to ignore Harding, it was left to Hoover to address Harding's place in history. Hoover ignored Harding's efforts to boost Marion and his electoral triumph but depicted Harding as a genial man and as a victim. Harding barely realized, Hoover said, that his friends had betrayed him: "these men had betrayed not alone the friendship and trust of their staunch and loyal friend but they had betrayed their country. That was the tragedy of the life of Warren Harding." Rather than praise the fallen president, Hoover argued that his weakness had allowed the nation to be betrayed. Hoover would not go so far as to call Harding corrupt, but nonetheless he stood on the steps of the Harding Memorial and condemned Harding.[55] President Hoover used the time and place when and where Harding's memory should have been the most sacred to explain to the nation why Harding should not be honored. Hoover's dedication served to purge the office of the presidency of the stain of his scandals. Harding's life became a tragic chapter in what was otherwise a triumphant national saga. Hoover's analysis was not substantially different than that of others who attacked Harding's character. This dedication summarized, for many, Harding's legacy. Hoover did not make Sawyer's distinction between true and false friends, nor did he depict Marion as the proof of Harding's virtue. National memorials often provide a way for communities to speak to the larger audience, to a national audience. The Harding Memorial allowed Marionites to proclaim their community's status as the hometown of a president. It did not, however, alter how the nation felt about that president.

Many of Harding's friends, both those who maintained the memorial and those who stood charged with corruption and failure, were in the audience as Hoover added betrayal to Harding's legacy, and some of them resented Hoover's comments. Daugherty, for one, felt it necessary to denounce Hoover in the introduction of his memoirs, and indeed he indicated that he took Hoover's address as a personal attack. Disregarding issues of morality or loyalty, Daugherty reminded readers that he had twice been found innocent of charges of in a court of law, argued that the attacks on Harding's reputation were "a passing phase," and concluded with the vague assertion that "Harding's place in history is secure."[56]

Memorials are meant to offer a solid, unwavering interpretation of history. While history is often messy and inconclusive, memorials should be the stuff of clear and sharp lines. While historians and locals struggled with Harding's scandals, the grand memorial stood as a silent reminder of the promise of past glory but did little to speak to the present. The Harding Memorial never overcame the reputation of the man for whom it was built; it never became a sacred place.

My Damned Biographers

This autumn a Mr. W. G. Harding, of Marion,
Ohio, was appointed President of the United
States, but Zenith was less interested in the
national campaign than in the local election. . . .
[Babbitt] was certain that if Lincoln were alive,
he would be electioneering for Mr. W. G.
Harding—unless he came to Zenith and
electioneered for Lucas Prout.

—*Sinclair Lewis*, Babbitt

The Harding Memorial stands in mute testimony to the unfulfilled story of Harding assuming a place in the pantheon of great
presidents. During the election Marion represented the civic
booster's ideal of a harmonious and prosperous community, a
place where competition and community, progress and nostalgia came together. Initially, it appeared that Harding's
legacy might continue those themes and equal the greatness
that his classically inspired memorial suggests. If Americans
had deemed Harding great, it would have done much to validate the self-image of Marion's boosters. However, after an
initial period of grieving, scandals left the Harding Memorial,
as Hoover declared, a place of tragedy. The memorial itself
demonstrated the Harding tragedy, its presidential grandeur
juxtaposed against the tawdriness of Harding's reputation.
The narrative of Harding's life as a tragedy served not only
the ends of his political opponents but also those of his fellow
Republicans. Harding's legacy was not so much abandoned, as
others have argued, as it was redefined. The now tragic Harding was reintroduced into the national narrative and it was
that narrative that Hoover echoed in his dedication.

William Allen White famously reported that Harding said, "I have no trouble with my enemies. I can take care of my enemies all right. But my damn friends, my God-damn friends, White, they're the ones that keep me walking the floors nights!"[1] Within the tragedy narrative, this confession has served to implicate him in the scandals and has continued to resonate with historians. For example, in the authors of the widely used textbook *The Enduring Vision: A History of the American People* place the Harding scandals within a historical context: "Like 'Watergate' in the 1970s, 'Teapot Dome' became a shorthand label for a sordid tangle of presidential scandals."[2] Harding's statement to White thus becomes a symbolic deathbed confession to one of the great scandals of the twentieth century.

If Harding's friends disrupted his sleep in life, his various biographers must have him rolling over in his grave. While academics have tended to neglect Harding, he has received significant attention in the public arena, with his contemporaries producing some of the most influential accounts. These works include F. Scott Fitzgerald's *Vegetable*, Samuel Hopkins Adams's *Revelry*, William Allen White's *Masks in a Pageant*, and Harry Daugherty's *Inside Story of the Harding Tragedy*. During the decade following Harding's death these authors played an important part in the transition of Harding's legacy from a beloved and martyred president to an incompetent slob who served tragically as leader.[3] In an indirect way, Sinclair Lewis's novel *Babbitt* also shaped Harding's legacy. Lewis's depiction of a small-town booster on the make, consumed by narcissism and materialism, has little to say directly about Harding. Indeed, Harding is mentioned only a few times. But many authors have echoed Lewis's critique of the 1920s, small towns, and boosterism when commenting on the booster-president.

Although they did not shy away from speculating about scandal, these authors were more interested in what Harding's presidency and biography said about American democracy and the log cabin myth. They followed two general themes. First, they turned Harding's biography into a morality tale in which the president's weak character was the cause of his failure. Second, they judged Harding's tragic fate as the result of the folly of having a common man as president. Although in some works it was suggested that the presidency held the potential to elevate a common man, the prevailing attitude was one of cynicism regarding the role of the people in the political process. Harding became an allegory for the corruption of democracy through the ignorance and the manipulation of the people.

Assertions that Harding had failed because of his small-town background and weak character were almost always accompanied by assurances that a great man could succeed in the presidency. In death, Harding was condemned for what, in life, had been hailed as his virtues—simplicity, loyalty, and calmness. His faithfulness to his friends, his hometown, and his political party were now seen as shortcomings. However, despite the doubts that many expressed regarding the log cabin myth, few would argue that the presidency and the political system it represented were broken. The argument, rather, was that these institutions had suffered from having the wrong person in office. At heart, the critique of Harding was a conservative one that portrayed Harding as an aberration, an exception, rather than as a product of a flawed system. The people, this critique went, had undermined the political system by elevating one of their own to the presidency.

Paradoxically, Harding was a scandalous figure who, as president, stood as an icon of American nationalism. To reconcile these conflicting realities, Harding underwent a virtual postmortem impeachment that served to separate him from the office of the presidency. Speculation as to whether or not Harding should have been impeached had he lived was nearly universal. One of the themes of this postmortem cultural impeachment was the condemnation of the judgment of the people who had elected and mourned Harding. Writers such as Fitzgerald found it difficult to separate Harding, with his common touches, from the people who had put him in office.

Impeaching the People

In 1923, F. Scott Fitzgerald weighed in on Harding with his play *The Vegetable, or, From President to Postman*.[4] The play was an attack on Harding, and not a very subtle one. As a Fitzgerald biographer writes, the play was "inspired by the pervasive stupidity, gross cronyism and rampant corruption . . . during the administration of the philistine president, Warren Harding." The play was a failure, opening on November 3, 1923, at Nixon's Apollo Theatre in Atlantic City and closing one week later.[5] Fitzgerald was the victim of poor timing, for his play appeared while the nation was still mourning Harding. Perhaps if Fitzgerald had waited his play might have better fit the mood of the country.

Despite the short run of his play, Fitzgerald foreshadowed the doubts that many intellectuals would express about Harding and democracy. Fitzgerald wrote in a letter, "I'm still a socialist but sometimes I dread that things will grow worse and worse the more the people nominally rule."[6] This is a theme that he, like many intellectuals and academics during the 1920s, would highlight in critiquing bourgeois materialism.[7] Harding, who was often described as a Babbitt, was an easy target. Echoes of Sinclair Lewis's *Main Street* (1920) and *Babbitt* (1922) can be found in many of the commentaries on Harding. Historian Niall Palmer points to the use of Lewis's *Main Street* and *Babbitt* in discussions of Harding. *Main Street*'s "impact lay in its iconoclastic depiction of those negative aspects of American society most often identified with small-town life—conformity, philistinism, bigotry, and smugness—which liberals, artists, and intellectuals most despised and against which much of the nation's youth rebelled during the 1920s." Palmer further notes that *Babbitt* "reinforced the association drawn by cynics between Harding and the narrow minds of Main Street America."[8]

Fitzgerald referenced an H. L. Mencken quotation from *Current Magazine* to explain the unusual title of his play: "Any man who doesn't want to get on in the world, to make a million dollars, and maybe even park his toothbrush in the White House, hasn't got as much to him as a good dog has—he's nothing more or less than a vegetable."[9] That Fitzgerald chose a Mencken quotation seems appropriate. Mencken's disdain for the masses and for Harding was well known. Interestingly, Fitzgerald's commentary on the log cabin myth did not feature a small-town businessman like Harding but rather Jerry Frost, a beaten-down railroad clerk whose ambition was to be a postal worker. Frost is surrounded by a cast of characters who mirrored qualities found in Harding's friends and family. To escape his life, Jerry drinks bootleg gin, only to awaken to find Mr. Jones, "the well-known politician," at his door. Jones tells Jerry he is the Republican nominee for president (54).

One of the difficulties of Fitzgerald's play is the convoluted message that emerges from his attempt to comment on all aspects of the period, a strategy typified by the use of Harding (or his fictional stand-in) as an icon of the period. Fitzgerald's only clear message is that Jerry fails as president because of his commonplace shortcomings. How did such an unqualified man become president? Fitzgerald suggests that the problem is not democracy but modernity; Jerry is selected as a candidate because of a psychological analysis he underwent at work. Money, politics, and morality mix when Jerry makes Dada his secretary of treasury. Dada, a religious Bible reader, destroys all the money because "it's easier for a camel to pass through a needle's eye than for a wealthy man to enter heaven" (95). Dada seems to be a parody of William Jennings Bryan. Then General Pushing, an obvious parody of Gen. John Pershing, informs Jerry that the army has voted for a war and demands money. Of course, there is no money for war. Fitzgerald clearly uses characters to represent many of the problems facing the nation in the postwar era. Jerry's nepotism combines with Dada's religious conservatism to create economic ruin.

Jerry's incompetence, not scandals, leads to an impeachment movement that has Fitzgerald, through one of his characters, proclaiming Jerry (Harding) to be the worst president ever. Senator Fish informs Jerry that the state of Idaho is calling for his impeachment. Perplexed, Jerry turns to his family for advice. Charlotte, a nagging wife in the mold of Florence Harding, counsels Jerry, "Well, all I know is that I'd show some spunk and not let them kick *me* out, even if I *was* the worst President they ever had" (77, emphasis in original). Ironically, it is corruption that saves Jerry's presidency. An opportunity to avoid impeachment presents itself when Jerry arranges a shady land deal to have the fictional nation of Irish Poland annex Idaho. Fitzgerald thus disposes of Idaho, part of the American heartland featured in many of the novels of the period. A frazzled Jerry declares that he does not want to be president. Pushing replies, "As a President you'd make a good postman" (112). Fitzgerald thus foreshadows what would soon be widely quoted Harding statements about not truly wanting to be president while at the same time reminding theatergoers of the role of patronage (the spoils of a postal position at the time) in politics.

Fitzgerald's play impeaches the common man and, more generally, condemns the idea of popular leadership. As president, Jerry is unable to understand complex issues. Relying on his advisors proves to be folly because they were chosen out of either family loyalty or political cronyism. Jerry is happy, and transformed, only when he achieves a position within his capabilities. Fitzgerald reverses the log cabin myth, where the common man rises to the presidency and is transformed into a bigger man (to use a common phrase of the day) who fills the office.

Among those who thought that Harding belonged in a small-town newspaper office and not the White House was Samuel Hopkins Adams. Like Fitzgerald, Adams entertained the idea that a scandal-plagued commoner turned president should have been impeached. Also like Fitzgerald, Adams stopped short of carrying through with his fictional impeachment. Adams, a muckraking journalist, was tremendously influential in shaping Harding's reputation. In 1926, Adams offered the American people *Revelry*, a fictional account of a presidential administration rife with corruption; several years later he published a nonfiction biography of Harding entitled *Incredible Era* (1939), which showed that he had not changed his mind about Harding. *Revelry* was a commercial success and did much to shape how Americans interpreted their experience with Warren G. Harding.

In *Revelry*, Adams addresses the relevance of the log cabin myth and, as is often the case with those dealing in fiction, he seeks authenticity if not necessarily accuracy. Adams presents the reader with easily recognizable fictional counterparts to members of the Harding administration: Harry Daugherty, Jess Smith, a presidential mistress, and an assortment of figures from the Ohio Gang, who drank and played poker with the president. Standing in for Warren G. Harding is President Bill Markham, a small-town politician who makes it to the big time thanks to his looks and his luck.

While clever and cynical in their politics, Markham and his crew are unsophisticated politicians whose small-town antics do not play well on the national stage. There can hardly be any mistaking the ambivalent but powerful role of women in the novel, a reflection of the uncertainty that the newly enfranchised women voters brought to the political process and the centrality of sexual scandal and domestic politics to Harding's legacy.

As Harding was accused of conformity and civic boosters in general were dismissed as pragmatic to the point of lacking in principles, Markham and his gang pride themselves on being practical politicians who have little patience for idealists and reformers. In a scene reminiscent of Lewis's *Babbitt*, Adams begins with a stereotypical scene of male bonding—a poker game that "any one hundred percent American would have recognized."[10] We are left to wonder if this is an observation or an indictment. We also see the president's charisma, as Markham's arrival "warm[s]" the atmosphere with "his personality." He is "a broad, sturdy, fair man, not more than forty-five or six." However, under Markham's eyes are "half-circles of the muddy lead-blue that tells of vitality-overtaxing excesses, quite as probably mental as physical" (12). So here is President Markham looking remarkably like President Harding, complete with the telltale signs of a life lived a little too well and the intellectual stress of being president.

Throughout the book Markham shuns fresh air and sunshine, a heavy-handed metaphor for the Harding's preference for dark, smoke-filled rooms. More like one of the gang than a president, Markham is in his element in the "thick" and "foul" atmosphere of the poker game. Markham's flouting of Prohibition laws is evidence of his cynical politics, and he does not worry because the newspapers don't "print personal stuff, scandal stuff, about the President" because the "newspaper boys [are] friends of his, too" (29). Markham, like Harding, places trust in his friends and, in the end, pays for that misplaced trust.

The parallels to the real First Family are obvious. Markham ducks out after the poker game to avoid returning to the White House. As he wanders the streets of Washington, Markham reflects on his life and his role as a husband. His reflections reveal that he is not altogether happy as a president or as a husband. The First Lady, Sara Belle, has guided him into the "White House, and then broken" and is confined to a sanatorium. Like the ailing Florence Harding she has an "eager, insistent mind and dominant will" but a weak body (26–27). Markham, like Jerry Frost (and presumably Harding) falls victim to his wife's nagging ambition. There is a direct connection between Sara Belle's illness and her ambition; we are encouraged to infer that Florence Harding also suffered from too much ambition.

Markham, however, does not suffer from ambition but from responsibility. Just as Markham's ailing wife has nagged him, so the presidential responsibilities she has brought him prove to be a burden. Markham reflects, "This business of being President! Pulled and hauled and pecked at, this way and that, by a thousand petty demands" (27). The henpecked Markham loves the people but dislikes the burden they have placed on him. Likewise, Markham is fond of his wife but dislikes the responsibilities she has placed on him.

Adams mixes the politics of class and sex when a drunken Markham stumbles upon Edith Westervelt, a cynical divorced heiress, who, in contrast to Sara Belle, is decidedly apolitical. Markham, the commoner, is immediately smitten with the aristocratic Westervelt (whose name sounds suspiciously like Roosevelt). The apolitical Westervelt approaches her friend Senator Peter Thorne to mentor her in the ways of politics in much the way that, it was argued, women voters needed to be schooled in the ways of government. Again, Adams echoes *Babbitt*, in which Lewis describes women entering the political arena as "wives uneasy with their new votes."[11] Thorne tells Westervelt that for women Washington usually means society but for her it has to be politics, because with her "power of influencing men" she has an opportunity to "become a real power if she play[s] her cards right." Westervelt rejects Thorne's advice, saying that for women, politics "usually means sex. I don't play that game."[12] Nonetheless Adams uses her as the apolitical and aristocratic voice of morality in the unraveling of Markham's presidency.

The interplay between Westervelt and Markham gives the reader a chance to contemplate the nature of politics. She is repulsed by Markham's booster clichés: "Business is the backbone of the nation"; "the word, American, is the proudest boast of history"; and Harding's own motto Boost, Don't Knock (97). When Westervelt attempts to insult Markham by telling him, "You must be what is known as a typical American," Markham misses the insult, replying, "You couldn't call me anything that would make me prouder." Echoing Harding and Babbitt, Markham states his ambition: "I like everybody and I want 'em to like me." Westervelt finds both the people and their president baffling, full of shortcomings (104–7).[13]

While Westervelt struggles with her feelings about politics, the people, and the president, the character Dan Lurcock exhibits few of these doubts. For Lurcock, politics means power and the president's popularity is a source of power. Lurcock is an amalgam of Harry Daugherty and Jess Smith, with a suggestive name for those aware of the rumors about the two men. Like Smith, Lurcock has "no official appointment at the Justice Department." Like Daugherty, Lurcock is believed to be a kingmaker. Lurcock takes advantage of Markham's great weakness, his loyalty. Lurcock is given a "free hand" because he has "made" Markham (40–41).

Adams makes no effort to disguise the story of how Daugherty discovered Harding. Indeed, the story has been transferred almost unaltered into Adams's novel, except for some of the places and the names. While in its initial form the story of Daugherty's discovery of Harding conforms to the log cabin myth—Adams gives the story a sinister turn. Lurcock spots Markham "sitting on the bootblack's high chair as if it were a throne." Markham has a "really noble profile" and cuts a "statesman-like" appearance (67–69). Adams's description of Markham passes judgment on Harding's character. Markham has luck and personal honesty, but "as a man and a politician" Markham is "torpid, good-humored, complacent, friendly, indulgent to himself, obliging to others, as loyal as a Samurai, full of party piety, a hater of the word No, faithful to his own code of private honor, reliable, and as standardized as a Ford car" (70). Markham rises to power not only because of these (negative) characteristics, but also because he is acceptable to the "oil crowd." Finally, Adams explains that "the job is too big for any individual. We crush our presidents under a mass of detail" (74–75). As Adams explains, the modern presidency can be handled only by great men.

For all Adams's denunciations of Markham, in his account the president remains an innocent tool of the grafters. In the novel, the Crow's Nest is the place where Lurcock runs the shadow government (41–42). This is an obvious reference to the Little Green House on K Street and the Little House on H Street in Washington D.C., which had featured so prominently in congressional testimony. Even as Lurcock and the others treat the presidency as little more than one of the spoils of victory, there remains some, but not much, respect for the office. As Lurcock admonishes his cronies, "Presidents don't graft." Adams assures readers (perhaps including those who voted for Harding) that Markham is "a tool of the grafters but not one himself" (77, quote 79).

For Adams, the key to understanding Harding is to understand the men around him. Like Harding's cabinet, Markham's cabinet is divided between the cronies and the best minds. When former senator Andy Gandy, a quack physician who resembles an amalgam of Charles Sawyer and Albert Fall, worries that Senate investigators might uncover his embezzlement, Lurcock reminds him that "they're all thinking of that record majority when they go up against the Chief, you bet" (55). Markham, for his part, is comfortable in the company of these questionable characters whom Adams uses to represent common politics. Westervelt, seeing no redemption for Markham in the American people, hopes that the "best minds" of the cabinet will save Markham. Thorne, a political insider, thinks otherwise, believing that the respectable cabinet members "can't get at him" because the president thinks of them as "'highbrows,' which is anathema" (66). Adams's Markham, like Lewis's Babbitt, rejects intellectual pursuits in favor of the practical and the common. In *Babbitt* the worst sin a man can commit is to be "highbrow."

Adams sees little virtue in the booster ethos that permeated the Harding campaign. Adams connects Markham's booster ethos with his vision of proper government, and the author uses that ethos to explain his downfall. For Markham, business should be done in the familiar ways of small towns. Adams has Markham fantasize about the cabinet he could create if he was given a free hand. He would pick "good fellows" with "broad gauge minds" who can play poker. Just as the 1920 election featured Harding's community, Adams conjures Markham's "ideal community" as one with "friendly faces" and "easy attitudes." The room would be full of smoke with "no damned windows open to blow a draft down your neck." Markham concludes, "To hell with the Best Element! They mostly played golf on Election Day and didn't know a primary from a recount" (175, 177). In Adams's telling, the people are unable to recognize the disinterested aristocrats and best minds. Instead, the people embrace Markham and his gang.

While the booster ethos fails him, Markham does have an opportunity to find salvation in the national civic religion by fulfilling the log cabin myth. It is not, however, the best minds that offer Markham salvation but rather Westervelt, who brings politics to a higher level. Just as Harding embraced "social justice" during the election to attract women voters, Markham tries to turn over a new leaf to impress Westervelt, the disinterested aristocrat. Markham judges that it is not the work that breaks presidents, "It's the weight of carrying the trust and confidence and well-being of your country." Markham finds renewed commitment to the presidency and, as he confesses, his haggard face takes on "a sort of dim ennoblement" (88, 136). Ironically, his conversion coincides with an attempt to seduce Westervelt into an extramarital affair. Markham's new love and desire to play on the level makes him uncomfortable with his old cronies because love is "a 'sissy' sort of thing; all right for artists and poets and those kind of inconsiderable people who didn't even have votes. Or perhaps they did but they didn't use 'em." Markham associates the franchise with men, but men who are appropriately masculine (109–110). Markham's attempt to seduce Westervelt (the aristocratic, reluctant woman voter) and his sexual double standard, which for Adams originates in Markham's small-town values, are as dangerous as his boosterism.

Markham's conversion does not make the nitty-gritty of politics go away. Lurcock has arranged for Markham, all the while in the dark, to profit from an oil deal (170). Lurcock is confident that intimidation and public apathy will prevent Senate investigators from uncovering his activities. Just as Harding sent a letter to Congress endorsing Fall's handling of the naval oil reserves, Markham sends a letter to Congress endorsing Gandy. Westervelt tries to stop Markham from making that mistake, but fails. Markham does not take her warnings seriously because she is a woman "meddling in politics" and "playing prettily at power" (213). In the end, the woman is right and the politician is wrong.

Adams continues to compare sexual and political morality, a discussion that features prominently in Harding's legacy. As it turns out, Edith Westervelt is not the only one who has to worry about her reputation. The joke on Harding is that it was a good thing he was not born a girl, because he could never say no. Likewise, Westervelt learns that the president's friends call him Easy Markham (288). Markham has no idea he is easy. Instead, he sits in the White House, "dreaming dreams of loftier things" (219). Markham finds it difficult to outlive his past, to rise above his friends, and to overcome his humanity. Adams tells us, "Presidents are people. They possess, though they must seldom yield to, the same frailties as folk of common clay" (234).

As Adams's novel nears its end, Markham's conversion to the civic religion is tested, but the nation's faith is preserved despite the parochialism, scandals, and incompetence of Markham's administration. Markham's world dissolves as he learns of Lurcock and Gandy's betrayal (239). As the investigators dig deeper into his corrupt administration, Markham turns to an aide: "Well, good God! Haven't I got any friends I can trust?" The aide replies, "Chief, a President can't afford friends" (264). Here was Adams's reply to Harding's confession about his friends keeping him awake at night. As the scandals surrounding Markham break and talk of impeachment begins, the best minds threaten to leave the cabinet, just as Markham needs them most.

In Adams's evaluation, a small-town politician can't rise to the level demanded by the modern presidency. Just as all seems lost, the "proverbial Markham luck intervene[s]," and the First Lady dies, granting Markham a political reprieve (266–68). However, with his renewed commitment Markham develops the symptoms of "White House breakdown" (269). Adams writes, "Poor Markham! The small-town politician in the giant's robe. It isn't his fault that he brought a ward heeler's mind and joiner's conception of politics to the biggest job in the world" (273–74).

Eventually the Markham luck takes a morbid turn and at this point Adams's account achieves the authenticity to merge with the real Harding reputation. Markham's escape is death. Earlier in the book Markham takes a bottle of sleeping pills from Westervelt to prevent her from committing suicide. Now, suffering from presidential insomnia, Markham stumbles into his bathroom in search of the pills. By accident he takes the "dark blue poison phial, the gift of Edith Westervelt's one surrender to him" (301). Upon learning of his mistake he does not seek medical attention; instead, he decides to die.

As with Harding, in Adams's novel the presidential death becomes a moment of national unity and a ceremony that honors civic religion. We learn that Lurcock, Thorne, and all the gang have been vigilantly standing by the president's deathbed (310). Westervelt now wishes she had given herself to him, but she realizes, "I never would have stayed to be tainted by his disgrace." Thorne says he will not save him even if he could. Why? "I care for the Party," he says, and he will not "cheat the great, sentimental, soppy-hearted American public." Markham's death will wipe out the "whole score," provided it is a "martyr's death and not a suicide's." Thorne concludes, "A president who dies in office is a hero" (311).

Adams compares the dying Markham with Washington, Lincoln, St. Paul, Socrates, and Christ. The nation keeps vigil as Markham is "dying at his post, a victim of the mighty office which he had lived up to according to his dim and flickering lights." Despite his negative portrayal of Markham and his politics throughout the novel, Adams embraces the themes of the early commemoration of Harding. The public mourns Markham as "the president, who was more of the people than any president since Lincoln, more simply human in his frailties and deficiencies." Markham wants his last words recorded as "Keep America on top" (315). Markham's last phrase, made noble by his death, is one of the clichés that Adams has ridiculed.

The novel features one last visit between Markham and Edith Westervelt, during which she tries to participate in the emotion that sweeps the nation. The aristocrat tells the common man that she loves him. He says, "Bless you for that lie. But I've loved you for the truth that is in you." Adams offers one last view of Markham through Westervelt: "She felt the shock of a suspicion that there was in this man something rarer and finer than her self-clouded vision had ever seen. Passionately and humbly she said: 'I would have been proud to love you'" (316). Finally, Peter Thorne offers the story's moral: "Friendship in politics undermines more principles than fraud, and gratitude is a worse poison than graft" (318). In this scenario, the nation is left with a false hero who pays for the betrayal of his friends with suicide. Markham's suicide preserves the dignity of the office and avoids the embarrassment of impeachment. Although Adams does not back away from his assertion that the presidency is too big for a common man, he does, in the end, pay homage to role of the common man in the national mythology.

Although Adams's account is obviously fictionalized, he claimed that his novel captures the essence of what he saw as a journalist while covering the Harding administration. His fiction, he argued, represents the truth behind the missing Harding facts. Harry Daugherty, to say the least, disagreed with Adams. Daugherty denounced *Revelry* as a "volume built on a foundation of falsehood." Daugherty ignored the fact that *Revelry* was technically fiction, asserting that it "is bad enough to attack a man when he is alive, but it is a terrible thing to attack him when he is dead." Like Fitzgerald and Adams, Daugherty found fault with the people. He blamed the people for the popularity of the scandal stories. They were "susceptible to scandal stories" because they did not understand the government. Still, Daugherty remained confident that the lies about Harding would unravel.[14] Since many considered Daugherty the mastermind of the Ohio Gang, he did not reassure many.

Fate's Tragic Mannikin

Intellectuals denounced Harding for failure and corruption, but they were joined by the influential voice of one of his fellow small-town editors.

William Allen White participated in the denigration of Harding and provided history, as we have already seen, with some of the most damaging Harding quotations. Harding and White shared a similar background. Both men came from the newspaper business and stood as icons of small-town America; White famously had edited the *Emporia (KS) Gazette*. Like Harding and so many other newspaper people, White embraced the "booster ethos" as the key to success in the newspaper business.[15] White also shared some personality traits with Harding. His biographer wrote that White "reveled in the masculine world of business and politics, yet he was forever dependent upon the ministrations of strong-minded women" (30). Like Harding, White had suffered a mysterious nervous breakdown, and both men tended to shape their rhetoric to meet their needs. As White's biographer wrote, by the 1920s White "had also become a figure on a larger national stage, transforming his typical performance into an archetypal one—that of the Small-Town Editor—well suited to the nostalgia of a newly urbanized society" (19). If anyone was qualified to comment on Harding as the president from Marion, Ohio, it was White.

White wrote a moderate evaluation of Harding's presidency not long after his death, that it was "an episode, a sort of intermezzo between President Wilson with his illusion of world peace unfairly negotiated and President Coolidge with his speculative boom."[16] In his later *Autobiography* (1946), White describes a meeting with Harding at the White House during which they discussed the newspaper business. Harding expressed a great deal of homesickness for Marion and the *Star*. Harding and White discussed the gentleman's agreements that governed county printing contracts. Harding then explained that he was meeting with some "decent" fellows from Ohio who were about to be indicted for violating conspiracy laws, but he could not see how it differed from the divvying up of patronage printing jobs, as he and White had done. However, Harding said he could not help his friends. Then, in this account, Harding delivered the famous line, "My god, this is a hell of a job! I have no trouble with my enemies. I can take care of my enemies all right. But my friends, White, they're the ones that keep me walking the floors at night!"[17] Here, Harding's statement is not so much a confession but a lament for his inability to aid his friends because of the standards of his office.

However, most do not use, or even remember, this account but instead turn to White's *Masks in the Pageant* (1928), a collection of essays on presidents he had known. In it White claims the Harding presidency failed because it rested on outdated small-town values and on Harding's weak character. White, the booster, attacks Harding, the booster, for lacking the foresight to bring progress to the national community. This attack is fitting, given that one of the most potent rhetorical weapons in a booster's arsenal is to accuse opponents of standing in the way of progress. White offers this dramatic prologue: "Harding in the White House was a protagonist prince of reaction. Not that his brain made the times; he had few and mediocre talents. The gods of the times created him out of the red Ohio mud and put him to dry against the fence outside the Executive Mansion; and when they breathed the breath of opportunity into his nostrils, he walked in— Fate's tragic mannikin."[18] White tapped into several common themes related to Harding's declining reputation, including denouncing Harding's small-town background. Still, White's opening paragraph labels Harding a "third-rater" in Ohio politics and a "henchman" (389).

While Adams and Fitzgerald had sought authenticity by using fiction to capture the shortcomings of the log cabin myth, White offered questionable stories under the veneer of journalism. White gained his authenticity because he was a journalist and a friend of presidents. White writes, in a "story which cannot be authenticated" but he nevertheless uses, that Ohio's masterful Republican boss Mark Hanna kicked Harding out of his office for acting as a "striker or fixer" for another political boss (389). White recounts Harding's life in brief, but not without mistakes. According to White, it was Senator Joseph Foraker who had organized the Ohio Gang and made Harry Daugherty its leader because he was "biddable." White writes that Harding defeated Cox for the governorship, when in fact he lost to Judson Harmon, and he attributes two children to Florence Harding (she had had a son with Henry De Wolfe before she married Warren). White also misidentifies Harding's background, writing that he "grew up as an average young American of the country town; no better, no worse than the common run of small-town sons of the upper and ruling class" (392–93). Perhaps White was thrown off by Harding's father's status as a physician or perhaps he assumed his politics meant he came from the "ruling class," but as we have seen Harding had a more humble origin and hardly had the temperament to be a striker.

White found a reason to damn most of the characteristics that had been praised during Harding's life. In doing so, White wrote a dramatic and a sensational account that was predictable, influential, and inaccurate. Reversing the arguments of such Harding boosters as Sawyer, White found that Harding's role in Marion foreshadowed his failure as a president. Of Harding's oratory, for example, White writes, "Harding, standing before a

Rotarian audience, or a Masonic conclave, or a Christian Endeavor convention, seemed to have almost human intelligence. He uses strange, etymologically silly words like 'common sensical,' 'normalcy,' 'citizenry,' and the like, which passed for erudition" (422). If Harding lacked human intelligence, it stood to reason that someone guided Harding through his career. Leveling a charge against Harding, one that was commonly made against many boosting newspaper editors, White wrote that the powerful men in Marion found that Harding was "easily handled." Further, White dismisses Harding's ability as a newspaper editor: "He has never written a line that has been quoted beyond the confines of his state, and has rarely taken a position which has attracted more than local notice. His paper is as impersonal as the town crier, from which the country newspaper was descended" (399). In the Senate, White writes, Harding had "the air of a Roman Senator" but "made no important record" (400–401). During the 1916 Republican convention, Harding stood "like an actor" at the podium, White says, adding that Harding was "a well-schooled senatorial orator, with his actor's sharply chiseled face," who had a "matinee idol manner" (394–95). Overall, White finds Harding to be an empty vessel that carried the worst traits of small-town America and celebrity politics.

Having denounced Harding and his background, White argues Harding was a tool of conservatives who hated Theodore Roosevelt, whom White greatly admired. White, like others, argues that Harding proved that great men needed to serve as president. He claims that there "can be no doubt" that "oil controlled the Republican convention of 1920" through the Senate cabal (404). Continuing his assault on Harding, White writes that during the election, the "word 'normalcy'" was the "only contribution which Harding has left for posterity." For White, Harding's legacy is a mispronounced word with a sinister definition: "His slogan, 'A Return to Normalcy,' meant, being translated, the return to respectability of those capitalistic forces of greed and cunning in American life which Roosevelt had routed and Wilson civilized. Only in this were they new forces—they stank of oil" (420).

White drew a line connecting Harding's lax morals to his hometown. White was among the first to hint at Harding's affair with Carrie Phillips, a reference that would help ensure that White's account would continue to be cited. White describes Marion during Harding's triumphant return after the Republican convention: "Every store front was a giant bloom of red, white, and blue; every store front but one. And when the reporters asked about it, they heard one of those stories about a primrose detour from

Main Street which Florence Kling, the Duchess, had chosen to ignore." Except for Carrie Phillips's cuckolded husband, however, Marion was fully behind Harding, because he "was their embodiment" (409).

White introduces several rumors that have entered into the historical narrative and are often accepted as fact. He writes, "Rumor said, probably apocryphally, that [Harding] had signed the order for the transfer of the oil reserve [at Teapot Dome and Elk Hills] when he was drunk" (430). White portrays Harding as saying, "This White House is a prison. I can't get away from the men who dog my footsteps. I am in jail" (431). White emphasizes the meeting between Harding and the wife of Secretary Fall for one hour at the Hotel Muehlebach in Kansas City. After the meeting with Mrs. Fall, Harding said to a friend, "In this job I am not worried about my enemies. I can take care of them. It is my friends who are giving me trouble" (432). White writes that Harding then asked Hoover and a few trusted reporters what a president should do who learned his friends had betrayed him (432). White does not hesitate to cite the apocryphal.

White's nonfiction account varies little in its conclusions from the judgments that Fitzgerald and Adams present in their fiction about Harding and the log cabin myth. White argues that Harding was not fit for the presidency, ignoring Harding's years in political office in his argument that Harding, used to life in Rotary and the chamber of commerce, "stood appalled" by his responsibilities as president. In words reminiscent of Adams, White argues that as the presidency began to transform Harding, his friends "saw in him strange moods; and they did, and spoke of what they saw—if his old poker pals in the Senate were first annoyed and then confounded by certain signs in the man, what they saw and felt was only the reaction of a kindly heart to a crushing sense of responsibility." Harding, however, would not complete the transformation into a great president because he continued to trust Daugherty and so his conversion was "superficial." He was not prepared for the presidency as it had been developed by Roosevelt and "perfected" by Wilson (412–14). As with Adams, White took the opportunity to equate politicians with prostitutes, with Harding being the prime example, because he had the "harlot's ingratiating familiarity which politicians imitate so well" (429). Harding failed as a president, according to White, because he "was to the last a small-town man, the Prominent Citizen of Marion, Ohio" (428).

White follows the pattern established by Fitzgerald and Adams of denouncing Harding and his small-town background, but then he inconsistently praised Harding as a gentle man unprepared for the presidency.

White, a famous foe of populism, found in Harding a man too common to be president.

Finally, White concluded that Harding was not fit to be included in the log cabin myth. White assesses Harding's legacy:

> Before the scandal had reached him men started to raise a memorial to him. A myth was born that he was a beloved President, a sweet and kindly man, like Lincoln. But—alas!— the myth was abortive. His friends, cronies, allies, and the Ohio gang were hauled into court. Death saved some, the prison took others, shame touched all. And Harding passed into contemporary history with a name so clouded that none would do it honor. Probably no other American President had to run the gauntlet of cruel malice and public odium as Harding ran it during the first four years that followed his death. Some day America will realize the tragic drama in which he moved, will realize how wickedly unfair the Republic was to pick up that man—weak, unprepared, with no executive talent, and with an unused mind—and pinnacle him in the most powerful place on earth. (434)

In his conclusion, White echoes Hoover, Adams, and others who saw Harding's story as a national tragedy, not recognizing the irony in arguing that in a republic small towns stood as a source of corruption and the average man was not fit to govern. White's romantic view of the presidency, his lax attitude toward facts, and his dramatic delivery foreshadowed what was to come with Harding's place in history.

Fate's Tragic Friendship

Thus far we have seen a great deal of tension between the notions that Harding came from the people to the presidency and the argument that Harding's background disqualified him from the presidency. Harding's legacy, it seems, held the potential to tarnish the log cabin myth. Of his alliances with his "damned friends," Warren Harding's association with Harry Daugherty has been, perhaps, the most damaging to his reputation. Daugherty and Harding had known each other for decades and had worked closely together. It was often assumed that Daugherty discovered and used Harding. As Adams wrote, "Harding became his [Daugherty's] meal ticket."[19] Daugherty's reputation was tied to Harding's and, more important, Daugherty damaged Harding's reputation even when trying to protect it and defend himself.

Daugherty served as attorney general under both Warren Harding and Calvin Coolidge and was indicted but not convicted for his activities in that position. Coolidge forced Daugherty and FBI director William Burns to resign in 1924 (J. Edgar Hoover replaced Burns as the bureau's head). Following the removal of Daugherty and Burns, the political pressure on the Coolidge administration gradually eased, leaving a "confused and inconclusive" end to the investigation. Even after the congressional investigation ended, however, Daugherty could not retreat from the public light as he still faced criminal charges for the illegal transfer of a German-owned American subsidiary company to an American syndicate under provisions remaining from World War I. Various bribes had helped to grease the machinery of government in approving the deal; Jess Smith had ended up with $224,000 from the deal. He deposited $50,000 of the money in an account known as Jess Smith Extra no. 3 at Washington Court House's Midland National Bank. Mal Daugherty, Harry's brother, owned the bank. Harry Daugherty blocked all attempts by investigators to look at bank records and ultimately destroyed the records. During the trials Daugherty refused to testify, leading one historian to conclude that no action "could have been more damaging to his already battered reputation."[20] Daugherty biographer James N. Giglio writes that in "a way unequaled until the capers of the Richard M. Nixon administration, Burns also misused his power by harassing prominent Congressmen and public officials who questioned Daugherty's official policies or who found Burns's actions intolerable." It remained "unclear," he continues, how "much Daugherty knew of the Bureau's myriad activities, but there is no question that when congressional investigations threatened his position, he was willing to use that power in retaliation."[21] So, in the end, praise from Harry Daugherty did not do much to help Warren Harding's reputation.

In 1932, Daugherty published *The Inside Story of the Harding Tragedy*, written with Thomas Dixon, author of *The Clansman: An Historical Romance of the Ku Klux Klan* (1905, the inspiration for D. W. Griffith's *Birth of a Nation*). To characterize Daugherty's memoir as self-serving would be an understatement. Although Daugherty comes to Harding's defense, he continues the argument that the Harding presidency was a tragedy. Daugherty does differ with previous writers, however, about the reasons for that assessment.

Daugherty's claim to authenticity came from his close relationship with Harding. But although giving lip service to the notion that Harding was his own man, Daugherty takes credit for nearly every one of Harding's accomplishments, including Harding's nomination and election, which reinforces the idea that Harding was a tool. Of the many others before who argued for their special insight, Daugherty is best situated to claim true insider status, a point he does not hesitate to emphasize: "I am, perhaps, the only living man who knows the facts."[22]

Daugherty defends his own record with two basic arguments. First, he claims to be a practical and fair man. His memoir has almost all the other players redundantly complimenting him on his forthright and manly conduct. Second, Daugherty portrays himself as the victim of a Communist plot to destroy him and the nation, deserving sympathy because so few realize that he saved the nation from a terrible fate.

One of the constant themes in the discussion of Harding was the comparison between the absent ideals of the Harding administration and the high-minded ideals of the Wilson administration. Echoing the supposedly nonideological booster ethos, Daugherty confesses, "I am, and always have been, a practical politician, though not a professional one." Daugherty does not view this as a cynical position but rather argues that his approach to politics places him within the mainstream of American history: "As I understand it, practical politicians created this Republic and make its continued existence possible." Conversely, he describes Progressives, a group he fought with often, as ineffective (4). For Daugherty, part of being practical was loyalty to party and to friends. Therefore, Daugherty confesses "to a leadership in the so-called 'Ohio Gang' for about forty years" (5).

Daugherty attempts to reclaim the log cabin myth, which had been used so effectively to promote Harding during the 1920 election but which more recently had been turned against Harding. In the captions to photographs in his book Daugherty persists in comparing Harding to Lincoln and refers to Harding as a great commoner. Even here Daugherty, for his own aggrandizement, accepts Harding's unflattering common traits. Whereas White and others saw the presidency as a grand office, Daugherty sees the tide of history diminishing the office and thus making it acceptable to Harding. Daugherty reassures Harding, "You're a man of the people. You're a typical average American. You're a Lincoln type who grew out of Ohio soil" (22). When Daugherty has Harding confess his fears that he was not big enough for the presidency, Daugherty explains the reality of the office: "the day of giants in the Presidential Chair is passed. Our so-called Great Presi-

dents were all made by the conditions of war under which they adminis-
tered the office. Greatness in the Presidential Chair is largely an illusion of
the people" (16–17).

Daugherty's praise of Harding, because of his need to elevate the latter's reputation, echoes the condemnation of his enemies. Throughout the
book Daugherty portrays Harding as a kindly, naive person who brought
people together. Daugherty writes, "Harding's method was always one of
conciliation." He "believed he could convert and win his enemies" (10). In
Daugherty's account, he protects Harding from his impulse to seek recon-
ciliation with his enemies.

If Daugherty was the kingmaker, what role did Florence Harding
have in Harding's rise? Was she the real power behind the throne? Daugherty portrays Florence Harding in a more traditional role than had become
customary, thus expanding his role in Warren Harding's rise to power.
Through Florence Harding, Daugherty visits the by-now common theme
of the presidency being beyond the ability of most men. Daugherty has Florence Harding say that she had no desire to become First Lady: "I've seen
the inside of the White House. I have a vivid picture of President Wilson
harried and beaten by the cares of office. The office is killing him as surely
as if he had been stabbed at his desk" (14). Daugherty thus foreshadows
Harding's own death as well as establishing Florence Harding as willing to
forego ambition (20). As First Lady, Daugherty says, the "real" Mrs. Harding "carried into the Executive Mansion the sweet spirit of her Marion
home life, and never attempted to play the 'Great Lady.'" Florence Harding was "simple and old fashioned" in "an age of jazz." Daugherty does
acknowledge her as a "close observer of public events, a student of men,
and one of the best-informed women in the country." However, he judges
that Florence Harding used her interest and knowledge appropriately and
that she was interested in her husband's work, but "never nagged" (162–63).
Daugherty challenged the prevailing notions regarding Florence Harding
and her marriage to Warren. Florence was typically portrayed as a nagging
shrew that drove Warren to power. Furthermore, much of the criticism of
Warren Harding grew from his inadequacies as a husband. Daugherty attempted to portray the Harding marriage, and Florence, in a more traditional light.

While there can be no doubt of Daugherty's importance in Harding's
rise, he took complete credit for Harding's success. In February 1920,
Daugherty made one of the most famous predictions in the history of
American elections when he told the *New York Times* that he expected the

convention to deadlock. Weary political bosses would agree to nominate Harding in the early morning hours. Harding and Daugherty, as it turned out, had a realistic view of the party. Daugherty's prediction that Harding would be nominated in a hotel room in the wee hours of the morning created a controversy in its own right. As for the infamous smoke-filled room that Daugherty's boasting had done so much to present in a sinister light, he writes, "We were told afterwards that Col. George Harvey met his friends in a smoke-fogged room in the Blackstone Hotel, decided on a candidate, and adjourned at 2 A.M. We paid no attention to these meetings, but sought out and gripped the hands of the delegates who were to vote" (39).

Daugherty had to address the charges of corruption, many of which involved his friendship with Jess Smith. Although he does not directly address the issue, Daugherty deals with the rumors that he and Smith were homosexual, referring to "sinister stories an army of liars would tell of my relations with this simple, loyal friend" (64). Daugherty deals more directly with Smith's role in the corruption of the Justice Department. Jess Smith, by some accounts, had operated out of the mysterious house on H Street, but Daugherty has a simple explanation: Daugherty had rented the house from Ned McLean when he moved to Washington so that he would not have to conduct political business from the Justice Department. Smith again came to his aid; Daugherty maintains that he "ran the house on H-Street for me with great skill." In addition to his legitimate political work, Smith had helped care for Daugherty's ailing wife: "No man could have dreamed at this time of the sinister interpretation enemies would put on this association with a helpful friend in my home and official life" (96). Daugherty takes refuge in the fact that although he was investigated by the House, the Senate, and the courts, "not one illegal or questionable act was discovered" (106).

Daugherty also addresses the issue of Harding's cabinet, which had been the source of so much controversy. According to Daugherty, Harding was in complete control of the cabinet selection and wanted no "yes men." However, Daugherty places himself at the center of decisions that resulted in a good selection, but counts himself blameless for appointments that resulted in scandal. Daugherty takes credit for arranging the deal that brought Hoover into the cabinet over the objections from the Senate in exchange for Andrew Mellon becoming secretary of the treasury. Daugherty wants to correct the record regarding his relationship with Albert Fall: "It is all but universally believed that Fall and I were inseparable chums in the Harding administration." He continued that "nothing could be farther from the facts" (71).

Both Harding and Daugherty came under intense criticism for their lack of respect for Prohibition. Harding, as we have seen, was often depicted as drinking while cynically backing Prohibition. Daugherty tries to clarify the issue. First, he makes the distinction between private and public acts. In a statement similar to the fictional words of Adams's attorney general, Lurcock, Daugherty endorses the practical politics of Prohibition: "We were not saints and did not pretend to be" (103). Daugherty also argues that it did not matter if he broke a law as long as he enforced it for other people. Such arguments hardly helped Daugherty's cause.

Daugherty had little praise for organized labor, but he did make some effort to portray himself as a fair-minded friend of labor. He also took credit for one of Harding's nobler acts, the pardoning of Eugene V. Debs. Despite claiming credit for the pardon in his memoirs, Daugherty had actually opposed the pardoning of Debs, writing to Harding that Debs's charm made him "a very dangerous man"[23] In an extended discussion in his book, Daugherty describes meeting with Debs to discuss a possible pardon. In the end, he has Debs say, "I just want to say that I thank you from the bottom of my heart for your generous and manly treatment of me in this meeting. No matter what you feel it your duty to do in my case, I'm grateful that we have met and I shall always respect you."[24] Unfortunately for the Harding legacy, Daugherty had clouded one of Harding's true acts of kindness.[25]

As Daugherty had explained earlier, presidential greatness came from dealing with an enormous crisis, such as a war. Daugherty explained how he, and Harding, had saved the nation from just such a crisis. Daugherty had been roundly criticized for seeking a nationwide injunction that brought a violent end to a wave of strikes in 1922. Criticism came not only from labor but also some of his fellow Republicans. Daugherty argued the strike was a threat to the existence of the nation. On the great strikes of 1922, Daugherty wrote that the United States had never "passed through a graver crisis." This was, of course, a rather exaggerated claim that played on the anticommunism of the day and the industrial turmoil that had followed World War I. Daugherty had discovered that "Zinoviev had sent from Moscow to his Communist agents in the United States" orders to strike (115). Furthermore, "Reds" threatened to take control of the railroads. He wrote, "If the roads were confiscated by the government, they would ultimately be turned over to the labor leaders to run. From that hour our time-tables and freight rates would be made out in Moscow, and the first step would have been taken in a revolution to overthrow our government and substitute a Soviet regime" (119). Daugherty reported to Harding, "We can't afford to proclaim a condition of civil war at this time, though we are actually in it" (127). Harding, while supportive of Daugherty, was distracted by Florence Harding's illness. What had caused her grave illness? Communists. The strikes had produced such anxiety in the First Lady that her health had broken (162–63). Daugherty, however, reported that he had saved the nation, with the support of the president, of course.

It was, according to Daugherty, his stopping of the Communist menace that was responsible for many of the attacks on him and that led his enemies to blame him for the scandals. He asserts that labor leaders, Reds, and their agents in Congress had moved to impeach him. According to Daugherty, "Big Bill" Dunne, a Communist associated with William Foster, had orchestrated the movement to send Wheeler to the Senate to get Daugherty (159). Daugherty informs his readers that the "furor raised over the Teapot Dome scandal brought to my I.W.W. enemy in the United States Senate the opportunity for which he was waiting" (188). Daugherty claims that Wheeler was the leading Communist in the Senate, that he was taking orders from Moscow, and that he was "no more a Democrat than Stalin, his comrade in Moscow" (203).

Daugherty attacks those who had written about Harding. He describes Samuel Hopkins Adams's novel *Revelry* as "a coarse, filthy screed in which he used fictitious names and shifted scenes to escape the laws of criminal libel." Daugherty asserts that "a more stupid and malignant lie was never circulated about a public official within my knowledge of American history" (186). Likewise, Daugherty has no kind words for Jess Smith's former wife, Roxie Stinson, who had been such a damning witness before Congress: "I did not know Roxie Stinson" (207). Daugherty dismisses the content or questions the motives of most of his critics.

Daugherty explains many of the attacks against him as the result of gossip mongers and says that "the Washington brand of gossip is the lowest, dirtiest, and most vicious small-town stuff." Washington was among the worst cities for gossip because it was "really a small town as American towns go" (217). Daugherty tries to explain why he had leased the Washington houses that became the setting for so many depictions of corruption. There were two houses associated with corruption in the Harding administration, the second being the Little Green House on K Street, which Daugherty characterizes as "another myth created by the tongues of Washington's scandal mongers." Daugherty writes, "I never entered this house in my life. I never saw it. Harding never entered it, nor saw it, to my knowledge" (221). Such vicious gossip was not new, he asserts, for the "same peddlers of dirt who had attacked Harding had pounced on his predecessor, Woodrow Wilson, the day after he entered the White House." According to the gossip of the day, Wilson had been a "devil with the women" before he was elected, and as president he "prowled" the streets of Washington (222).

Daugherty concludes his account by explaining that he helped Harding work on his will before the Alaska trip. Daugherty maintains that he did not go on the trip because Harding wanted him to remain in Washington to manage the government. Daugherty was undoubtedly responding to reports made at the time of Harding's Alaska trip, and afterward, that he was falling out of favor with Harding as Harding learned of Jess Smith's corruption and became suspicious of Daugherty's activities.

Daugherty's memoirs did not do much to boost either his own reputation or Harding's. His exaggeration of the threats he faced during the 1922 strike did not help but, more important, Daugherty does not offer a portrayal of Harding that was radically different from the one offered by Harding's critics; Daugherty's Harding was a man not in charge. Daugherty does maintain that Harding was an upright man and says Harding was in charge, but at every important moment Daugherty explains that it was he who saved the day. Daugherty was only one of many to claim to present the true inside story, but his claim had been watered down to the point of having almost no value. More than anything else, Daugherty seeks to redeem his own reputation and expresses his hope that the historical respect for the offices of president and attorney general will shelter him and Harding: "It is the glory of our Republic that in all its history no dishonest or disreputable man has ever been President of the United States" (1).

Given that Daugherty characterizes the attacks on Harding as Washington gossip, it is perhaps fitting for Alice Roosevelt Longworth to have the final word. Furthermore, given all the commentary about Harding and the log cabin myth, it seems equally fitting that the aristocratic daughter of Theodore Roosevelt, wife of a prominent congressman, and cousin of Franklin Roosevelt offer her insights into Harding's place in history. It was, after all, Roosevelt and Wilson to whom Harding was most often unfavorably compared. While she may have been an eyewitness to the presidential administrations of her father and of Wilson, she was more famous for her witty and snide commentary. She has contributed some of the best-known barbs of the twentieth century. In her autobiography, *Crowded Hours,* Roosevelt Longworth describes Florence Harding as a "nervous, rather excitable woman" who was "strident." She was shocked to see how Harding and his cronies violated the Eighteenth Amendment by serving "every imaginable brand of whisky" in a White House study while they played poker. She concludes, famously, "no matter what Harding's failings may have been, nothing more contemptible and distorted has ever been written than the gossip books that have been published about him. The assertions or implications that he was murdered, or killed himself, are of course without a vestige of foundation, though I think every one must feel that the brevity of his tenure of office was a mercy to him and to the country. Harding was not a bad man. He was just a slob." She concludes that Harding's discovery of what was going on around him and the worry and shame it caused him contributed to his death.[26]

Here again is another famous quotation that has often been taken out of context or remained unexamined. One representative example can be found in a popular essay on Harding by Morton Keller, who writes that it "seems unlikely that the cruel judgment of Alice Roosevelt Longworth, T. R.'s trenchant daughter, will ever be replaced: 'Harding was not a bad man,' she said. 'He was just a slob.'" While those who quote Roosevelt Longworth usually pass along her statement that Harding was a slob, rarely does any reference to her denunciation of the gossip accompany the rest of her statement. By 1933, when her book appeared, Harding's reputation was so bad that calling him a slob seemed somehow to elevate his status. The book was certainly kinder than Hoover's dedication of the Harding Memorial. Although many aspects of Harding's life vindicated the log cabin myth, a consensus was reached that his presidency was a tragic shortcoming, if not an outright betrayal of American institutions and values.

The Harding family moved to Caledonia, Ohio, in 1870 and lived there until Warren was five. The 1920 election featured representations of Harding's Ohio background in what was a modern equivalent of a log cabin campaign. *Courtesy of the Ohio Historical Society*

Like much of the country, Crawford County did go Republican for Harding in 1920. Harding emphasized local history in many of his campaign speeches. *Courtesy of the Ohio Historical Society*

Harding the newspaperman-turned-candidate meets with reporters on the steps of the "press house" built in his backyard for the election. Most stories about Harding were positive, in large part because journalists viewed Harding as one of their own (notice the newspaper tucked under his arm). *Courtesy of the Ohio Historical Society*

Harding poses with a hot-off-the-presses copy of the *Marion Star* during the 1920 campaign. The campaign emphasized Harding's role as a small businessman, newspaper owner, and booster. *Courtesy of the Ohio Historical Society*

Reproduced from the *World* of August 6th.

STANDARD PRESS, COLUMBUS, O.

dal KRONER

COX

LEAGUE OF NATIONS

AMERICA FIRST

Issued by Republican State Executive Committee
GEO. H. CLARK, Chairman
187 South High Street   Columbus, Ohio

UNDER WHICH FLAG?

Please Post

A campaign poster from 1920 illustrates the choice that Harding and the Republicans presented to the public. Democratic candidate James Cox raises the flag of the League of Nations while Harding stands before the American flag. Harding successfully contrasted his hometown patriotism with the Wilsonian internationalism of the Democratic Party. *Courtesy of the Ohio Historical Society*

The America First! poster from the 1920 election was created by Howard Chandler Christy. Harding's America First pledge symbolizes the traditional interpretation of Harding as rejecting progressivism and embracing isolationism. *Courtesy of the Ohio Historical Society*

Florence Harding (*right*) chats with two women during the front porch campaign. Because the 1920 election was the first following the ratification of the Nineteenth Amendment, the Harding campaign sought ways to attract women's votes. Also, in the campaign the front porch represented both the public realm of politics and the intimacy of the home. *Courtesy of the Ohio Historical Society*

Candidate Harding with the actress Blanche Ring. The Harding campaign was the first to use Hollywood celebrities to polish the candidate's image. The appearance of glamorous stars in small-town Marion underscored the campaign's mix of old-fashioned community values and an embrace of modernity. Florence Harding stands in the background. *Courtesy of the Ohio Historical Society*

President Harding's funeral procession in Marion in 1923. Harding died a popular president. The national mourning of Harding reflected the nation's need to heal following the First World War. The commemorative efforts borrowed themes from the 1920 election, including an emphasis on Harding's ties to Marion. *Courtesy of the estate of Walter M. Lauffer*

Planning for the Harding Tomb began shortly after Harding's death in office. The elaborate classical tomb reflects Harding's prestige in 1923. However, by the time the tomb was completed, members of the Harding Memorial Association had difficulty arranging a dedication, and President Hoover did not dedicate it until 1931. *Courtesy of Jeff Johnson*

The Shadow of William Estabrook Chancellor

He knew that there was scarcely a detail in George's book that was precisely true to fact, that there was hardly a page in which everything had not been transmuted and transformed by the combining powers of George's imagination; yet readers got from it such an instant sense of reality that many of them were willing to swear that the thing described had been not only "drawn from life," but was the actual and recorded fact itself.

— *Thomas Wolfe,* You Can't Go Home Again

The shadow is a metaphor commonly used to discuss a legacy. For example, we speak of a person standing in his or her predecessor's shadow, or alternately for a person to be overshadowed. William Leuchtenberg has written about Franklin Roosevelt's legacy casting its shadow on his successors. David Greenberg titled his history of Richard Nixon's image *Nixon's Shadow*. With more sinister connotations, Francis Russell writes of Harding living in the shadow of his birthplace, Blooming Grove, Ohio. In a reversal of the log cabin myth, Russell finds in Harding's birthplace a dark secret that cast a shadow on Harding's life. By this, however, Russell is not invoking the typical denunciation of Harding's small-town ways (although he does that as well) but rather is referring to the persistent rumor that Harding had African American ancestry. Harding's reputation developed during a period when Americans were divided over conflicts concerning urbanization, religion, race, gender, and generally what it meant to be American. During the 1920s race riots were common, the Ku Klux Klan flourished, and immigration laws reflected racial nationalism.[1] Harding's presidency and his legacy did not escape these conflicts. Race plays a substantial part in understanding Harding's legacy.

Whereas Harding's boosters and detractors emphasized his mid-western small-town background (to different ends), the issue of Harding's race suggests the nationalization of a vernacular reputation apart from the booster ethos. By *vernacular reputation,* I am referring to an aspect of Harding's image that was grounded in the local community and believed by a significant number of people but did not become part of the national commemorative story. That the Harding family was black or that it included a mixed racial background was widely believed in Marion, Blooming Grove, and other parts of central Ohio. As Harding became a national figure, this local memory took on increased importance. Sociologist William Estabrook Chancellor was the individual primarily responsible for transforming this vernacular memory into a national scandal. The story that Harding was black was granted authenticity because it came from Harding's hometown and because of the authority conferred by Chancellor's academic credentials.

During the 1920 election William Estabrook Chancellor, then a sociology professor at the College of Wooster, became obsessed with tracing Harding's ancestry and set out to investigate and publicize his findings. Chancellor argued that the Harding family had black ancestry and that such ancestry constituted a moral stain that should have kept Harding out of the White House. Chancellor failed in his effort to ruin Harding and instead ruined his own reputation; the College of Wooster fired him from his professorship, the federal government suppressed his biography of Harding, and he was forced into temporary hiding. Chancellor's work would go on, however, to become an important part of the Harding legacy. But Chancellor's argument was a shaky one, based largely on racial stereotypes, particularly stereotypes regarding the immorality of black men.

Looking at Chancellor brings us back to the president's hometown. As it turned out, Marion, like Harding, had its dark side, a story that boosters did not want to tell. However, to understand the Chancellor affair and the impact it has had on Harding's legacy, it is necessary to look at two different but related stories: first is Chancellor's argument regarding Harding's ancestry, which was granted legitimacy by his standing as an academic. Second is the local context of central and northeastern Ohio, in which he conducted his research.

The second story involves Marion, Ohio, in the violent year of 1919. Harding's 1920 campaign evoked a quiet, idealized Main Street of yesterday, but Marion was not as idyllic as it appeared; it had many of the problems that made Americans yearn for normalcy. World War I had fostered industrial growth and the ensuing influx of people had disrupted the community. In the early months of 1919, Marion exploded in a violent race riot. During its course, white Marionites drove almost the entire black population from the town. When Chancellor appeared to conduct his research on the candidate and his family, he found a white population charged with racial tension and community boosters who hoped the riot would not damage the town's good name. That riot, so important to the context of Chancellor's research, has been largely forgotten or ignored by historians.[2] Throughout Chancellor's work and Marion's experience with the race riot ran the common themes of citizenship in the community, morality, and race.

Chancellor's Shadow

Chancellor was the first of many scholars who would fixate on issues of race and morality when it came to Harding. Because Harding was president, he became a vehicle through which Americans discussed race and identity. Whether acknowledging it or not, they would all build on Chancellor's work. Although the claim of black ancestors in the Harding family has wide currency, it has not been substantiated. Despite the lack of direct, concrete evidence, the belief that Harding was black, or of mixed racial ancestry, has not gone away. The origins and persistence of the rumor shed light on the way in which history is created. The belief is not confined to fringe elements but can be found in widely read mainstream works. Francis Russell is the historian most responsible for spreading the rumor. Russell organizes his book *The Shadow of Blooming Grove* (1968) around two important and interconnected themes: the possibility that Harding was black and the exploration of his extramarital affairs. From Russell we learn that the shadow that followed Harding from his birthplace in Blooming Grove was the rumor of black heritage. In pursuing this shadow, based on Chancellor's work, Russell makes an indirect but important connection between the belief that Harding was black and the belief that he was sexually promiscuous.

Even as Russell uses the metaphor of the "dark shadow," as he calls it, throughout his biography, he dismisses Chancellor and notes that Chancellor's "white-supremacy obsessions" drove him to the point of endangering his "own mental stability." Russell's dismissal of Chancellor as unstable or insane is typical. In 1999, Robert Ferrell said that Chancellor was "nothing less than a nut."[3] Fellow Wooster citizen Edwin Abramson describes Chancellor not as a scholar but as a fanatic who brought the most "national attention that our fair city of Wooster has probably ever received."[4] Russell describes Chancellor's lectures at the College of Wooster as a "rant against the blacks."[5] Yet Russell also helps validate Chancellor's claims: "With the author's obvious paranoia and scurrility of his approach, it is not to be wondered at that no historian has tried to sift the facts from the fantasies. Yet facts are there. While in Marion Chancellor picked up the story of Harding's liaison with Carrie Phillips and made the sole printed mention of her name until the discovery of her long-hidden love letters in 1963" (529).[6] Russell metaphorically uses the possibility of mixed ancestry and accepts Chancellor's discoveries regarding Harding's extramarital affairs but makes no effort to further investigate the Harding family tree, surely an issue of some importance, given the topic. While it is understandable that Russell would highlight the possibility of Harding being the first black president while at the same time distancing himself from the obviously racist work of Chancellor, it is regrettable that he goes no further in finding out whether such rumors have any factual basis but rather accepts much of what Chancellor wrote.

Following the publication of *The Shadow of Blooming Grove* and, more important, the changes accompanying the civil rights movement, scholars have used the issue of race to reinterpret Harding's legacy, at least in part. J. A. Rogers's *The Five Negro Presidents* (1965) featured on its cover a drawing of Harding with a black man who Rogers claims was Oliver Harding, the paternal granduncle of the president. Rogers relies on Chancellor's work in his discussion of Harding. However, unlike Chancellor and others who made use of Chancellor's work, Rogers has a larger point. Rogers's short book is a critique of the way in which race has been defined, particularly the assumption—common throughout most of American history—that one drop of black blood made a person black, an assumption that permeates Chancellor's work. He writes, "That, therefore, these American Presidents might have had some Negro strain is possible. Did some persons who knew the intimate details of their ancestry tell of them? There are many instances of whites being exposed as Negroes."[7] Rogers becomes a starting point for an ongoing discussion of the possibility of Harding and other presidents being of a mixed race ancestry and what that might mean for national identity. Sociologist Gary Allan Fine suggests that if Harding was the first president who had African American ancestry, that heritage could be the basis for a more positive interpretation of Harding's career. Auset BaKhufu offers a more radical approach in *The Six Black Presidents,* wherein she argues that Harding was one of many presidents who were black. She enlists Chancellor's work in an effort to demonstrate that African Americans have held the highest office in the land. What for Chancellor disgraced the presidency and for Russell provokes ambivalence is now enlisted by BaKhufu in the cause of black pride. She relies primarily on evidence collected by Chancellor and cited by Russell to argue that it was "widely documented, and a well-known and definite fact to many White and Black elders in Harding's hometown, that Warren G. Harding was a Black man." She also repeats Harding's often-quoted reply when asked about the rumors, "How should I know? One of my ancestors might have jumped the fence." Like Russell, BaKhufu offers no substantial proof that Harding was black but instead relies on Chancellor.[8]

Popular historian Carl S. Anthony has argued that Harding's legacy should be reassessed, considering his relatively enlightened attitude regarding race relations.[9] Anthony writes that with "the credibility of a later sociology professorial post at Wooster College in Ohio," Chancellor "got people to talk." Anthony acknowledges that "the material he [Chancellor] most sought—genuine evidence of Harding's ancestry—never materialized as reliable information," but he notes that in the "process of his search over the years, [Chancellor] opened a Pandora's box of truths about both Warren and Florence: facts such as the Carrie Phillips affair, Warren's precarious heart condition, Florence's De Wolfe relationship and treatment of Marshall that were known by only to those closest to the Hardings in Marion."[10] Chancellor became one of the commonly used sources on intimate, and intimately scandalous, aspects of Harding's life, but because Chancellor's conclusions were mired in racism, people often dealt with Chancellor from a distance.

Given the prevalence of race as an issue in Harding's biography and the central role that Chancellor played in emphasizing racial issues, certain questions remain to be answered. Where did Chancellor get his information? If Chancellor was deranged, then what about the people whom he interviewed and cited in his work? These are questions that Russell does not attempt to answer. While Russell lists racial background as one of the "four mysteries" of Warren G. Harding, conducted research in Marion, where he discovered the long-lost Carrie Phillips letters, and notes the "scurrility" of Chancellor's approach, he failed to investigate the environment in which Chancellor conducted his research.[11] With deeper local research, Russell would have discovered that Chancellor's work revealed more about the conditions of race relations in central and northern Ohio than about the Harding lineage. Russell stresses Harding's connections with

Marion and much of his book was an attempt to puncture the tranquil façade of Harding's front porch campaign by exposing the scandal and corruption lying beneath the all-American image. In this respect Chancellor's work served him well. Russell failed to discover, however, that the president's hometown was deeply divided along racial, religious, and ethnic lines.

The Historical Record

The Harding family genealogy was mundane, but entering the election of 1920 there was no clear public record of the family's background. As the Harding family moved and prospered, Warren's father, George, as one historian has written, "constructed an ancestry occasionally based on fantasy instead of fact." During the election of 1920 both George and Warren Harding further embellished the family background with tales of frontier heroism.[12] These constructed tales of frontier ancestors fit nicely with the log cabin myth, which was so important to the front porch campaign and gave Harding's partisans a way to point to Harding as a great commoner.

Chancellor's revelation that people from the candidate's hometown believed he was not white represented a danger to the Harding campaign. The Republican Party's response to Chancellor's activities only added to the confusion. As the issue of Harding's race exploded later in the election, the chairman of the Ohio Republican State Committee informed Daugherty that the story was everywhere. Suggesting the connection between race and gender in this first national election in which women voted, he worried that the story was "affecting the woman vote." To counter the impact of the story, Republican leaders had the Wyoming Historical and Geological Society of Pennsylvania prepare an elaborate, lily-white Harding family tree for distribution to the press. Samuel Hopkins Adams wrote that the electorate was confused by these rather high-handed claims for the "folksy Harding." The electorate, he maintained, did not care if the "Hardings came across the Atlantic Ocean on the *Mayflower* or down the Ohio River on a flatboat." Senator Boise Penrose, who was often described as a political boss of Pennsylvania and one of the Senate cabal that nominated Harding, was credited with giving the instructions "Don't say anything about it [the story that Harding was black]. We've been having a lot of trouble with the negro vote lately."[13]

Following Harding's death the evidence became even scarcer; Florence Harding destroyed many of the presidential papers in 1923 and the Harding Memorial Association hid the remainder. As we saw in the previous chapter, in the absence of evidence Chancellor's work was one of several alternative and not altogether accurate biographies that emerged to fill the void.

Professor Chancellor

Despite what has been written about Chancellor, contemporaries did not view him as mentally unstable or deranged. It was only later that locals would seek to distance themselves from Chancellor by labeling him a fanatic and discounting his academic credentials.[14] Chancellor had been superintendent of schools in Washington, D.C., before joining the faculty at the College of Wooster. Wooster was less than eighty miles from Marion, providing Chancellor with a base from which to investigate the various towns that were important for the Harding family. Chancellor held an endowed chair at the college. His work had impressed college president Louis Holden, who wrote that Chancellor "was nothing if not stimulating to the student mind. He got students to thinking and asking questions of many kinds, and they liked him." Even after the passage of many years, Chancellor retained his reputation as a challenging teacher. A historian of the college described Chancellor as "a lively and progressive thinker, one who effectively challenged the students' family faith in long underwear, castor oil, and the Republican Party." He did not remember Chancellor as "obsessed by racial questions." In addition, Chancellor was a widely published scholar, with books that included *Our Presidents and Their Office* and *The United States: A History.* Chancellor was respected enough that Champ Clark, Speaker of the House, wrote the introduction to *Our Presidents.* He was an ardent Wilsonian Democrat who was among the most vocal in the Wooster community in supporting American involvement in the Great War and the League of Nations. He wanted to discredit Harding as part of an effort to preserve Wilson's legacy. In 1919 the Democratic governor of Ohio, James Cox, soon to be the Democratic presidential nominee in 1920, appointed Chancellor to represent Ohio at the anniversary of the landing of the Pilgrims at Plymouth Rock.[15] When Chancellor embarked on his crusade to ruin Warren Harding, he did so from a respected position.

Chancellor's attendance at the 1920 Republican national convention was the first step in his campaign to destroy Harding's presidential bid. Here, Chancellor warned the delegates of a grave threat, as he saw it, with flyers declaring that the presidential candidate from Ohio was a mulatto. Harry Daugherty, who as Harding's convention campaign manager was probably at the height of his political power, later described Chancellor's activities as a "vicious and outrageous personal attack" that backfired on the Democratic Party. Daugherty pointed out that Chancellor brought no new information to the convention. The Republican executive committee had long been familiar with the "ancient lie" that had been raised in every Harding campaign since he won a seat in the state senate in 1898.[16]

Daugherty set the tone for defending the Harding family: "no family in the State had a clearer or more honorable record than the Hardings, a blue-eyed stock from New England and Pennsylvania of the finest pioneer blood, Anglo-Saxon, German, Scotch-Irish and Dutch" (56). Daugherty also offered an origin for the mulatto story. In a schoolyard fight between the Hardings and the Applemans, he wrote, the latter began hurling insults at the Hardings, with the Appleman children calling the Hardings, among other names, niggers. A family feud developed and others in the community soon joined in, thus spreading the story (56–57). After Harding's death, Joseph DeBarthe offered another explanation for the story. DeBarthe was a Marion physician who wrote *The Answer,* a point-by-point defense of Harding that was intended to counter the various charges made against Harding after his death and the appearance of Nan Britton's book in 1927. According to DeBarthe, the rumor had started when Harding's grandfather, who was a "pronounced and enthusiastic abolitionist," aided escaped slaves on the Underground Railroad. The local pro-slavery element began the story to discredit the Harding family. DeBarthe also assured the American people that "nothing but the purest Caucasian blood has ever flowed in the veins" of the Harding family.[17]

Whatever its origins, the story followed Warren Harding to Marion, where his enemies seized on the issue to block his rise as a newspaper publisher and politician. James Vaughn, a rival newspaper publisher, attacked the Harding family while Warren Harding's *Marion Star* was still a fledgling venture by pointing out the "woolly head of Doctor George T. Harding." Later Vaughn, perhaps at the prompting of Amos Kling, Florence's father, dedicated a full page to the rumors of mixed ancestry in the Harding family. Kling, Harding's father-in-law, had long disapproved of his son-in-law. As part of this long-running feud, during the 1910 governor's race Kling declared that he hoped never to live to see Ohio have a black governor. One Marion resident recalled that the *Marion County Democrat* had published a black silhouette of Harding; the editors explained that Harding's color prevented his features from showing.[18] The story of whether or not the Hardings were of mixed ancestry had been politicized and muddled for some time before Chancellor stumbled upon it.

The Ancient Lie

Chancellor did indeed tap into the ancient lie, as Daugherty called it, in the geographic heart of Harding's political support. Chancellor did not create his broadsides or his later biography of Harding from whole cloth. Rather, he used his position as a professor to research, albeit one-sidedly, to prove his theories regarding Harding's race. Chancellor spent months interviewing people throughout central and northern Ohio in small towns that had been disrupted by racial, religious, and ethnic tensions. Chancellor collected sworn depositions from the people he interviewed.[19] He proved that some people believed that the Harding family was racially mixed but did not point out that those beliefs were built on stereotypes.

Chancellor was hardly alone in his belief that a person's race and moral character were reflected in his or her appearance. Samuel Hopkins Adams, in *Incredible Era* (1939), refers to the connection between Harding's appearance and his character: "Nowhere in that countenance would a physiognomist find anything symptomatic of the man's innate weakness and softness of fibre, though possibly in his carriage, for he slouches a little as he moves. True, the face is slightly asymmetrical, but that is no indication for a criminologist, being only the outward and visible evidence of an inward and comforting cut of tobacco, snugly tucked away in the pouch of the cheek."[20] Adams, like Chancellor, relies on dubious logic and pseudoscience in making connections between Harding's appearance and character. This analysis seems even more confusing given the near constant refrain that Harding looked like a president, unless we understand this as an attack on one of Harding's seemingly irrefutable political virtues, his appearance. That is, Adams is saying that the public voted for Harding because of his superficial appearance and ignored his lack of substance.

Chancellor, who was steeped in the scientific racism of the day, had no difficulty in finding others who shared his beliefs about the Harding family and the state of race relations in America. Calvin G. Keifer, a forty-five-year resident of Galion (a town some twenty miles northeast of Marion), swore under oath that Warren Harding had "negro blood" and that others shared his belief.[21] Seventy-three-year-old Elias Shaffer, a resident of Akron and a lifelong Republican, had attended school with George T. Harding, Warren's father, and swore that he was black. Shaffer made several points that were often repeated as evidence of Harding's mixed heritage. First, talk of the Harding ancestry was common and open and "none of the Hardings every [*sic*] denied it." Second was the issue of appearance. Shaffer said that

Phoebe Harding, an aunt of Warren's, "was decidedly of Negro appearance." Third was a reference to the mixing of the races and lax morals. Shaffer testified that Phoebe Dickerson's (that is, Warren's mother's) brother had opposed her marriage to George T. Harding because he was "a descendent of a Negro and had colored blood in his veins."[22] George W. Cook, a former treasurer of Marion County and a resident of the city of Marion, repeated, as Chancellor summarized his testimony, that "this report and statement [of black ancestry], though repeatedly made and talked of, has never been denied publicly or privately to his knowledge." As further evidence, Cook cited the opposition that Amos Kling had raised when his daughter, Florence, announced her plans to marry Warren. Kling, "publicly on the streets of Marion at the time of his daughter's marriage to WGH, declared in the presence of a great many people, and in the presence and hearing of the [family], that Warren G. Harding is a negro." Again, no denials came from the Harding family.[23] The feud between Florence and her father was commonly known and became an important part of the local lore in the story of Harding's rise.

The level of crudeness in the affidavits varied even as the sentiments stayed the same. Ninety-three-year-old Montgomery Lindsay of Marion swore that the Hardings were "niggers." Lindsay had been a student of Rosslindy Harding, swearing that she "had the features and color and resembled a negro." Lindsay, apparently white, did not explain how he came to have a black teacher. He went on to recount a story from his school days: George T. Harding "was a colored man of very high coloring and on one particular day he came to the school to take his sister Rosalindy [*sic*] Harding home and the children were scared of him, he being the first colored man they ever saw." Lindsay went on to ascribe to Warren G. Harding what he saw as black characteristics. He had employed the teenage Warren Harding, then a neighbor lad of sixteen or seventeen, to cut corn on his farm. In Chancellor's narration, Lindsay recounted how he paid Harding "two cents more on the shock for the reason that the Harding family was very much in need of help at that time and it was his intention to help them out by employing W. G. H. at a higher wage than the other help. At this particular time Warren G. Harding did not complete cutting one shock but quit, saying the work was too hard for him." He attributed the family's poverty and Warren's unwillingness to engage in hard work to a black background. Here would be another theme in Chancellor's various biographies: that Harding did not like to work hard.[24] As additional proof, Lindsay repeated Amos Kling's accusations and Harding's refusal to deny it.[25] Lindsay's account was not consistent with other details about the Hardings, who were not poor. Accounts vary as to how hard Warren and the rest of his family worked. Harding's sister Charity ascribed Warren Harding's later health problems to his working too hard as a teenager, writing that "such heavy work (when so young and developing so rapidly) was not conductive to a strong physical foundation for after life. He was too tired to rest and sleep at night." Having found what he wanted Chancellor made no effort to verify the details presented by the people he interviewed, or to reconcile the various accounts.

Having failed to prevent Harding's nomination, Chancellor worked to prevent his election. Central to his attack, and no doubt for his own protection, Chancellor insisted that he was simply reporting the results of his scholarly research. Chancellor produced a series of broadsides, all of which made essentially the same claims even if they were not always consistent in the facts. In one of his broadsides he describes, not very accurately, Warren Harding's family:

> His father is George Tryon Harding, obviously a mulatto; he has thick lips, rolling eyes, chocolate skin.
>
> His *wife* was Phoebe Dickerson, a midwife by trade. She died several years ago. They had two sons and three daughters, and W. G. W. B. [Warren Harding] was born when G. T. [George Harding] was only twenty years old.
>
> Nothing is known of the family or ancestry of this Phoebe Dickerson. One daughter was black with kinky hair; only one daughter ever married. The names were Abigail, Carrie, and Mary.
>
> The parents of G. T. Harding were:
>
> Amos Harding of whom almost nothing is known, he was a white man from New York State, and Mary Ann Dickerson or Dixon Harding a black woman, but when they were married, if ever, no one knows. They had this son G. T. in the year of 1844.
>
> The brother of May [Mary] Ann was Mordecai Dixon or Dickerson, of whom his children, all Bucyrus has a tale. He sat in the corner of the Baptist Church reserved for Negroes; was often on his feet in prayer meetings, etc. He was a cooper by trade and had a large and rather wild family. Mordecai was born in 1813 and died in 1901.

By Professor Wm. Chancellor
Professor of Political Economics of Wooster University[26]

In another broadside Chancellor outlines the Harding family:

> Harding Family Tree
> Amos Harding
> (White from New York)
> Father: George Tyron Harding
> (mulatto)
> Mary Ann Dixon
> (negress)[27]

In the accompanying text, Chancellor offers as a key piece of evidence the fact that Amos Harding had seventeen children and ninety-eight grandchildren. While Chancellor does not openly state that young marriage (although one could hardly consider being married and having children in their twenties unusually young) and large families were immoral, through context he makes it clear that he viewed them as signs of moral depravity and of being black. It is also likely that Chancellor was playing on fears of white "race suicide" by discussing high birth rates among African Americans and further playing on white fear by linking race to a presidential candidate who would be the nation's ruler and head of state.

Ultimately, Chancellor's "proof" of Harding's black ancestry came from the local context. Chancellor explains that he had "spent twenty-two days in Blooming Grove, Galion, Bucyrus, Marion, Caledonia, and the countryside where the thousand descendants of Amos live. He spoke French and came from the French West Indies via Virginia in 1820." Chancellor, it seems, had changed his mind about Amos Harding and now decided that he was not a white man from New York. Chancellor then proclaims that "Harding is entitled to be considered mostly white, part red, part black. He is hybrid, mestozo, mulatoo-creale." According to Ohio law at the time, if Chancellor's description is accurate, Harding would have been considered black because all that was required was "one drop" of African American blood for a person to be classified as black.

Chancellor tried to use Harding's own statements as veiled warnings of what a Harding victory would bring. "As Harding himself says," Chancellor writes, for example, "one race is as good as another in America." As final proof of his claims, Chancellor includes two postscripts, one informing readers that Blooming Grove was a station on the Underground Railroad and another noting that he, Chancellor, had been superintendent of schools in Washington, D.C., from 1905 to 1915. Chancellor would make repeated references to Blooming Grove's role in the Underground Railroad without ever specifying the significance of this association and without giving precise examples. For Chancellor, it was self-explanatory and damning of Blooming Grove that its citizens had been involved in the antislavery movement. Chancellor would add to his own list of credentials that, on his father's side, the Chancellor family was descended from "old Virginia slave-holding families." In his later biography of Harding, Chancellor described the area around Marion and Blooming Grove as Little Africa: "Little Africa consists of three counties, where for a hundred years has raged the feud between the whites and the mestizoes. In it live a thousand descendents of Amos Harding and ten thousand other hybrids." He also writes that "few in Blooming Grove are white all through." Finally, Chancellor is always careful to emphasize that "Marion citizens" had told him that "Warren Gamaliel Bancroft Harding (as he was baptized) is an octoroon."[28]

Chancellor's correspondence with contemporaries reveals results from his investigation that do not appear in the broadside. In both his private and public pronouncements, Chancellor's version of the Harding genealogy is ever changing. His correspondence also illustrates the connections between Chancellor's racism and the prejudice against other groups that was common to the period. In particular, Chancellor's racist views made it difficult for him to accept the success of any African American in business or politics. To reconcile Harding's success with his supposed ancestry, Chancellor turned to anti-Catholicism and again to the local context. Marion Republicans, "both men and women," who knew Florence Kling DeWolf Harding, as Chancellor referred to her, "tell me that they voted for Harding against Tim Hogan, believing that an octoroon is preferable to a Roman Catholic but they will never vote for him as President." Tim Hogan, a progressive Democrat who had some success in cleaning up state government as attorney general, had been Harding's opponent in the 1914 senatorial race, which Harding had won. The Ohio Guardians of Liberty, an anti-Catholic group, aided Harding's victory by waging a campaign against Hogan on the grounds of his Catholicism.[29]

While conducting his research locally, Chancellor justified his crusade in national terms; he was working to preserve the office of the presidency and Woodrow Wilson's vision of America. While I have not found any direct connection between Wilson and Chancellor, Chancellor was clearly motivated by his desire to support Woodrow Wilson's administration. Declaring his lack of interest in the "race question," Chancellor writes that he favored Cox because "he is FOR the League."[30] Chancellor assured one correspondent that he was not interested in the race question but had a preference for white statesmen "if possible." He then outlined what he claimed was the Harding genealogy and the connection between the Underground Railroad and Blooming Grove, this time adding that George Harding, who practiced homeopathic medicine, "was never able to support his large family or compete with white doctors."[31] Marion provided Chancellor with the material that he believed would ruin Harding and preserve Wilson's legacy. Chancellor closed one letter with, "Leave it to Marion to work the landslide to Cox!"[32]

What did Chancellor find in his investigation? Without a doubt he found people who believed that the Harding family was, at least in part, black. He also found people more than willing to gossip about Marion's leading citizens, providing gossip that was destined to become some of the most famous in American history. Chancellor also found a community beset by racial tensions that persisted after their peak, reached in 1919, in the form of a violent race riot. The riot came in the wake of the turmoil that accompanied World War I and as a reaction against the migration of black southerners northward in search of wartime industrial work.

Leave It to Marion

Imagine, if you will, William Chancellor not as a deranged lunatic stalking the streets of Marion but rather as a distinguished professor from a nearby college. Also, imagine what he found in Marion. By the time Chancellor arrived, Marion's African American population had already fled the town to escape white mobs. Chancellor conducted his investigation in a virtually all-white town whose citizens were fully captured by the tensions gripping postwar America. Chancellor found Marion to be a fitting place for Harding, writing that it "never was a clean city, and Warren felt at home in it."[33]

Certainly Chancellor's description conveyed a different impression of Marion than America had received during the election of 1920, with Harding campaigning on a tree-lined avenue—at that time Marion appeared to be a very clean city. By 1920 Marion had experienced several decades of rapid industrial growth, and it appeared that the vision of Marion's civic boosters was coming to fruition. Fittingly for a town served by both the Pennsylvania and Erie railroads, the *Star*'s editorial page was titled the Hub of Commerce. The expansion, however, was not without its costs. The influx of people had unsettled Marion's sense of community. The booster emphasis on harmony becomes that much more understandable when one realizes how little harmony Marion had had just one year before the election.

Marion's postwar tensions led to violence, and the murder of Belle Scranton, on the night of January 29, 1919, served as the catalyst. Belle Scranton was a resident of the working-class West Side, with a husband who worked for the Erie Railroad. She had been murdered while walking home from the train station. She was returning from Bucyrus, where she had attended the funeral of a friend whom she knew through the National Protective League, an anti-immigrant organization. Scranton's murder shocked Marion's citizens; the *Marion Star* referred to the attack as one of the "most atrocious crimes" in Marion's history.[34]

The police, perhaps inadvertently, led Marion down the path toward violence. They hoped to track down the assailant by tracing Mrs. Scranton's stolen jewelry and, since Scranton's clothes were covered with grease, officials looked for a man who worked with his hands, leading police to the rail yards. The police began systematically arresting black men who worked for the railroads, although they found no evidence to incriminate any of the suspects and offered no explanation as to why they targeted black men.[35] The arrests of black men marked the beginning of what would eventually escalate into a riot. Civil unrest seemed a certainty as the *Star* ran the bold headline "Would Burn Him Alive," while reporting that railroad workers were maintaining a fire for that purpose. To prevent vigilante justice, local police and railroad detectives increased the pace of arresting black men, though the *Star* conceded, "there is little evidence to fasten the crime to any of them," and assured readers that "every precaution to protect the men under arrest" would be taken.[36]

The *Star* editorialized that the "horrible crime" cried out for punishment while simultaneously asserting fear of the consequences of vigilante justice. Rather than turning to violence, the crime brought to light the previous neglect of Marion's West Side by its police force and the need for "greater and more effective police protection for the western part of the city," where railroad lines offered "easy ingress and egress" and a lurking place for the unsavory element.[37] Adopting the first-person booster tone of speaking for the people, the *Star* explained that it was time for citizens to realize that "we have grown out of the village class; that we have become a city with, we regret to say, the disadvantages as well as the advantages which go with a city." A few decades earlier, "almost every Marionite knew almost every other Marionite, and a bad citizen was a marked man because the entire community knew him to be a bad citizen."[38] While the analysis appearing in the *Star* seemed reasonable, there was no indication of which citizens were the bad ones or of how many citizens might abandon the old ways of the village for the new, impersonal ways of the city. Having offered a diagnosis, the *Star* and authorities called for the citizens of Marion to re-main calm. The rumors, the *Star* warned, must stop because the "lynching of an innocent man would be a frightful way in which to avenge the mur-der of Wednesday night."[39] Despite these statements, the messages sent by Marion's authorities were clear. The police offered, by their actions, a defini-tion as to which citizens were bad, and the *Star*, in seeking to restore calm, suggested that lynching was not a solution.

The Scranton murder and investigation were but the first steps toward the civil unrest that authorities feared. The community's anger and fear ex-ploded only after a second crime: Margaret Christian was attacked on Sunday evening, February 2, 1919, only four days after the Scranton murder. Ac-cording to the *Star*, she was hurrying to her West Side home when "a colored man grabbed her by the throat."[40] The *Star* noted that the incident, "on the heels of the attack and murder of Mrs. Clyde Scranton, last Wednesday night, caused great commotion in the city, Sunday night and early this morning."

The attacks increased the anxieties of Marion's residents regarding industrial growth and migration. Following the arrests the police and the *Star* would become more precise in their definitions of the bad citizens as a way of explaining the disruption to the community. The police arrested George Washington Warner in connection with the Christian case, and the *Star* immediately declared him all but convicted of the murder. Twenty-two years of age and searching for work, Warner had recently migrated from Kentucky to work for the Erie Railroad. Police concluded that Warner fre-quented the Strawstack Hangout, a shelter for transient black men just north of the Erie roundhouse. They based this conclusion on the traces of oats and straw found on his clothing and on the direction he was running. More important, police concluded that Warner might have been involved in the Scranton murder because the Strawstack was about three hundred yards from where her body had been found. The police conducted several searches of the straw for Scranton's stolen jewelry and other evidence that might link Warner to that murder, but to no avail.

Impatient with the police investigation, a lynch mob of two hundred formed outside police headquarters, a development the *Star* noted despite a reluctance to acknowledge the purpose of the mob. Unable to find

Warner, the crowd dispersed. Most members of the mob went to the West Side, where they attacked a saloon owned by James Hagan, an establishment frequented by black men. There the mob was dispersed by police officers, but it regrouped and later that night broke into smaller groups that roamed the West Side, breaking the windows of homes belonging to black families and ordering the families to leave Marion.

With mob violence now a reality, the *Star* and city officials sought to protect the city's reputation with a slight shift in rhetoric. Gone were thoughtful essays on the nature of growth and pleas for peace. In their place came a concern for order and the need to excuse the mob's action. Mayor A. J. Sautter arose at 4:30 in the morning and acted "in every way possible to keep Marion's name clean of any mob violence," the *Star* reported. Upon the advice of the sheriff, the mayor's first act was to close all the saloons. The *Columbus Dispatch,* more honestly, reported that Marion had been placed under "semi-martial law." The *Dispatch* coverage offers an important corrective because Columbus was the closest major city, about fifty miles from Marion, and also the state capital. The mayor then met with black leaders and police regarding the request, as the *Star* called it, for the black residents to leave the city. According to the *Star,* many of the city's black residents were "property-owners and . . . residents of good standing and reputation and they were advised that there would not likely anything result from the threats and orders made to them, it being the opinion that the men in the crowd are desirous of ridding the city of a certain class that has come from the South during the past two years to do railroad work and do not claim Marion as a place of legal residence." Again, the *Dispatch* published a slightly different version—one not based on property ownership as a requirement for citizenship and protection by the local government. The Columbus paper plainly labeled the crowd a lynch mob and reported that the "few colored families who remained in the city Monday night were barricaded in their homes."[41]

To protect Warner, Sheriff James Ullom transferred him to the town of Mount Gilead, only a short drive to the east. The sheriff acted just in time; upon his return to Marion he faced another crowd, this time of around three hundred, which the *Star* described as orderly. The crowd had formed outside the jail only to be frustrated because Warner was not in the jail. The following morning Sheriff Ullom announced, in a spirit that the *Star* would appreciate, that the men were "not in an ugly mood and complied with his requests." That night, however, the mob had reformed and, now "baffled," regained its direction when word "leaked out" that Warner was in Mount Gilead. Twelve leaders of the mob, several of whom were recently discharged from the military and still in uniform, raced to Mount Gilead. Marion judge Grant E. Mouser, a close friend of the Harding family, attempted to prevent vigilante justice by telephoning the leaders of the mob in Mount Gilead to warn them not to use violence. Again the mob found Warner gone.[42]

Local officials placed a high priority on restoring order and protecting the town's name. The next morning, February 3, 1919, Judge Mouser announced the creation of a special grand jury to investigate both the charges against Warner and conditions on the West Side. The special grand jury was clearly designed to placate the crowd (that is, the mob) and restore order. The judge promised to consult with members of "last night's crowd" in the selection and composition of the jury. To this end, Mouser requested that the members of the mob who had been arrested be released from the Mount Gilead jail.[43] The *Star* reported that the following night, Monday, February 4, 1919, was quiet. To prevent another outbreak of violence in Marion, Police Chief J. W. Thompson brought in "outside police assistance," which included the entire Erie Railroad police force and officers from nearby towns.[44]

While the large law enforcement presence undoubtedly contributed to the peace of the city in the aftermath of the mob violence, Marion's quiet was also the result of the mob's success in accomplishing its goals, which had included a campaign of terror against most of the city's black citizens. On the morning after the riot, signs were found throughout the West Side with the warning TNT—Travel Nigger Travel. On Monday morning, the *Star* reported that a "general exodus" of the town's black residents had taken place overnight. Officials estimated that over two hundred black families fled the town before daylight. The Erie Railroad discharged about one hundred men who worked at the roundhouse and transfer station, some of them "so scared that they feared going after their pay." Many black residents fled so quickly that they left behind furniture and other possessions too big to easily carry. The few black people who remained in Marion were "keeping off the streets for the time to avoid any outbreak." The *Star* reported, "several close observing persons remarked at noon, today, that they had not seen a colored person on the streets this morning." One saloon owner complained that his business was now ruined because black men employed by the Erie Railroad made up the preponderance of his customers. After Marion officials announced that they anticipated no further violence, Mayor Sautter allowed the saloons to reopen.

The outbreak of violence in Marion had been particularly fierce and in many ways fit established patterns of white violence against blacks. Despite half-hearted protests from the *Star* and the sheriff's efforts to maintain order, almost the entire black population of Marion had fled, leaving the white community in which Chancellor would, in a few short months, be conducting his interviews. The *Star* had tried, without success, to differentiate between long-standing propertied black residents and industrial workers who were defined as transient and thus outside the community. The plea for order was by and large unheeded and, as civic leaders feared, state officials in Columbus took note of the violence.[45] Notices continued to appear on homes and businesses warning black residents to leave and to notify others of their "tribe" to go with them. The sheriff reported that "lifelong" black residents had been receiving notices to evacuate the city "voluntarily" or face the use of force.[46]

In the end Marion officials were able to link Warner to the Scranton murder, although their evidence was based on the testimony of a man the sheriff publicly called a "mental defect." The Scranton murder and the subsequent riot would eventually become forgotten moments in Marion's history. The investigation by state officials had attracted a great deal of publicity and, of course, residents of nearby towns noticed the black citizens fleeing in terror. These events would soon be overshadowed by the nomination of Harding, which attracted William Estabrook Chancellor to Marion.

What was the significance of Chancellor conducting his investigation in Marion? First, the Marion of 1919 was consumed with racial tensions and, by 1920, with the nomination of Warren G. Harding. Although it was less visible during the celebration of Harding's successes in 1920, the racism of 1919 did not simply go away. Consistently, town boosters were concerned with image—with keeping Marion's uglier side out of the public arena. Chancellor's, and later Russell's, goals were opposite of those of the boosters. Why did Chancellor choose to not expose the riot, which would have damaged Marion's name? Clearly, Chancellor did not have a high opinion of Marion, but he also shared in many of the assumptions regarding citizenship and race that were evident in the public discourse during the riot and its aftermath. Both the *Star* editorialists and Chancellor avoided the more vulgar and violent side of racism but clearly linked morality, race, and citizenship in a way that, as Chancellor had phrased it, preferred white leaders to black. They shared during this debate over citizenship an underlying assumption that blacks tainted the community. Chancellor disliked Marion but found there the dark shadow that Russell and others would so exploit in their writings on Harding. He did not expose the riots, perhaps, because he agreed with the goals of the rioters and approved of the actions of the mob.

Conclusion — Marion

In 1919, Marion had garnered statewide attention for the race riot. Although he made no mention of the riot, it was almost inconceivable that Chancellor could have been unaware of the conditions there while living in nearby Wooster and while investigating Harding. The local story, however, was not over. In the early to mid-1920s, sociologist Frank Bohn found in Marion a classic case study of the rise of the Ku Klux Klan. Bohn was drawn to Marion because the town had seemed so typically American during Harding's front porch campaign. Bohn was clearly and bluntly sympathetic to the Klan movement, particularly admiring its rise and influence in the Midwest and praising Marion's white, Protestant population. Perhaps Bohn found the Marion Klan so tempting to study because the Klan had taken to having events at the Harding Memorial even as it was under construction, with the memorial offering the dramatic patriotic symbolism favored by the Klan. Even more ironic, in death Harding, who had been reviled by some racists as our first black president, was claimed by others as a member of the Ku Klux Klan.[47]

Despite the interlude of harmony that came with the front porch campaign of 1920, by the mid-1920s Marion County politics and business were again divided along ethnic and religious lines, with either opposition or support by the Klan as a centerpiece of politics. The Klan of the 1920s focused its hatred on blacks, but it also targeted immigrants, especially Catholics and Jews. During the 1924 mayoral election the Klan supported Reverend Buckley, of the Disciples of Christ Church. A Republican, Buckley won easily. However, Buckley won without the help of the Republican City Committee. The division could also be seen in business, as Protestants and Catholics boycotted each other's establishments. The Knights of Columbus built a brick market house and reserved it for use only by Catholics. The Klan organized a boycott and ruined the market financially, then purchased the building (390).

Bohn, Chancellor, and the Marion Klan all shared common beliefs regarding nativism, racism, and fear of moral decline. This should not be surprising. Nor should it be surprising the Marion had an active Klan and experienced racial and religious tensions during the 1920s. The decade following World War I was a high-water mark for racism, especially violent racism. The interesting thing is that from this environment Warren G. Harding, even with the rumors regarding his race, became a popular civic leader and elected official. In 1938 Harold F. Alderfer discovered that Marion residents still believed that Harding was partially black. He quoted a *Star* reporter: "It was generally believed that there was negro blood in the Harding line, but that W. G. had outgrown it."[48]

Conclusion — Chancellor

The ancient lie at the heart of Chancellor's work reflected the locality of Marion and the acceptance of racism at the time. It was more than the act of a deranged lunatic or a political dirty trick. During the election Chancellor, armed with research gathered in Ohio, distributed flyers with the title *The Right of the American People to Know*. To this date no one knows how Chancellor financed his expensive campaign. Republicans suspected Democrats, but the Cox campaign denied any involvement in the affair. Joseph P. Tumulty, Woodrow Wilson's private secretary, told Samuel Hopkins Adams that a stranger had presented him with proof of the allegations but that Tumulty had turned him away. According to Tumulty, the Democratic National Committee would not touch the material—"Suppose Senator Harding is elected. What a terrible thing it would be for the country if it came out that we had a President alleged to be part negro!"[49] Edward L. Doheny, the oil millionaire who was later implicated in the Teapot Dome scandal, offered $25,000 to publish full-page pictures of George and Phoebe Harding to show America their whiteness. Most newspapers suppressed the story. Harding made no comments on the issue, a decision that reportedly came at Florence Harding's request (184).

The College of Wooster attracted national attention because of Chancellor's activities, but it was not positive publicity. The college's president, the Reverend Charles F. Wishart, called a special meeting of the board of trustees in which they questioned Chancellor. Chancellor admitted to having done the genealogical research but denied having put it into print. He argued that Harding's nomination was part of a plot for "negro domination" of the United States. The trustees demanded his resignation and so Chancellor left his position (183). In an ironic twist, Chancellor was attacked in Wooster after the announcement of Harding's victory by an angry partisan mob crying, "Get Chancellor! Lynch him!" A group of four students protected him by literally barricading themselves in his house.[50] Chancellor and all the students escaped, but Chancellor was now leaving behind the status of a reputable educator and becoming an outcast.

As a story circulated that Chancellor had threatened to assassinate Harding, the Secret Service placed Chancellor under house arrest. Locked in his house, Chancellor began working on the monograph that was to be the culmination of his research. *Warren Gamaliel Harding: President of the United States* was, as stated in its introduction, "an account of the ethnological experiment at Blooming Grove, a main Ohio station in the underground railroad, formerly called Harding Corners, and of the six months' investigation into the ancestry of the President including a report as to whether his parents were ever married; and if not why not."[51] The publishers insisted that the book would be an "exoneration and vindication" of Chancellor. The book was a subscription book, sold door-to-door. Secretary Gree of the Ohio Democratic Committee described the salesmen as "tough-looking fellows." Howard Lowry, who had investigated the affair, noted that the publisher, Sentinal Press, was a "Dayton printing firm that kept well hidden," operating undercover as it poured out Ku Klux Klan literature.[52] There is some confusion here: according to the title page the book was published by Sentinal Press, but Lowry and others refer to a Sentinel Press, a Klan operation out of Cincinnati. The Reverend Samuel Snepp, the brother of the Dayton attorney who worked with Chancellor, recalled that two men from Cincinnati negotiated with his brother regarding the Chancellor research.[53] The biography, attributed not to Chancellor but to his research, was to be a tour de force of the supposed sins of the Harding family, a defense of Wilsonianism, and an explication of the scientific racism of the day.

Chancellor's hopes for vindication were dashed, however, when the federal government suppressed the book. In *The Strange Death of President Harding*, opportunist Gaston Means claimed, in typical fashion, to have been part of the dramatic roundup of the books that were then burned at the McLean residence. Samuel Snepp, the Dayton lawyer who had helped Chancellor arrange the book's publication, wrote to Adams that government officials had terrorized and intimidated him.[54] It is ironic that this book, which almost did not see the light of day and had a small circulation, went on to have such a strong influence on Harding scholarship.[55] Samuel Hopkins Adams concluded that scholars will never know the whole truth of the Chancellor affair or the Harding ancestry. He also concluded that Harding's ancestry really was not an important issue: "If negro blood there were in his line, he honorably and courageously lived down the handicap."[56]

Adams, of course, offered little praise for Harding and that, despite its of-fensiveness to modern ears, amounted to praise from him. Harding scholars would find kernels of truth in Chancellor's work even as they denounced him. However, they rarely questioned his evidence. Writers such as Adams and Russell found it easy to use Chancellor's work, perhaps, because he documented his research in a way familiar to academics and because for most of the period when Harding's legacy was being discussed the claim that he might be black simply remained another scandal, another taint on his legacy. Furthermore, we cannot discount the influence of Chancellor's focus on Harding's private life (and in particular his sex life), which he pur-sued in the name of defending Wilson. Chancellor was hardly alone in this impulse to use Harding's private life for public politics.

Chancellor gained some fame—along with Gaston Means, Nan Britton, and others who offered insight into the seamier side of the Harding admin-istration—and some sympathy after the suppression of his book. He was eventually able to resume his academic career, joining the faculty of Xavier College in 1927 and later returning to the College of Wooster. He would later deny having written the Harding biography, telling Mark Sullivan, au-thor of *Our Times*, an influential account of the 1920s, that he had not writ-ten the book or the broadsides but rather that a black man trying to elect Harding was responsible.[57] Chancellor died in 1962; his obituary in the *Wooster Alumni Bulletin* made no mention of the scandal. He never saw his work become the shadow in Francis Russell's biography of Harding.[58]

Like so much else in Harding's legacy, Chancellor's trail led back to Marion. Marion would be remembered as the president's hometown, even after the Harding scandals had made that distinction somewhat du-bious. Forgotten, however, was Marion's own scandal and how it had pro-vided William Chancellor with the information that would so damage Harding's reputation.

Harding, Our First Black President

So here we have Warren Harding, weirdly enough, as both a black presi-dent and a member of the Ku Klux Klan. Sociologist Garry Alan Fine ar-gues that it would be possible to reinterpret Harding's place in history if he was viewed as our first black president.[59] Could Harding's reputation rise if we thought of him as a black president? Put another way, would Harding's new racial identity serve as justification for his shortcomings as president? That would certainly be in line with Chancellor's own reasoning and is suggested by Rogers's argument that Harding had to overcome racism to succeed. The reality, however, is that insufficient evidence exists to convincingly argue that Harding was black or of mixed race. It is possible that Harding can be considered black as determined by Ohio's one-drop law, but the belief that Harding was black is based primarily on Chancellor's dubious work, which is not supported by less-creative family genealogies. The most pervasive argument that Harding was not white is based on the persistence of the rumor of black ancestry, combined with the fact that Chancellor did stumble on Harding's affair with Carrie Phillips and published it before most journalists or scholars were willing to. The exception was William Allen White, who discussed Harding's detours off Main Street without naming names, but who was obviously referring to Carrie Phillips. The reasoning, therefore, is that since Chancellor, whatever his personal issues, was able to uncover one embarrassing secret about Harding then it makes sense that he could have done likewise with the possibility of black ancestry.

While it is unlikely that Harding could be revised as a black president, the prospect does point to other issues. Briefly, that Fine could argue that interpreting Harding as a black person would improve his reputation points not only to the poor quality of Harding's reputation but also to the substantial improvements in race relations that have taken place since the 1920s. More intriguing, the discussion of race raises the issue of whether Harding's reputation could be revised based not on his own race but rather how he dealt with the issue of race as president. Was racial harmony a component of normalcy? Given what almost everyone has written about Harding, one would expect him to be a joiner and go along with the Klan. It seems intuitive that Harding, the politician who joined every civic club and talked of old-fashioned patriotism and America First, would join yet another organization that wrapped itself in old-fashioned values and over-the-top patriotism. Harding, who was so much a part of Marion, would seemingly want to join the Klan, an organization that was powerful and popular there during the 1920s, just as it was throughout many other communities in the Midwest and the South. Surely Main Street led Harding to the Klan.

Was Harding a member of the Klan? The rumor that Harding was a Klansman, and had joined the Klan in a White House ceremony held while he was president, has gained academic currency. For example, anthropologist Pem Davidson Buck cites Harding as cooperating with the Klan.[60] However, in his biography of Florence Harding, Carl Anthony dismisses the idea that Warren Harding joined the Klan. Instead, he argues, Harding joined the Shriners and in his acceptance speech made a strong statement against hate groups. The press reported his speech as an attack on the Klan, which was then holding a rally near Washington. Anthony speculates that, in retaliation for Harding's attack, the Klan itself spread the rumor that Harding had joined the Klan, when in reality he had joined the Shriners. Alton Young, the Klan's imperial wizard, said, "Harding agreed to be sworn in as a member of the Ku Klux Klan. A five-man 'imperial induction team' headed by Simmons conducted the ceremony in the Green Room of the White House." Young said that the delegation had forgotten their Bible so Harding provided one of his from the White House living area. From here the story spread rapidly, despite Harding's denial. When queried, the president's secretary replied that in "some quarters it has been represented that the President is a member of this organization. Not only is this untrue, but the fact is that the President heartily disapproves of the organization and has repeatedly expressed himself to the effect."[61] This would seem a clear denial of Klan membership and a rejection of the organization's values.

Harding's public record on the Klan and race relations was mixed. However, historians Eugene Trani and David Wilson conclude that Harding "was unwilling to commit himself even on the resurgence of the Ku Klux Klan." They note that blacks began considering abandoning the party of Lincoln because Harding's record was "unsatisfactory." Harding's "sympathetic hearing early in his administration made disillusionment the more bitter" because his "words were not matched by deed." They do recognize that it was "perhaps unfair" to "expect more of Harding" given "the times."[62] Perhaps they should have also mentioned that Harding's actions, limited as they were, amounted to more than those of the presidents who came before and soon after him and that Harding died in office without completing his term, thus leaving many of his promises unfulfilled. Trani and Wilson thus interpret Harding's denouncement of the Klan as a failure to take a stand against racism.

So what were Harding's words and deeds? During the campaign Harding had promised to support an antilynching bill, and in his first message to Congress he did just that. The bill passed in the House but was filibustered in the Senate. He also proposed the creation of a race commission that would "formulate, if not a policy, at least a national attitude of mind calculated to bring about the most satisfactory possible adjustment of relations between the races."[63] Why did Harding give an early sympathetic hearing to black voters? Was it because he was black? Was it because he himself had repeatedly been called nigger? The standard interpretation is that Harding desired to create a two-party system in the South. To that end, the Republican Party would need black voters to remain loyal and regain their ability to vote in a solidly Democratic South whose leadership was committed to maintaining Jim Crow. While this might not have been high-minded, Harding was at least interested in ensuring that African Americans could vote.

On October 26, 1921, Harding delivered his best-known speech on race at Birmingham, Alabama, on the celebration of the semicentennial of the city's founding. Harding's Birmingham address is important for his legacy because, as Robert Murray concludes, this address was also "the most important presidential utterance on the race question since Reconstruction days and, regardless of motivation, required considerable courage."[64] Harding's speech was dismissed by blacks and whites alike, each of whom found something in it to dislike. Harding received death threats from white supremacists after the speech. Harding's speech echoed the times as he struggled with his own needs as a national leader and a party leader. Harding did not transcend his times, but neither did he descend to the level that he could have. While Harding's call for changes in American race relations may seem tepid today, he did, at least, address the issue. More important, unlike Wilson, Harding did not embrace the ugly racism found in movements like the Klan, in movies like *Birth of a Nation*, or the race riot in his own hometown.

Harding's speech reflected his own booster background and belief in progress. In his pronouncements you can find elements of the booster ethos: a call for economic prosperity and harmony, fairness, republican virtue, and a belief in business leadership. Standing in one of the South's premier industrial cities, Harding began his speech by praising its economic development as a testimonial to southern progress, "since slavery was abolished and the rule of free labor and unfettered industrial opportunity became the rule of all of our great Republic." The Civil War, Harding argued, "marked the beginning of that diversification of industry which has made the South of to-day an industrial as well as an agricultural empire." According to Harding, in true booster spirit, this was the important story. He urged historians of the Civil War to move away from the study of the political and military and to focus instead on industrial development.

Harding then moved on to more contemporary events but continued with his theme of wartime transitions. Harding said that "the World War brought us to full recognition that the race problem is national rather than sectional" because of the "great migration of colored people to the North and West." The Great Migration forced the South to realize its dependence on black labor and "made the North realize the difficulties of the community in which two greatly differing races are brought to life side by side." Although Harding made no mention of his hometown, one has to wonder if he had the people of Marion in mind, people who could testify to just how difficult and ugly race relations had become. Harding then discussed black soldiers who had served in Europe during the Great War, lamenting that many of them now wanted to live in Europe; one black soldier told him that being there had given them their "first real concept of citizenship." Searching for a solution to the problem of race in America, Harding went on to argue, "Politically and economically there need be no occasion for great and permanent differentiation, for limitations of the individual's opportunity, provided that on both sides there shall be recognition of the absolute divergence in things social and racial." Suggesting something akin to Booker T. Washington's Atlanta Compromise, Harding said the members of both races would "stand uncompromisingly against every suggestion of social equality." Therefore, the answer was to have it "accepted on both sides that this is not a question of social equality, but a question of recognizing a fundamental, eternal, and inescapable difference." In the political realm Harding said, echoing Lincoln, "Let the black man vote when he is fit to vote; prohibit the white man voting when he is unfit to vote." He then appealed to the "self-respect" of blacks and to their desire to improve their position in society. He would "insist upon equal educational opportunities for both," although he qualified this with a caveat that equal education might not occur within several generations.

Harding proceeded to mildly scold the South, "both black and white," informing southerners that the "time has passed when you are entitled to assume that this problem of race is peculiarly and particularly your problem." Asserting again that race was a national problem, Harding went on to broaden the context even further: "more and more it is the problem of Africa, of South America, of the Pacific, of the South Seas, of the world." Striking an attitude very different from Wilson's vision of a community of nations, Harding continued that race "is the problem of democracy everywhere, if we mean the things we say about democracy as the ideal political state." Americans, Harding argued, wanted to avoid class and ethnic divisions, and he lamented the growth of divisive voting blocs along the lines of class, race, and ethnicity. This was not solely an issue of political ideals. Harding argued that it was of the "keenest national concern that the South shall not be encouraged to make its colored population a vast reservoir of ignorance, to be drained away by the process of migration into all other sections," as had been the case in "recent years."

In true booster fashion Harding disavowed self-interest even as he argued for something that would benefit him. He declared that he did not want blacks to be "entirely of one party." He wished that the "tradition of a solidly Democratic South and the tradition of a solidly Republican black race might be broken up." Harding could foresee a time when blacks "vote for Democratic candidates, if they prefer the Democratic policy on tariff or taxation, or foreign relations, or whatnot; and when they will vote the Republican ticket for like reasons" with full citizenship. With these goals Harding urged southerners to "take advantage of their superior understanding of this problem and to assume an attitude toward it that will deserve the confidence of the colored people." He then pleaded with his own party not to use blacks as a "mere political adjunct." The way to rid the nation of hatred and "dangerous passions" was to persuade blacks that under both political parties "they would be treated just as other people are treated, guaranteed all the rights that people of other colors enjoy, and made, in short, to regard themselves as citizens of a country and not of a particular race." Much as Harding had urged women to become involved and partisan during the election, Harding argued that blacks with the vote could act independently.

Reflecting the racial nationalism of the day, Harding transitioned from a discussion of race and citizenship to a discussion of immigration and republican virtue. The essence of Harding's discussion was how to create a harmonious and virtuous community. As a small-town booster, Harding had linked conformity to progress, as a president he would link assimilation to patriotism. Harding argued that the country needed a better education system that would not create an overabundance of lawyers and a shortage of laborers. Related to the issue of labor was the perceived problem of a rapid increase in the national population that, he rationalized, would be curbed by recent immigration restrictions. As the immigrants "Americanized," Harding said, there would be "less rapid multiplication." This, he reasoned, would create a need for people to do the "simpler, physically harder, manual tasks" that had been done by immigrants. He said, however, "I don't think it has been good for what the old Latins called the national *virtue*" for old-stock citizens to push the unwanted jobs on immigrants. Harding called on American national virtue, "a word I have always liked, employed in the Roman sense" to "raise honest, hard, manual work to a new dignity if we are to get it done." Harding was evoking the nation's old republican traditions of a virtuous citizenry as the cornerstone of representative government and the free labor ideology that had been prominent in the early days of the Republican Party as a solution to the nation's social problems. Harding's speech continued the themes of boosterism and progress that he raised on Social Justice Day during the campaign.

Harding would not have been Harding if he did not end his speech on a positive note. Returning to his theme of progress, he said that the "march of a great people is not a blind one" for a people who "wish to be more than apace with progress." He praised Birmingham's advances over the past fifty years and concluded that if "we are just and honest in administering justice, if we are alive to perils and meet them in conscience and courage, the achievement of your first half century will be magnified tenfold in the second half, and the glory of your city and your country will be reflected in the happiness of a great people, greater than we dream, and grander for understanding and the courage to be right."

As was typical of Harding, the Birmingham speech wove together themes of historical destiny, progress, and nationalism. What Harding proposed was not that far removed from Booker T. Washington's Atlanta Compromise; he was advocating economic and political rights for blacks while "acknowledging" differences between the races. Harding added to that message a strong dose of the booster ethos and an evocation of the old Free Labor ideology of earlier days, in recognition of the virtue of manual labor, which he argued blacks would be doing. Harding's proposed course of action would not be acceptable for an American president after the civil rights era; his vision was much more in line with nineteenth-century civic boosters and leading citizens. Interestingly, Harding clearly asserted that the Civil War was a triumph of northern values over southern values not only in economics but also in race relations, and no doubt his message was reinforced by his presence in one of the great industrial centers of the New South. Race, according to Harding, was a national, not a regional, problem and the proper solution was citizenship, suffrage, and progress. Harding tied together the march of economic and democratic progress with the need for a change in race relations. As Harding explained it, the South could not stand behind regionalism and federalism on this issue and so there was in Harding's speech an implicit, and again delicate, discussion of national action to improve race relations. Although Harding's speech was not as pointed as some would like, in large part because of his propensity to seek compromise, he was the first president since U. S. Grant to suggest the need for national action to improve race relations.

Harding reinforced the message presented in his Birmingham speech on at least two other occasions. Before he left the South, he gave an address in Atlanta in which he praised Henry W. Grady, a spokesman of the new industrial South and the newspaper editor who had coined the term New South. Grady and Harding both understood the booster ethos. In his Atlanta address, Harding praised Reconstruction as a time that paved the way for progress, even if there were some mistakes.[65] Harding addressed the legacy of slavery and the Civil War again when he dedicated the Lincoln Memorial in May 1922. Harding praised Lincoln as a martyr, a commoner, and the Great Emancipator, arguing that the

> supreme chapter in history is not emancipation, though that achievement would have exalted Lincoln throughout all the ages. The simple truth is that Lincoln, recognizing an established order, would have compromised with the slavery that existed, if he could have halted its extension. Hating human slavery as he did, he doubtless believed in its ultimate abolition through the developing conscience of the American people, but he would have been the last man in the Republic to resort to arms to effect its abolition. Emancipation was a means to the great end—maintained union and nationality. Here was a great purpose, here the towering hope, here the supreme faith.[66]

Here again we see Harding's desire to create the harmonious community. He embraced the unification of the country under Lincoln but waffled on Lincoln's role as emancipator. Although praising Lincoln as the Great Emancipator, he noted that Lincoln's greater "purpose" lay in maintaining the union. In this juxtaposition we see Harding's own search for a compromise that would bring political rewards for his own party but that would also benefit the nation as a whole through the march of progress in the United States.

Harding got little credit from his contemporaries for his stance against the Klan or his thoughts on race. Murray writes that "Harding's courageous attacks on the politically powerful Ku Klux Klan did not impress Negro leaders as they groused about appointments." Harding became exasperated and wrote to a friend, Malcolm Jennings, "Negroes are very hard to please." The Dyer Bill, the antilynching act that Harding had called for, passed the House but was temporarily stopped in the Senate Judiciary Committee. A lynching in May 1922 prompted Harding to push the bill out of committee. However, Harding moved slowly, fearing reprisal from southern senators. The bill did not reach the Senate floor until November 1922, where it was killed by a southern-led filibuster. Likewise, Harding's request for a commission on race died in committee. Murray concludes that there was "little question that during the twenties the Republican Party completely bungled the chance to align growing numbers of northern Negroes behind its banner. Still the fact remains that Warren Harding was the only president between the Square Deal and the Fair Deal who examined the question of race relations in a fresh way." Harding's meager achievements were not entirely his fault, Murray writes. Only "in the matter of patronage could he be held culpable, and even here there were extenuating circumstances. In the area of race relations, Harding deserved more credit than he received."[67]

Harding, unlike his progressive predecessor Woodrow Wilson, viewed Republican efforts during Reconstruction not as a tragedy but as a flawed but positive step in national progress. Wilson famously described the movie *Birth of the Nation,* with its pro-Klan interpretation of Reconstruction, as tragically true, and as "history written with lightning." Harding, on the other hand, rejected the popular interpretation of the Civil War as an act of Northern aggression that brought an end to an elegant Southern way of life based on a humane, and certainly not evil, system of slavery. Harding was fundamentally at odds with the prevailing interpretation of history, both inside and outside the academy, as well as the general mood of the people. For Harding, progress had meant that slavery needed to end. Progress also demanded that racial tensions needed to lessen. Here, Harding stands in positive contrast to Wilson, who supported segregation and expanded it during his time as president; to Theodore Roosevelt, who made his Progressive Party lily white for fear of alienating southern voters; and to William Estabrook Chancellor, who called Harding a black man while bragging of his own family's slaveholding tradition.

Chancellor's crusade against Harding took a significant but minority strand from the vernacular culture of central Ohio and transformed it into a part of our national memory. What was lost in the various commentaries about Harding's race and whether or not it amounted to a disgrace to the presidency was an understanding of the context. Indeed, the lack of context defined the story as public memory and not as history, despite its appearance in many history books. Placed in context, Chancellor's crusade and his sources reveal how important, and divisive, race was to Americans of the 1920s.

He-Harlot

There is a vast difference, ladies and gentlemen
of the jury, between reputation and notoriety,
and the seeker after the later is generally
amply repaid for efforts to secure it.

—Joseph DeBarthe on Nan Britton

If ever there was a he-harlot,
it was this same Warren G. Harding.

—William Allen White

To this point we have seen enough scandal to ruin the reputation of any public figure. At the nexus of Harding's reputation
stood his hometown, which was closely related to his character. Commentary on Harding came in many forms: some was
fictional, some factual, and some spurious. With the release of
The President's Daughter in 1927 Nan Britton dealt the final,
fatal blow to Harding's reputation, ensuring that Harding's
legacy would forever be mired in tabloid-style sensationalism.
The Britton scandal, much like the Chancellor affair, produced a public memory lacking chronological context but
steeped in regional and personal context. Since its release,
Nan Britton's book has dominated Harding's legacy, changing
the central question asked of Harding. Instead of debating
the extent of Harding's knowledge of and involvement in political scandals, interested parties focused on a new question:
did Nan Britton and Warren Harding have a child? The Harding marriage, with the Britton story, would become a central
concern of reputational entrepreneurs.

True Romance

In addition to its obvious sensational appeal, this question has also retained its vitality for over three-quarters of a century because a definitive answer has remained elusive. The question has no national political significance but it has provided endless opportunities for those wishing to exploit the scandalous nature of Nan Britton's story. It also illustrates the rise of celebrity-driven tabloid-style scandals. In many ways this is an obvious but overlooked aspect of Harding's, and Britton's, legacy. The twentieth century saw the rise of popular literature and journalism that often focused on the sensational and the titillating. The twenties, as a decade of rapid transition from Victorianism to modernism, meant that the sexual revolution and the new woman played out in cheap fiction and middlebrow culture. Nan Britton's book reflects the existing social tensions that were also present in the popular literature of the period, especially stories aimed at women readers. In short, Britton's overwritten accounts of professions of true love, clandestine romance, and contradictory moralizing were part and parcel of the period. The Britton controversy intensified the cynical connection that commentators made between modernity, relativism, sexual promiscuity, and political immorality.[1] Literary stereotypes abounded in the Harding-Britton story (the powerful man with a younger mistress, the innocent girl, the nagging wife) and themes (trips to Europe, betrayal, social wrongs) that readers would have found in magazines and newspapers.

Most of those who commented on *The President's Daughter* soon after its publication focused on whether they should believe Britton. Despite the numerous and heavy-handed references to flappers and prudes in the various accounts, no one took the analysis further. Even Frederick Lewis Allen, who examines the new morality of post–World War I America in *Only Yesterday* (1931), does not make the connection between flappers and Britton, even though Britton herself identified with issues important to the new woman. Allen writes that Harding's "private life was one of cheap sex episodes" and explains that he came to this judgment by reading the "confessions of his mistress." He is "struck by the shabbiness of the whole affair; the clandestine meetings in disreputable hotels, in the Senate Office Building (where Nan Britton believed their child to have been conceived), and even in a coat-closet in the executive offices of the White House itself." Allen goes on to explain that "doubts have been cast upon the truth of the story," but then asks by way of verification, "Is it easy to imagine any one making up out of whole cloth a supposedly autobiographical story compounded of such ignoble adventures?" Thus, the ignobility of the story becomes proof of its truth. How did this reflect on Harding? According to Allen, through Britton's account "one sees with deadly clarity the essential ordinariness" of Harding.[2]

Even scholars more interested in the politics of the decade have addressed the issue of Britton and Harding's paternity. Robert Murray, in *The Harding Era,* does not come to a conclusion regarding the paternity of Britton's daughter. He accurately describes *The President's Daughter* as "replete with syrupy poems, fervid embraces, secret meetings, breathless remarks (such as 'Isn't this g-r-a-n-d?' and 'What rapture!'), numerous pictures of an eight-year-old girl who looked like the dead president, and a dedication to unwed mothers." (Although Murray does not make this conclusion, his description could apply to much of the popular literature of the time.) Murray goes on, "at no time did she [Britton] evidence any trace of guilt and she displayed a hopelessly romantic view of illicit love triumphing over all obstacles." Murray, as he often does, comes right to the point: "the enormity of her wrong, or that of Harding's, if true, simply never fazed her." Murray finds incredible Britton's claim that many people could know of the affair and not talk. He also notes that her claims had "enough authenticity" to confirm suspicions, and says that Britton's story had some plausibility for residents of Marion who knew both Harding and Britton. Murray finds the acceptance of Britton's story by Harding's sister Abigail to be the most convincing piece of evidence.[3] Still, Murray does not definitively come down on one side or the other.

In *The Strange Deaths of President Harding* (1996), an academic defense of Harding, historian Robert Ferrell seeks to disprove Britton's claim. Ferrell accepts Britton's story of a childhood infatuation with Harding, citing as evidence the doodles about Harding that Britton sketched in her schoolbooks. However, Ferrell accepts little beyond that. He argues that Britton's book was intended as a money-making scheme. As Ferrell interprets her story, Britton had an illegitimate child and saw an opportunity to blackmail the Harding family. When Dr. George Harding, the president's brother, stopped the payments that their sister Abigail was sending to Britton, Ferrell argues, Britton hit on the idea of the book. Ferrell maintains that Britton did not write the book; he cites the testimony of Earl Hauser Smith, who helped prepare *The President's Daughter* for printing, and claims that Richard Wightman, her partner in the Elizabeth Ann Guild (an organization to aid illegitimate children), wrote the book. Ferrell speculates that the Elizabeth Ann Guild was staffed by ghost employees whose salaries were channeled to Britton and Wightman. According to Ferrell, "the ultimate purpose of publishing *The President's Daughter,* which was to assist in raising the legal position of illegitimate children, received little more attention than to write letters. Had Ms. Britton wished to help the mothers of these children she might have spent much more money on the task."[4] Ferrell and Murray failed to recognize that calls for the reform of marriage and family were standard parts of twenties' lowbrow women's literature.

Carl S. Anthony makes use of Britton's account in his 1998 biography *Florence Harding: The First Lady, the Jazz Age, and the Death of America's Most Scandalous President.* Anthony accepts Britton's account and places a great deal of emphasis on the state of Florence and Warren Harding's marriage. In addition to mentioning Nan Britton, "the most famous of his mistresses," and the "tempestuous" Carrie Phillips, Anthony provides a rather lengthy list of Harding's mistresses, real and alleged. Other presidents, he notes, "were accused of affairs, but with Harding there was tangible documentation."[5] While one cannot discount the various political scandals that mired Harding's administration, Harding's marriage and the private scandals have been at least as important in establishing his poor reputation among scholars and the public.

For those who believed it, Nan Britton's story offered proof of the link between the Harding scandals and sexual promiscuity. To complain that politicians have loose morals is hardly an original critique, but with Harding, critics emphasized the connection between political and sexual promiscuity. Harding could seduce both women, innocent or not, and the public. In his autobiography William Allen White describes his first impression of Harding: "He was a handsome dog, a little above medium height with a swarthy skin, a scathing eye, and was meticulously clad in morning clothes with a red geranium as a boutonnier [*sic*], and he had the harlot's voice of the old-time political orator."[6] Rather than noting that Harding looked like a Roman senator (a comparison often raised by other contemporary commentators), White paints Harding as a somewhat unsavory dandy, a male harlot. As Adams implies in his novel, Harding was easy. Adams makes the same point in his biography of Harding, recounting the anecdote of George Harding telling his son that it was a good thing he was not born a girl because he could not say no.[7] Harding was, to use one of his nicknames, a he-harlot.

The Britton scandal also points to the cultural expectation that a president be the patriarch of the country. Underlying the Britton scandal were the related assumptions that Harding's character was not the stuff of either a good president or a good husband. It is interesting that at this moment of intense public debate over the nature of the family, the patriarchy of the presidency was challenged by Britton and others. For Harding's legacy, the loss of status as a patriarch undermined attempts to defend him. White feminized Harding by referring to him as a harlot. The story about Warren Harding not being able to say no was similar in that Harding was compared to a girl, or rather than he lacked the morality to be a proper girl. Britton's book took the allegations that Harding was promiscuous from insider gossip to a full-blown public discussion. No longer would it be necessary to use fictional names to discuss what previously had been protected by presidential privilege. Unlike Teapot Dome and its related scandals, where Harding stood as a patsy for his corrupt friends, Britton depicts him as his own man who chose to cheat on his wife and who lacked the character to be respected as a patriarch. In historical memory, Harding is left to meander through the pages of history stripped of any presidential clothing that might have concealed his flaws.

The Britton story contains several elements that are found in contemporary women's novels, "sob sister" journalism, and modern media scandals. Historians and commentators have tended to condemn Britton rather than Harding, ignoring that, if the story were true, both Britton and Harding stepped beyond the bounds of what many Americans accepted as moral at the time. They have condemned Britton along many of the same lines that rising middlebrow culture was critiqued: feminine, sappy, and questionable. Britton justified this transgression by appealing to modern sensibilities in a manner that would have been familiar to readers of popular fiction. Rather than seek forgiveness for her affair, Britton condemned Victorian standards of marriage and embraced moral relativism as a way to establish her embrace of modernity.[8] Rather than condemning them both, Americans who discussed Britton's story were urged to take sides, to choose not only between Warren Harding and Nan Britton but also to choose between Britton and Harding's wife, Florence. Discussions of the Britton scandal often included comparisons between Florence Harding and Nan Britton, the contrast between the Victorian and the New Woman, which highlighted familiar cultural stereotypes. In this period—when the "nineteenth-century conception of marriage as an institutionalized arrangement whereby husband and wife were expected to fulfill certain socially defined obligations toward one another was giving way to a more 'modern' notion which regarded marriage as a personal relationship between two individuals for the achievement of mutual happiness and emotional fulfillment"—middlebrow culture, including movies and popular novels, explored these themes of marriage and sexuality.[9] Clear parallels existed between the story Britton told and those of the popular women's novels of the day.

In an age of middle-class concern for morality in the wake of scandals in baseball and Hollywood, Britton's book was shocking not only because of its allegations but also for its frank discussion of sexuality, reproduction, and marriage. With *The President's Daughter* subjects that were once taboo but now emerging in the general popular culture became political discourse. Indeed, Britton's book appeared amid other books that explored themes of marriage and the sexual revolution. Many of these novels sold very well and some, like *The Sheik* (1921) and *Gentlemen Prefer Blondes* (first serialized in 1925), became hit movies.[10] Even the printing of *The President's Daughter* was dramatic and defied convention. The police seized the printing plates and copies of the book, acting on the complaint of John S. Sumner, head of the New York Society for the Suppression of Vice, who deemed the book to be "obscene, lewd and indecent."[11] The Elizabeth Ann Guild, established by Britton to publish the book, brought suit and recovered the books, plates, and $2,500 in damages. Nan Britton's story was thus launched in controversy.

Britton's book was not political in the conventional sense. It was, however, as we see with the attempt to suppress the book, political in other ways. Britton used the First Family as an example of the failures of traditional marriage, in fact beginning her account with an attack on marriage: "In the author's opinion wedlock as a word quite defines itself. Often a man and woman are locked at their wedding in a forced fellowship which soon proves to be loveless and during which the passions of the two express themselves in witless and unwanted progeny." By contrast, Britton told of her "life-long love" for Warren Harding, explaining "*the need for legal and social recognition and protection of all children in these United States born out of wedlock.*"[12]

Britton's rejection of conventional values helped her justify what would appear to be her betrayal of Warren Harding and cast her story between a series of dualities: her role as the young, modern, fertile woman versus the older, power-hungry woman; her calls for understanding as a woman versus her male attackers; modern versus Victorian marriage. Britton attempts to legitimize her cause by using Harding as an example of a responsible father of an "illegitimate" child. Furthermore, Britton argues that because of Harding's prominence, the "man-character" she calls him, the story of their affair and child would become public knowledge (ii). She understood that her "fact story," as she called it, would create an uproar; she writes that Harding "may be misjudged," but she knows "in her heart that these revelations cannot but inspire added love for him after his trials and humanities are perceived and acknowledged" (iii). Harding's trials certainly attracted the public's interest, but they hardly inspired love.

Mr. Harding's Bride

The President's Daughter was an autobiography that began with Nan Britton's 1896 birth in Claridon, Ohio, a rural town near Marion. Her father was a physician and her mother was a schoolteacher. Very early in her life, the family moved to Marion, where her father became friends with Warren Harding, periodically contributing to the *Star.* In high school Nan Britton was in Abigail Harding's English class. Nan developed a crush on Marion's leading citizen when he ran for governor in 1910. Even as Britton was weaving her story of an adolescent infatuation, she was foreshadowing her affair with Harding. In the book's early pages Britton develops the theme of girlish innocence that she carries throughout the book.

Just as Chancellor's discussion of Marion's racial difficulties had challenged Harding's depiction of small-town Ohio, Britton's story of forbidden love struck another blow to the booster's image of a harmonious community that Harding wove so carefully during the election and that members of the Harding Memorial Association tried to recreate after his death. Britton followed the by-now established convention of introducing local gossip to a national audience. She referred to rumors of Harding's affair with a woman who was, in all likelihood, Carrie Phillips. Even as a child, Nan Britton heard the gossip but, she says, it did "not move *me* to condemnation of either Mr. Harding or Mrs. Arnold [Carrie Phillips]." As an adult, she writes, "I sympathize with her in her regard for him, for I could conceive of nothing save a very high-minded friendship existing between him and anybody" (11, emphasis in original). This was truly a bizarre statement coming from a woman engaged in a detailed confession of her own role as Harding's mistress. Britton walks a fine line in her account between maintaining her innocence and her credibility (24).

Following her father's death Nan moved to New York City, where she trained at the Ballard Secretarial School for Girls. It was at this point that the story leaves behind the mundane but also introduces the theme of Nan as a modern young woman looking to make her way in the big city. Britton contacted Senator Harding and asked for help in finding a job. As the two corresponded, Britton read between the lines: "Under the cordial phraseology of his letter there was more than the mere desire to offer assistance to me" (29). Britton saved Harding's letters, and they reveal that his tone with Britton was friendly but professional. Harding offered his help in finding her a job in Washington: "I will go personally to the war or navy department and urge your appointment on personal grounds, as well as political." Harding then evoked the memory of her father: "I remember full well that your esteemed father belonged to the party now in power, and that will help."[13] He did ask a "personal favor" of Britton. He inquired of her training to be sure she met the requirements of government employment.[14] Harding's letters reveal a cordial tone but little beyond that. However, in Britton's book the letters become the first step in her seduction.

Britton attempted to confer legitimacy to the relationship she claimed with Harding by using the symbols of marriage. Although inconsistent and not always clear, Britton contrasted her desire for a companionate marriage with Harding with his actual Victorian marriage with Florence Harding. Closely related were her juxtapositions of her virtues as a woman with the shortcomings of Florence Harding. She offered Warren Harding what Florence Harding could not: a young, fertile, modern partner. Although Britton depicts Florence Harding as lacking the necessary femininity to be a good wife, Florence was modern in her own right, with her involvement in politics and business. Britton sent mixed messages that potentially allowed readers to draw conflicting interpretations. She explicitly linked money and sex. Britton describes meeting with Harding at the YWCA where she was living as innocent, but then says Harding later arranged for them to meet at the Manhattan Hotel in New York City. Britton's account of this meeting in *The President's Daughter* is interesting. As it turned out, hotel rooms were in short supply and Harding was forced to take the bridal chamber. She writes that between "kisses we found time to discuss my immediate need for a position." She continues that Harding did not want her to move to Washington; he "frankly confessed to me, he preferred to have me in New York where he could come over to see me and where he would feel more at liberty to be with me." Although Britton's prose is suggestive, her ambiguity allowed it to fall within the confines of the description of flappers in popular literature. Britton and Harding petted (to use the slang of the day) but went no further. She assures readers that there were "no intimacies in that bridal chamber beyond our very ardent kisses." Still, Harding "tucked $30 in my brand new silk stocking" to help pay for a trip to Chicago.[15] Not only did Britton and Harding discuss her future employment and his ability to clandestinely visit, according to Britton, Harding also slipped her money in a manner that suggested that he had less than high-minded motives.

Contradictorily, Britton enlisted Harding in her condemnations of traditional marriage, foreshadowing her argument that she was the proper "wife" because she better fit what some called companionate marriage, even as she argued that she was better able than Florence to meet Warren's needs.[16] In a story that foreshadowed the controversy over Harding's paternity of her child, Britton writes that Harding had told her of German experiments "to create children by injecting male serum, taken at the proper temperature, into the female without the usual medium of sexual contact." Harding denounced this as "German madness" and affirmed his belief that "children should come only through mutual love-desire."[17] Britton does not have Harding proclaim that children should be the result of marriage, but rather through the type of relationship they were entering. Furthermore, given that part of the paternity controversy would involve claims of Harding's sterility, she has him denounce artificial means of insemination. Britton makes the point that the prospect of her having his child "did not occur to me." However, she speculates that it was "not unlikely that even as early as that very first visit Warren Harding was entertaining the possibility of becoming the father of a real love-child" (36). By having Harding approve, Britton downplays and displaces the burden of illegitimacy.

In Britton's account, Harding gradually becomes a patron for the Britton family, helping Nan get a job at U.S. Steel in New York, beginning in July 1917, as a secretary, and helping her mother secure a teaching position in Cleveland. On one hand this patronage seems paternalistic and hinting of a Victorian double standard, as the powerful man not only kept a mistress but aided her family. However, as Britton tells it, it also reflects a modern woman's desire to advance her career. Writing on Senate Committee of Commerce stationery in May 1918, Harding addressed a letter to "My Dear Miss Britton" in New Philadelphia, Ohio, advising her on how to secure employment for her mother in the school system. He enclosed letters of introduction to Frank T. Spaulding, the superintendent of schools, and to Mr. Mark Thomson, president of the board of education.[18] Harding remains appropriately friendly but not intimate: "I was interested to note of your visit to Marion and hope you had an enjoyable visit there. I have not been in the old town myself since early in last February. I wish you would remember me very cordially to your good mother and be assured of my very abiding esteem for yourself."[19] In December 1918, Harding was again replying to "My Dear Miss Britton," offering her yet more career advice. This time he focuses on ambition. Nan Britton, we can gather from Harding's response, wanted to move up from her position at U.S. Steel. Harding thought it unwise.[20] Harding's correspondence reveals an interest in Britton and her family, but motivation beyond helping the daughter of an old friend is difficult to determine.

In Britton's telling, the more experienced Harding led her down the path to temptation. According to Britton, Harding rationalized his actions by telling her that it had been "many years since his home situation had been satisfying." He also made distinctions between male and female morality, telling Britton that "he knew of *no* man except his brother 'Deac' who married, having had no previous experience with woman."[21] Britton, through Harding, almost calls into question "Brother Deac's" masculinity and certainly questions his worldliness (45–46). Ironically, Britton uses Deac's Victorian values to justify both her affair and her story of male libidinousness and female purity.

As Britton tells it, the affair carried with it commentary on the president's virility and masculinity. Britton recounts that Warren Harding confessed his desire to have a child, possible through adoption, but she says that Florence had blocked his wishes. Florence Harding was older than her husband, a point that Nan Britton makes repeatedly, perhaps by way of explaining why Florence Harding did not want children (74). (Florence had a child, Marshall, before marrying Warren.) Britton maintains the innocence of her early contact with Harding: "I was deliriously happy to lie in close embrace with my darling, I just could not even yet permit the intimacies which would mean severance forever from a moral code" that her parents had taught her. Harding, by contrast, was not so easily satisfied. According to Britton, Harding argued that "if people were to know that we had been together intimately without indulging in closest embrace they would not credit the story. In fact, he said to me with something like chagrin that the men would say, 'there certainly must have been something wrong with Harding!'" (48). Following what could be a standard sexual script from romantic fiction, Britton gave in to Harding's advances and the affair became sexual. Britton argues that their having sex was akin to the consummation of a marriage with her rather than a betrayal of his marriage vows. Britton wrote: "Mr. Harding's bride—as he called me—on that day" (49).

Having rationalized her affair with a married man, Britton then describes conceiving Elizabeth Ann in Harding's Senate office. Her after-the-fact discussion of the conception of their "love child" has several controversial dimensions. First, there is simply the issue of the child being fathered outside marriage by a prominent politician. Britton, as we have seen, deals with this by arguing that she was fulfilling a procreative role that compensated for Florence Harding's failure. Second, there is the issue of birth control, a controversial issue in the 1920s. Britton bluntly discusses birth control (although she usually uses a euphemism, such as *precautions*). In her account, while in Harding's Senate office they have forgotten birth control and "of course the Senate Offices do not provide preventative facilities for use in such emergencies." She continues, "For a second time in less than two weeks, having none of the usual paraphernalia which we always took to hotels, and somehow not particularly concerned about possible consequence, we spent a most intimate afternoon" (75–76). Having described the most important and controversial part of her story, Britton immediately offers an explanation about why she did not have proof of Harding's paternity, writing that both she and Harding had agreed to "destroy all love-letters." She writes that Harding kept his letters in a locked desk drawer in his Senate office and had instructed George Christian to destroy them in the event that "anything happened to him" (77).

Now pregnant, Britton takes the reader into a world that was not discussed as part of a presidential legacy. It is also this part of her account that has been largely ignored. Britton felt that Harding wanted her to have the child rather than for her to "handle" the problem otherwise, but "of course our difficult situation called for a discussion of an operation, or other means of procedure" (79). She "pretended" to be interested in an "operation" (an abortion) because her sister Elizabeth was anxious for her to have one. Elizabeth arranged for Britton to visit a doctor who told her, after an examination, that she was of "such a nervous temperament" that he did not want to perform the operation. Elizabeth, however, continued to want to end the pregnancy and so consulted a friend who helped her "prepare some 'bitter apple' medicine," but Nan could not bring herself to take the concoction. Britton, of course, informed Harding of all this (84–85). Britton, again, has herself and Harding discussing a highly controversial topic, abortion, in such a way that confers validity on her controversial statements.

Britton continued to argue for the legitimacy of her relationship with Harding. Upon her decision to have the child, Harding bought Britton a ring and then, "We performed a sweet little ceremony with that ring, and he declared that I could not belong to him more utterly had we been joined together by fifty ministers" (87–88). Harding arranged for her to have the baby in New Jersey (88–89). Britton is as blunt, and dramatic, in describing the pregnancy and birth as she is when writing about the conception. After recovering from giving birth, Britton and the baby, Elizabeth Ann, moved to Chicago to stay with her sister. Britton writes that Harding provided for the child and discussed who could raise her. He returned to the possibility that Florence Harding might die before he did, in which case, "I'd take the baby myself and make her a *real* Harding!" (127–30, emphasis in original). Nan Britton struggled financially to keep the child. Harding arranged for Nan's sister and her husband to adopt the baby, and for a while Nan lived in Chicago with them, pretending to be the child's aunt. She wanted, however, to claim Elizabeth Ann as her own.

Harding's political success, in Britton's view, further legitimized her relationship with him and her status as the mother of his child. During the 1920 Republican convention, held in Chicago, Britton unsuccessfully attempted to convince Harding to meet her at a park so that he could see Elizabeth Ann. Harding tried to "seriously discuss with me plans for financially caring for my situation and for Elizabeth Ann's, but, though I finally changed the topic, saying, as always, that I didn't want to discuss those things." Britton, meanwhile, took pride in the glory of being the "mother of Warren Harding's only child!" (102, 130, 131, 135, 136).

After Harding won the election, Britton wrote that she had visited him several times in the White House, one visit comprising the infamous episode when they reportedly hid in a closet to avoid being discovered by Florence Harding. Britton explained that she and Harding had worked out an elaborate plan for writing letters and sneaking her into the White House with the help of a trusted Secret Service agent. In her book Britton describes what might appear to be an effort to get her out of the country so as to avoid scandal. Harding paid for her to visit Europe. Interestingly, Republican leaders were also supposed to have paid for Carrie Phillips to travel out of the country during the campaign. The story of a powerful man having the "other woman" travel to Europe was a common one. For example, it is central to the novel *Gentlemen Prefer Blondes*. Britton was traveling in Europe when she learned of Harding's death and wrote that she was forced to rely, as she cryptically describes it, on the kindness of a series of men to return to the United States.

Nan writes that when she found out that neither she nor Elizabeth Ann was in Harding's will, she approached his sister Abigail, who was sympathetic. She also approached Tim Slade, the Secret Service agent who she says had sneaked her into the White House. Abigail's cooperation ended after a meeting she arranged between Nan and Dr. George Tryon Harding III (Warren's brother), who demanded that she produce evidence that supported her claims. In trying to understand his attitude, Britton evokes changing values when she recalls Warren Harding's words, "Brother Deac is the only man I know who never slept with a woman prior to his marriage." She could not produce evidence. Importantly, there is a vague discussion of some mysterious physical problem with Harding (398–99).

Britton again brings the discussion back to Harding's legacy and reputation, contrasting her argument that Elizabeth Ann was Harding's heir with the Harding family's concern for his reputation. In particular, Britton relates a conversation regarding changing the name of the high school where Abigail Harding had taught for years to Harding High School. According to Britton, Abigail said, "If this [news of the affair] should get out, Nan, they would take the Harding name away from the high school!" (403). Britton concludes her book by explicitly linking Harding's death, service to his country, and patriarchy:

> According to materia medica, Warren Harding died as a direct result of a cerebral hemorrhage and indirectly from ptomaine poisoning. But I, the mother of his only child, have never for one moment entertained such a thought. I believe that under the burden of fatherhood which he revered but dared not openly confess, combined with the responsibility of the welfare of the nation he loved, the twenty-ninth President of the United States truly laid down his life for his people. He died of a broken heart. And through the voice of the child he loved may there arise a diviner and more lasting memorial to his memory than any reared by human hands,—the answer to the plea from the heart of a mother,—*social justice for all little children!* (439, emphasis in original)

The difficulty of evaluating Britton's story, then and now, is the lack of evidence. Many readers, however, have found the intimacy and familiarity of Britton's account persuasive. Britton maintained her authenticity, paradoxically, by establishing herself as an innocent child, mistress, champion of social reform, and, later, mother. She took the moral high ground, saying that she had written the book out of love for her daughter and for

Warren, professing her love even as she provided much of the information that would contribute to the final destruction of his reputation.

Legacies

Britton's story, obviously, did not end with the publication of *The President's Daughter.* If Britton had never decided to write a book, her story would have remained one of the unproven stories that haunt Harding's legacy. As it is, Britton achieved a high degree of notoriety and for a number of years dedicated herself to telling her story. Britton followed *The President's Daughter* with a sequel, *Honesty or Politics,* in which she recounts her efforts to secure funds from the Harding family and, failing at that, her decision to write and publish *The President's Daughter.* Britton also returned to her theme of championing unwed mothers, comparing her cause to those of earlier reformers, including abolitionists. Even as Britton was engaged in a fierce struggle with the Harding family over Harding's legacy, she called upon history for legitimacy. In *Honesty or Politics* she directly compares *The President's Daughter* to Harriet Beecher Stowe's *Uncle Tom's Cabin* and uses quotations from abolitionist William Lloyd Garrison to deflect the charges of those who called her a gold digger.[22] As Britton explains it, she had the force of history behind her cause for children.

Britton begins *Honesty or Politics* by juxtaposing the plans to build Harding an expensive memorial with her life in New York City, where she shared a small apartment with her six-year-old daughter and her mother (3). Britton lived in New York because she hoped to become a writer. However, to support herself she worked as a secretary for "Mr. Norman Pickway" (an alias for Richard Wightman) of the Bible Corporation of America (12). In the interim Britton ran out of money and had to send Elizabeth Ann to live with her sister in Chicago. Desperate, Nan Britton turned to her employer for help in getting her story out.

Honesty or Politics conveys Britton's awareness of her place in Harding's reputation. Nursing her bitterness over sending Elizabeth Ann away, Britton read about the laying of the cornerstone for the Harding Memorial, funded with pennies given by children to "erect a magnificent marble-pillared mausoleum for the Twenty-ninth President of the United States,— whose own little girl was denied maintenance by her father's family!" She had waited a year for the Harding family to establish a fund for Elizabeth Ann, and now explained that her "conception of a fitting tribute" to Harding was not an "inanimate marble" but "a vibrant flesh-and-blood child—

his own little girl" (23). Although Britton calls Elizabeth Ann a "living memorial," she fails to note that the children of presidents are rarely treated as living memorials or legacies but are more likely to serve as protectors of their father's legacy. Furthermore, Britton's evocation of her child as a living memorial seems feminine or motherly in the masculine world of presidential commemoration. Britton's argument becomes even more problematic when we consider that Elizabeth Ann was illegitimate. Elizabeth Ann, even if she was openly acknowledged as a Harding, was very unlikely to become a living memorial.

Britton's mixed messages continue throughout the book. On one hand, Britton describes a relationship with Wightman that was similar to the relationship she had attributed to Harding, including accusations that Britton became Wightman's mistress. On the other hand, Britton continues to claim that her work was to bring about social justice for women and children.

In her second book Britton addresses some of the controversy that had developed around *The President's Daughter,* revealing her view of how her book fit in with other books that had been written about Harding. Britton writes that Wightman had cautioned her to excise some of the more controversial statements from the book. She describes her later regret for doing so because one of the parts she had cut detailed the "particular physical trouble" that she discussed with George Harding (60–61). As it would turn out, the "physical trouble" was Warren Harding's supposed sterility, which became a center of the defense of Harding and attack on Britton. Britton described the reaction that T. R. Smith, a representative of a publishing house, had to her manuscript as he turned it down, lamenting, "We're passing up $100,000—and we know it!" Smith's firm had published Adams's *Revelry* to great protest. Smith said, "This book is dynamite. *Dynamite!* You're dealing with the private life of a President of the United States!" (65; emphasis in original). After several publishers had rejected the book, Britton explained how she and Wightman established the Elizabeth Ann Guild and the Elizabeth Ann League. Once published, *Honesty or Politics* attracted the attention of tabloid reporters and con men hoping to make some money but was met with "journalistic silence" by the reputable press (145). Britton determined that the "newspaper fraternity" was boycotting her book and that booksellers were in conspiracy against it; her break came when H. L. Mencken praised Britton's book (148–49).

Whatever Britton's motives for writing *The President's Daughter,* she touched a nerve among struggling single mothers. In *Honesty or Politics*

Britton received hundreds of letters from unwed mothers. For example, she heard from "Claire," whose story was similar to her own. Through Claire, Britton learned of institutions where pregnant women who were unmarried would go and, upon giving birth, would then leave the child at the institution, never to see him or her again. In Britton's dramatic telling, such babies often died of neglect. Britton also tells of a nurse who helped "girls in trouble" have their babies. Britton offers this shocking account of a visit to the apartment of the nurse: "On the occasion to which I wish to refer— I shall never forget it!—this nurse held up for my edification a glass jar, inside of which as the fully-formed, unbelievably tiny and perfect body of an infant, in the curved position in which it had such a short time before lain living in its mother's womb." Britton exclaimed that it was murder and the nurse agreed, "Of course it is" (188–91).

Having published her two books, Britton began exploring other opportunities. Interestingly, Britton turned to middlebrow venues, merging notoriety, fame, and reform. She began public speaking and looked into having her book adapted for theater and motion pictures (283). According to Britton, top Republicans stopped the production of a play based on her story. Similarly, she explains, Will Hays of the Motion Picture Producers and Distributors of America blocked efforts by producers to turn her book into a movie. In contrast, Britton argues, Hollywood continued to "emanate reel after reel of sex levities and vulgar inanities, and our prohibition laws are held up to the ridicule of the millions" in films (287). As Britton saw it, Hays was "depriving the Twenty-ninth President of his right to immortalization through the use of his name in sponsoring a cause unexcelled in righteousness" (288). We might ask what form this immortalization would take.

As historian Robert Sklar has observed, World War I was an "unsettled period when late-Victorian mores persisted side by side with an emerging image of a 'new woman'—it could only have been disconcerting to respectable Americans to see photographs of determined young women in ankle-length dresses, high-button shoes and broad-rimmed hats standing in long lines outside a Hollywood casting office."[23] As we have seen, commentators had long noted Harding's movie-star good looks. Now, Nan Britton completed the image. For Americans who were unsettled or titillated, how different was a Hollywood casting office from Harding's senatorial or presidential offices? Sklar's observation on the movie industry applies equally well to Harding's scandals: there "is no way to show a cause-and-effect relation between Hollywood's pleasure principles and the gradual unloosing of sexual restraints in American life; perhaps the two go together as symptoms of social change which affects them both" (81).

Britton concludes *Honesty or Politics* with a discussion of the $800,000 memorial to Harding that had been built in Marion. Britton argued that when "history shall have recorded for posterity the achievements of our Twenty-ninth President, our grandchildren shall learn also of his dear humanities." According to Britton, Harding's reputation would be redeemed when she triumphed in her cause.[24]

The Answer

While Britton compared Elizabeth Ann to the Harding Memorial in an attempt to claim Harding's legacy (and, perhaps inadvertently, undermined the efforts of the Harding Memorial Association to dedicate the memorial), it fell to Marion to defend Harding's reputation. Not surprisingly, given that both Britton and Harding were from Marion, the controversy over *The President's Daughter* became a dialogue about Marion. Britton discussed her life in Marion, identifying those who now sided against her as well as with her. For example, she wrote of her friendly relations with Judge Grant Mouser's daughters, although he had denounced *The President's Daughter.*[25] That book brought forth those boosters who defended the intertwined reputations of Harding and Marion. However, their defense now had a distinctly shrill and unpleasant tone.

Britton could not escape noticing the appearance of a book with the long-winded title *The Answer to 'The President's Daughter' and other Defamations of a Great American* —more commonly shortened to *The Answer* —by Dr. Joseph DeBarthe. DeBarthe was a former editor of the *Buffalo (NY) Times* and a self-taught physician. Like *The President's Daughter, The Answer* was a self-published book (the title page simply reads, "The Answer" Publishers). DeBarthe seems to have received financial backing from prominent local residents of Marion.[26] DeBarthe's purpose was to "deny and refute the scandals and untruths" told about Harding and to defend the president's character.[27] Oddly enough, DeBarthe intended his book to be an argument before the court of public opinion, but only a few Marion merchants sold the book. It is likely that *The Answer* would have had only local influence had not DeBarthe's accusations prompted Britton to sue. *The Answer* is best understood as not only a defense of Harding but also as an attempt by local boosters and Harding partisans to reclaim Harding's legacy and Marion's image.

Boosters often aimed their rhetoric at their fellow citizens, hoping to convince others to accept their vision. Boosters raised comparisons that were unflattering to other towns or urged people to rally to protect the reputation of their town. While Harding's backers could not stop the degradation of his memory nationally, they could sway local opinion. While we can see this developing in the Harding Memorial Association through Sawyer and Donithen, it fully became part of Harding's legacy in the battle over Nan Britton's claims. DeBarthe exemplified the us-versus-them attitude that was developing.

Central to DeBarthe's case is that Harding could not have fathered Nan Britton's child. Harding, DeBarthe argued, was sterile. DeBarthe's story takes a familiar turn: he had no evidence for his startling revelation. He explains that medical "ethics preclude the presentation to the readers of this volume substantiating affidavits from physicians to whom Mr. Harding applied for relief from his trouble." Rather, DeBarthe argues that it was true because Britton could not prove it false: "The element of truth found in this presentation cannot be controverted by anything which has appeared or may hereafter appear from the pen or lips of the Complaining Witness [as he referred to Britton throughout *The Answer*] or any of her associates" (7). DeBarthe directs readers to the conversation between Britton and Harding's brother concerning a "particular physical trouble" in *The President's Daughter*. As DeBarthe interprets the meeting, Britton was fishing to see if George Harding knew of the president's sterility. As further evidence, DeBarthe points to Warren and Florence's childless marriage of thirty-two years. Because Florence had had a child during her previous marriage, it must be that Warren was at fault for their lack of children, a condition "he deplored," according to DeBarthe (11–14). DeBarthe carefully notes that sterility is caused by conditions beyond a man's control. He wrote Harding was "a perfect man physically in every other way, this one defect, the result of the before mentioned surplus glandular trouble in his youth, absolutely precluded the possibility of fatherhood on his part" (37).

DeBarthe casts doubt on the entirety of Britton's story, going so far as to contest her "claims" to be from Marion. He compares her actions to a "prospector's vain search for a mineral-bearing lode" (19). He dismisses Britton's call for help for unwed mothers and children as a "sop" (22). DeBarthe is not entirely above reproach in his own use of logic and evidence—for example, contradicting his earlier denial that Britton was from Marion by admitting that she had lived part of her childhood in Marion and referring to the friendship between Dr. Britton and Harding. The friendship, as he sees it, was further proof of the falsity of her story: "That this defendant, whose chief fault and failing was his loyalty to his friends, forgot, as is alleged, the obligations due his (then) dead companion, debauched this daughter of his friend, and suffered her to bear, unprotected and unprovided for, the pains of motherhood and the penalties of an unhallowed love!" (69). DeBarthe took the argument that Harding's unquestioning loyalty had allowed the scandals of his administration and used it against Britton.

DeBarthe adopts parts of the narrative of Harding as a tragic president. As with other writers, DeBarthe finds fault with the people. He argues that for the first time in history American citizens sat "supinely" and watched an "aggregation of sex perverts" attack the memory of a president with "deliberate villainy." Instead of watching, Americans should have prosecuted the perpetrators. The press had been equally inept, "stricken dumb by the avalanche of vituperation and filth these conscienceless miscreants have had the audacity to put into print." DeBarthe laments that no one had risen to defend Harding, who "died a martyr on the altar of treachery" (27).

Although, he writes, ethics prevented him from offering proof of Harding's sterility, he expresses no ethical reservations in offering his opinion of Britton. DeBarthe hoped that by proving that Britton was a woman of loose morals he would undermine her credibility, ignoring the logical assumption that such an accusation, if true, might only make it more likely that she would serve as a powerful man's mistress. This was a difficulty for DeBarthe. Britton had denounced the conventions that DeBarthe used to judge her, and Britton, by her admission, had had an affair with an older married man and felt no guilt.

Although DeBarthe writes that he would prove Britton's degeneracy by putting "important acts and truths before the public," his account relies heavily on rumors and stereotypes to make his case (33–34). He explains that Britton was a weak-minded woman "whose imagination and sex obsession had always swayed and controlled her" (42–43). He maintains that Britton's behavior was guided by lesions of the brain that caused insanity and was "bred in the bone" (15–16). DeBarthe argues that the affair, if it did take place, must have been Britton's fault; she shamelessly tells of throwing herself at a married man (73). He contrasts Britton with Florence Harding, praising the First Lady as a mother and casting doubt on the validity of Britton's motherhood: "Would a normal flesh and blood mother cast the pestilence of a bawdy house upon her innocent offspring to gain her own financial independence?" (173–75). DeBarthe runs through various options and repeatedly comes back to an assault on Britton's character.

What of Warren G. Harding's character? Having depicted Britton as little more than a prostitute, DeBarthe then has to rely on Harding's good character to prove that he was a man who would not associate with such a woman. Given Harding's public reputation, this was a difficult case to make. DeBarthe expands on Harding's qualities, using many of the familiar points: "He possessed at no time in his life one solitary earmark of greatness." He was a "good fellow" who enriched the "human herd." He was "true to every friendship he made. Therein lay his greatest political defect; his most grievous fault" (78–79). Regardless of his fault, DeBarthe claims he deserved respect because "he *was* President of the United States" (83, emphasis in original). DeBarthe concludes, "Scandal is the weapon of the ignorant, the malicious, and the cowardly, and no person in public or private life, no matter what the standing of the person nor what his circumstances, is free from these poison shafts." Even Lincoln, DeBarthe notes, was maligned as a president (185).

Although Britton lost the lawsuit, DeBarthe's effort to redeem Harding's reputation was not successful, in part because the debate over Britton's story still centered on the question of whether or not it was true. Samuel Hopkins Adams, in what was otherwise a very negative account of Harding, describes DeBarthe's effort as a "gallant failure."[28] Historian Robert Ferrell argues that there might be some substance to DeBarthe's story. DeBarthe's sources remain a mystery, but Ferrell speculates that one of the chief sources was Dr. George T. Harding, Warren's brother. According to Ferrell, Harding biographer Randolph Downes learned that one of the president's nephews had proof of the president's sterility. Harding told an acquaintance, "I have never been able to be the father of children, and no human in the world is as crazy about little folks as am I."[29]

DeBarthe is correct in noting that Lincoln was maligned as a president, but he ignores the reality that the debate over Lincoln's legacy did not revolve around whether or not he was sterile, corrupt, or unfaithful. The unfolding saga of Britton and her impact on Harding's memory was about to become even more personal and, if possible, bizarre.

Another Strange Death

In her second book, *Honesty or Politics,* Britton links her story to several other sensational, and questionable, accounts of Harding's life. As we saw in the previous chapter, *The President's Daughter* was part of a web of books and conspiracy theories that fueled the fervor over Harding's legacy. Chief among them was *The Strange Death of President Harding*, by Gaston Means. Means, who had worked for the Department of Justice, had first achieved notoriety while testifying before Congress during the investigations into Teapot Dome. Means served a prison term for his part in the corruption at the Justice Department. With *Strange Death*, Means reemerged into public view as the author of a controversial book. Thus Means was a familiar figure with credibility as an insider. In *Strange Death*, Means relies on Britton's story of forbidden love to validate his claims. The stories in Britton's and Means's books merged in the public memory of Harding.

Britton tells of a mysterious visit from Gaston Means, who was looking for a coauthor. Although Britton turned him down, she recounts a later visited from May Dixon Thacker, Means's eventual coauthor. In Britton's telling, Thacker asked questions that indicated she had information that could help Britton, and Means claimed that he had stolen Britton's letters from Harding. Britton professed her disinterest, even after Thacker urged her to read the manuscript. Thacker continued, "It is—to say the least—a vindication of you."[30] As it turned out, Means's credibility was worth little. Thacker later confessed that the book was fictitious.

Daugherty, in his memoir, challenged Gaston Means's credibility, saying Means was one of three hundred investigators whom Daugherty "never saw." (Daugherty saw him but two times.) Because Daugherty had fired Means, Daugherty explains, Means had allied himself with the congressional plot to get revenge on Daugherty. According to Daugherty, Means's inference that Florence Harding had murdered her husband was the "one that cut me deepest and that I can never forgive in this world."[31] Scholars have clearly established that Means was a fraud. Robert Murray claims, "The Means book delivered a final blow to the Harding image," although it "apparently mattered little that President Harding had never met Means or that Means was a perjurer, a thief, a convict, and a swindler."[32] Francis Russell describes Means as a "swindler for the joy of swindling, a liar proud of the credibility of his lies, a confidence man able to make his cheats and deceptions works of art." Means had "half-persuaded Americans that their President had been murdered."[33] Russell's gleeful discussion of Means's shortcomings does not, however, prevent Russell from describing the scene of Harding's burial in such a way that left open the possibility that something was amiss (603).

Why would people believe a confessed and convicted criminal? The forming of historical reputation often begins with public opinion, whether it is based on cold, hard facts or on something more whimsical. Means simply gave the public what they expected. His account neatly fit into the prevailing view of Harding. By 1930, when the book appeared, it would have been more difficult for the public to accept a positive interpretation of Harding. Samuel Hopkins Adams testifies to this in his *Incredible Era* when he justifies using *The Strange Death of President Harding* as a source. Adams writes that he used the book "not because it can be accepted as authentic or reliable (the author was straining every nerve to establish his thesis that the President was poisoned by his Duchess and that jealousy of Nan Britton was a contributory motive), but as indicating a considerable possibility of the domestic situation." Adams states, "If one could believe Gaston B. Means, an excess of credulousness against which precaution is always advisable, it was about this time that he was employed by Mrs. Harding to investigate Nan Britton."[34] Here we see Means's story entering the historical narrative, not because it was factual but because it met the preconceived public view of Harding, particularly those views related to the private lives of Warren and Florence Harding.

Before the court of American public opinion, Means's reputation served as primary evidence of the authenticity of his story. Means did not have to establish that there was corruption in the Harding administration (he himself was the evidence of that corruption); rather, he expanded on the existing scandals. Means's claims were outrageous, but it had already been alleged that Harding had committed suicide, was black, had joined the Ku Klux Klan, was a drunkard, had many mistresses, and was a political thug. Means's reputation as a criminal made his condemnation of the Harding administration all the more damning. As Means depicted them, the private lives of Warren and Florence Harding were clearly outside the accepted social boundaries as defined even by a criminal.

In contrast to DeBarthe and other Harding defenders, Means reminded readers that he respected women, the family, and the American household. Thus, he defended Nan Britton and justified himself: "I do not fight women or children. I would never do anything that would hurt a woman or a child. I would never degrade a woman or besmirch an innocent. Had Nan Britton not already told her story, I would remain forever silent. But what I have to say now—cannot in any way reflect on Nan Britton or her daughter."[35] Means's explanation contrasts with the actions of the many of the leading citizens of Marion, especially members of the Harding family who were engaged in a very public and ugly fight with Britton.

Strange Death also contributed to the image of Warren G. Harding as a puppet. Means portrays Harding as under the sway of those who sought to control the power of the presidency. According to Means, the struggle for control of the president took place between Florence Harding and her two rivals, Harry Daugherty and Nan Britton. Although he earlier claimed that he did not attack women, Means depicts Florence Harding with the worst stereotypes available for an ambitious woman; he repeatedly discusses her unattractiveness, her emotional outbursts, and her delusions of grandeur. As we have seen, these were, by now, very familiar portrayals of the First Lady.

As Means tells it, his first assignment, given to him by Charles Sawyer, was to recover damaging correspondence between Florence Harding and Madame X, a Washington soothsayer. Madame X was Madame Marcia, a soothsayer whom Florence Harding consulted. Again, Means builds on pre-existing claims, in this case following headlines created when Marcia claimed that she had predicted Warren Harding's election and death in office.[36] Her story reinforces the prevailing attitude that only the strongest of men could survive the presidency. Instead of the recovering correspondence with Marcia, Means claims that he had unearthed letters from Charles Sawyer to a Mrs. Whiteley revealing their extramarital affair. Means professes his disgust and explains that he had turned the letters over to Florence Harding.[37] Conveniently, as with Means's other claims, the evidence disappeared.

Through this account, Means now became part of Florence Harding's plan to regain control of the president. Means focuses on two people, Florence Harding and Charles Sawyer, who were dead and who had few defenders of national stature that could refute his story. According to Means, by turning the letters over to Florence Harding, he gave her leverage over Charles Sawyer even though, in reality, there is no reason to believe that Florence Harding and Sawyer were enemies. In Means's tale, Florence Harding believed she was the one who should control Warren. Means has Mrs. Harding explain her reasoning: Madame X "tells me that I [Florence Harding] am a 'Child of Destiny!'" (48).

Following in the footsteps of Britton and Adams, Means emphasizes the impropriety of corruption in the White House. Means has Florence justify her actions to preserve the "sanctity of the home," but according to Means, Florence Harding was not concerned with the traditional family but with political power. The home, in this case, was symbolized by the White House: "The White House typifies *the 'home' of the nation*. It must be protected from any slander or any shadow of scandal," Florence Harding supposedly told Means (51, emphasis in original). Florence Harding's quest for power stood in stark contrast to her failures as a woman. Means explains that Florence Harding was "an old woman: withered, nervous, high strung—tenaciously holding on [to] the illusion of youth and fooling nobody but herself" (55). Ultimately, Means's depiction of Florence provides justification for Warren's infidelities. Warren Harding could "no more resist a pretty girl or woman than he could resist food, when hungry" (56). As he did in his congressional testimony, Means places Daugherty at the center of the corruption and tells us that Jess Smith was Harry Daugherty's "man Friday." Means hints at a homosexual relationship between Daugherty and Smith: "Just what his relationship to Mr. Daugherty was, no one ever knew, except as a faithful and confidential friend."[38] Means and Smith knew each other through their work at the house on H Street, where (according to Means) Harding and other high-ranking members of the government drank and cavorted with "dancing girls" (60).

In Means's telling, Florence became increasingly unstable as she disclosed more of her plans. Florence Harding's lust for power revealed an ugly side: "Our earnest little suffragettes who strived so long and hard for the mere right to vote,—to have a single voice in the government of our nation, might do well to recall that in the latter half of the 16th Century all Europe was governed by women." Means has Florence Harding go on to attack the public for mistreating women: "America needs to be taught a lesson. 'First Lady of the Land' shall take upon its silly misnomer, a regal dignity. I am a 'Child of Destiny.'" Clearly, Means meant for this depiction to be unflattering—a deranged woman with delusions of grandeur and royalty.

Means continued to borrow themes from the Britton controversy. The Florence Harding of Means's book was determined to have a second term, but first she had to deal with Nan Britton; Means explains that Daugherty and the gang were using Britton to blackmail the president into signing oil leases (128). Florence Harding revealed to Means that all his work had been building up to ending that threat. Florence Harding had trouble believing that the affair was real. More important, she believed Harding was sterile: "Warren Harding is not capable of having a child, therefore he is not the father of Nan Britton's child. That's logical, isn't it?" she asked Means. As proof she offered, "We have no children. I have demonstrated my ability. I've had a living son by a former marriage" (139).

Means claimed that he stole four diaries from Britton and letters from the president that proved the affair and Warren Harding's paternity, and the press immediately began to speculate that Britton was having difficulty presenting proof in her legal battles because Means had stolen it. Means directly compares Nan Britton and Florence Harding. He describes Britton as an "attractive young woman: blonde, fresh, vital" (148). Britton was a "delightful little modern woman" whose heart was enthralled with the "glamours of the 'King,' [who was] old enough to be her grandfather." She was "young, eager, panting,—calling for sex-fulfillment, dazzled by his masculine beauty and his position,—determined, flattered, seductive." By contrast, Means could not understand what Warren Harding had seen in his wife "for thirty-two years!" She was a "little, drab, strong-minded, self-willed woman, years older than he, clinging with tenacious ferocity to the illusions of youth,—seeing no reason at all why she was not as attractive as any young girl!" Florence Harding, he continues, had consulted a "soothsayer to find mystic ways and means to enhance her attractiveness." She felt "secure— because of her mental equipment!" Florence Harding was condemned for her intellect as Warren Harding found in Nan Britton freedom from the stigma of sterility (149–50). Means builds on the themes that Britton had begun and takes them a step further. He crassly contrasts the reproductive abilities of Britton with the older—and, by his emphasis, power hungry— Florence. Florence's attempts to appear feminine, as Means portrays her, seem unnatural.

Means writes that he delivered the proof of the affair to Florence, who confronted the president. Means then contrasts Warren and Florence and editorializes on their marriage. Warren was a "prince of a man—an Apollo— an Adonis. He was a likeable sort of a man, as both men and women agreed." On the other hand (and here Means nearly repeats himself verbatim), Florence was a "little drab woman, strong-minded, self-willed, older than her husband by nine years, 'twas said—clinging with tenacious ferocity to the illusions of youth, deceiving nobody but herself. Ambitious, worldly, greed for power" (162). Whereas Warren was a natural man—whom no woman could resist—Florence was an unnatural woman because she had overly developed masculine traits. As Means saw it, Florence did not even know how to properly confront the president with the evidence of his affair. Warren now became Florence's victim: "Nag! Nag! Nag! If only she would let him alone. He had always been loyal to the Party. That was the most important factor in his career." Finally, Means decides it was Warren and not Florence who had been betrayed. He concludes that a "private life that ignores the demands of conventional society with regard to marital fidelity does not necessarily preclude the possibility of a public life devoted to the service of the country. Does it,—I asked myself? Such dual personalities are by no means unknown in our 20th Century civilization" (165). Means presents a complicated moral vision that separates public life from private, but also makes the philanderer the victim of his faithful wife.

Means reflects on the Harding scandals but also de-emphasizes the political scandals such as Teapot Dome, the Veterans' Bureau, and related administration misdeeds in favor of the personal scandals. He maintains that everything was for sale in the Harding administration. Teapot Dome was "old stuff, but even so,—it has yet to be excelled in criminal annals for sheer thievery and deviltry" (195). Means turns back to the melodramatic life he had constructed for the First Family. After the First Lady catches Nan Britton in the White House, Means has her declare, "My love for Warren Harding has turned to hate" (239). In Means's fictional confrontation, Warren Harding threatens to reveal all, be impeached, and leave town with his child. Furthermore, he denounces their marriage: "I never loved you. You want the truth. Now you've got the truth" (242).

Rather than dwelling on a possible impeachment, Means has Florence Harding plan to take control during the Alaska trip, ominously declaring, "I am a 'Child of Destiny.' I must fulfill that destiny. *The President is to die first.* He will die in honor: the stars have so decreed" (249, emphasis in original). Means was in Washington when he learned of the president's death, but he recounts that a friend of his who was in contact with the presidential party reported, "Circumstances of his death appear shrouded in mystery" (256).

Upon her return to Washington, Florence Harding called for Gaston Means and explained that "[on the trip], I learned of dangers of which I had not dreamed. From all directions,—they came" (260). Means has Florence Harding describe the now famous death scene: "I was alone with the President . . . and . . . only about ten minutes. It was time for his medicine. . . . I gave it to him . . . he drank it. He lay back on the pillows a moment. His eyes were closed. . . . He was resting. . . . Then—suddenly—he opened his eyes wide . . . and moved his head and looked straight into my face. I was standing by his bedside." The former First Lady paused. Means asked, "You think—he knew?" Means says she asked him if she could stop an autopsy. Means replied that she could. She had prevented the making of a death mask. In their final exchange, Means claims, they acknowledged what each understood: "'Mr. Means—there are some things that one tells—nobody.' To which I replied, 'Mrs. Harding,—there are some things—it is not necessary to tell.' And from that instant, we understood each other"

(263–64). Thus, without saying so explicitly, Means implies that Florence Harding has admitted murdering the president. Of course, Means's account is fictional. In the end, he provides no evidence for his accusations, and a close reading illustrates that he had made no direct accusations regarding the president's death.

Warren Harding's death completed the somewhat plausible but fictional account supplied by Means. That people accepted that story demonstrates how far Harding's reputation had degenerated—to the point that his themes of tragedy, possible impeachment, corruption, and political and sexual promiscuity resonated. Means's story seemed to validate Nan Britton's story and so the two accounts were taken as confirmation for what many had suspected or had used fiction to speculate about.

A Question of Evidence

Most of the evidence either for or against the validity of Britton's story is indirect. A good deal of it is circumstantial, based on recollections or character judgments. Samuel Hopkins Adams, who conducted research in the late 1920s in Marion, writes, "I have talked with high-school classmates of Nan Britton who knew her well until after she left Marion, and they are unanimous in giving her a good character and reputation." In addition to citing the judgment of fellow Marionites, Adams goes on to call Gaston Means's account a "fairly convincing testimonial (if true) of her illicit monogamy."[39] However, others who knew Harding denied Britton's account. Patrick Kennedy, the doorkeeper at the White House, said he "never had heard of Nan Britton" and that "no strange woman ever came to see President Harding." Ike Hoover, the White House usher, bluntly stated, "There was never a gadabout by that name or any other name in the White House. Nan Britton is a liar." Harding's close friend Ed Scobey said, "I never heard of this woman and I know a great deal of that book is untrue."[40]

Harry Daugherty, calling upon his own close relationship with Harding, denied the validity of Britton's story. Daugherty discussed the new will that Harding had written shortly before his death, explaining that Harding "could not have passed through this solemn hour with me without the frankest discussion of all the facts." Harding could have made a "deed of trust that would have made ample provision for Nan Britton and her child, outside the terms of his regular will."[41] Daugherty concluded that Britton was a "fake." Daugherty saw Britton's story as part of a tradition of "scandalous tattle about a President of the United States," a tradition that he noted included Washington, Lincoln, Arthur, Harrison, Cleveland, Roosevelt, and Wilson (249).

Now we turn to the familiar pattern in the public debate over Harding's legacy: Harding partisans, mostly from his hometown, attacked Britton, but neither side painted the former president in a particularly favorable light. Furthermore, the nature of evidence quickly became a central part of the debate. From Marion, DeBarthe attacked Britton as a liar and a sexual degenerate and, in turn, Britton took legal action. Unable to sue DeBarthe because he had died after falling down a flight of stairs, she instead sued Charles A. Klunk, one of the book's sponsors, in December 1928. Britton asked for $50,000 in damages.

The case did not reach trial until October 1931, in part because of the desire to wait until after the dedication of the Harding Memorial. John M. Killits presided over the case in the federal district court in Toledo, Ohio. Britton hired William Fish Marsteller as her attorney and Klunk was represented by Judge Grant E. Mouser. Again, with this critical turn in the story of the Harding legacy we are left with missing evidence, as historian Robert Ferrell explains:

> Proceedings in the courtroom should have been interesting, considering their subject, but unfortunately it is not possible to discover much about what happened. No stenographic record survived. In the case files presently in the Chicago branch of the National Archives there is evidence that a record was taken and transcribed. Probably Judge Killits kept it until he finished with the case—after it ended Marsteller moved for a retrial—and then somehow the record was lost, with the possibility that Killits destroyed it, because during the trial it was clear he considered the subject of the case lewd and degrading.[42]

Killits also closed the trial to reporters until the very end. Ferrell discussed the scanty evidence that remains from the trial, the most important piece being a hotel register that Marsteller introduced. However, it did not contain Harding's or Britton's names and was inconclusive. Not unlike the public debate, the case quickly became a series of testimonials by residents of Marion and others (but not Britton) as to Britton's character and reputation. In the end Britton lost the case (72–73). However, remember that the case originated as libel suit against Klunk (and the deceased

DeBarthe). While Britton failed to prove her case, it is also true that Mouser failed to disprove Britton's claims.

So where does this leave us? We are substantially no closer to determining whether or not Harding fathered Elizabeth Ann than before. We know that Harding met with Britton and helped her secure employment. We also know that he aided the Britton family and that Britton was, in fact, a close friend of Warren's sister Abigail. Abigail Harding believed Nan Britton's story. Does this mean that Harding and Britton had an affair? No. But it seems likely, based on the evidence, that they did. Britton's desire for celebrity and her claims to be a reformer only further clouded the issues. In her books Britton consistently comes back to her desire to be a social reformer, but she would never leave behind the status as of presidential mistress, perhaps because it was her role as a mistress that had brought her attention and celebrity. Whatever the validity of Britton's claims, and Harding's paternity, a great deal of the debate was framed in terms familiar to readers of popular middlebrow literature. The Harding and Britton scandal helped mark the waning of Victorianism and the emergence of modernity.

While the question of whether or not Warren Harding and Nan Britton had a daughter together can be compelling, it is also of limited importance. We know that Warren Harding was unfaithful to Florence Harding. The question is, was Nan Britton one of the women that Warren Harding was unfaithful with? Ultimately, as far as Harding's reputation is concerned, Nan Britton's story damaged it beyond redemption. Regardless of the protests from residents of Marion and a small number of sympathetic scholars, Harding and Britton are now and forever linked in the public's memory. More important than the issue of paternity is the nature of the scandal. The Britton scandal is important because it came during a transition in social and cultural morals. On one side of this social divide stands Florence Harding, unfairly characterized as a prudish Victorian, and on the other side stands Nan Britton, superficially characterized as a floozy and flapper. This national narrative puts Warren Harding in the middle, hoping that the double standards of the old Victorian ways would allow him to have it both ways. Most important, perhaps, the Britton scandal confirmed for many the link between lax personal morals and unsavory politics as Harding demonstrated that one could be a harlot in both the private and the public spheres.

Harding Alley

Reddy, we must be loyal to Warren
and preserve his memory.

—*Florence Harding to Maj. Ora M. Baldinger,
while destroying the Harding papers*

I think that there's enough dynamite in those
letters to blow up the Harding Memorial.

—*Francis Russell, after his first examination
of Harding's letters to Carrie Phillips*

On a rainy day in October 1963, Francis Russell drove into
Marion to begin research on his planned biography of Warren
G. Harding. As he approached the town, the rain stopped and
the Harding Memorial appeared on the flat landscape. Russell
describes Marion in terms that would have pained boosters: "a
small city with nothing to distinguish it from any other town in
the central Ohio plain but the columned marble drum of Alex-
andrian immensity at its outskirts that is the Harding Memorial;
that, and the mystery still attaching to the name of the most
disparaged of American presidents." As for the memorial, still
wet from the rain, as "curious an architectural amalgam as it
was, it managed somehow to be harmonious. An outer ring of
columns without fluting was what I suppose would be called
Tuscan. This was balanced by an inner ring of smaller Ionic
columns, and within that inner ring an unroofed garden area
spread out, with two polished dark granite slabs making the
graves of Harding and his wife, whom he called 'the Duchess.'"[1]

Russell traveled on to the Harding Hotel, "another memorial of sorts." There he was greeted by a "portrait of Harding"

in the lobby and by a lawyer "connected with the entrenched older circle that controls the affairs and social life of any such small city." Russell asked this man about the department store whose owners had refused to decorate for the campaign in 1920. The building, famously described but left unnamed by William Allen White, was the Uhler-Phillips department store; Jim Phillips, the store's owner, was married to Carrie Phillips, who had had an affair with Harding. According to Russell's unnamed informant, "anybody who'd been around a little" knew about it. Rumor had it that Hoke Donithen had arranged for the Republican National Committee to pay Phillips for her silence. On reflection, he recalled that Carrie Phillips's attorney was rumored to have some letters that Harding had written to her. Thus began the reemergence of Marion as a center of national scandal.[2]

The Harding Memorial stood as an impressive piece of architecture, but it could not answer the charges made against Harding nor give the public a reason to honor Harding's memory, as Russell realized on that rainy afternoon. While locally the memorial stood for a lost moment of greatness, nationally it conveyed an ironic message—here stands a memorial to a failure. That ironic message, however, was not immutably written in stone. The memorial literally had no words beyond those typically found on a common headstone and thus was a blank slate for contested interpretations. Russell's visit to the memorial represented the potential for change because he was the first of many historians who had a renewed interest in Warren Harding. These historians discovered, as had the writers and biographers who preceded them, that Harding's reputation was tied not only to national events and conceptions of the log cabin myth, but also to the boosterism still to be found in the Harding Memorial Association.

The leaders of the association were also aware of the potential for a change in Harding's reputation in the early 1960s. The association not only had at its command the great marble structure and the famous front porch, it also served as the guardian of Harding's papers. More than the marble memorial, these papers attracted Russell and other historians to Marion. Here was an opportunity to go beyond the tragic legacy of incompetence and betrayal that Hoover had articulated during the dedication. Here was the chance to escape the shadows of Britton, Chancellor, and Fall.

Presidential papers often serve as a catalyst for reconsidering an administration. Certainly the availability of presidential papers can lead to more sophisticated and nuanced interpretations that in turn will influence the interplay between academic and popular history by adding texture to the flatness of public memory. Harding's papers had not influenced what was written about Harding between 1923 and 1963 because the association did not allow researchers to use the papers. However, in the late 1950s the Sawyer family—who ran the Harding Memorial Association, which had custody of the papers—began a slow process of preparing the papers for release. More than any other people, the Sawyer family, beginning with Charles and then his son, Carl, controlled the association.

The Sawyers and other Harding partisans discovered that controlling the writing of history was easier said than done. While they perceived themselves as protecting Harding's reputation in the decades since his death, the reality is that Harding's reputation had almost assuredly cemented during their years of inactivity. It would prove difficult to convince historians, either popular or academic, to reconsider the received wisdom on Warren G. Harding's place in history.

When the association did make the papers available to the public, it met with obstacles that were of its own making. First, most people believed that all the Harding papers had been destroyed during the 1920s. Furthermore, the papers that survived were tainted by decades of censorship, and there was no assurance that all the extant papers had been released. Finally, the discovery of the letters that Harding had written to Carrie Phillips during their affair overshadowed the release of the presidential papers. As Russell notes, Harding's letters to Phillips included enough dynamite to explode the few positive remnants of Harding's reputation. What started as an attempt by the association to rehabilitate Harding became yet another effort to censor history in the midst of a sensational scandal.

We Must Be Loyal

The story of the Harding papers went to the heart of the formation of history and memory, illustrating the interplay of the historical record with the political and cultural forces that shape how that record is used and abused. Kenneth W. Duckett, the Ohio Historical Society archivist who oversaw the acquisition of the papers, called it "one of the great stories in American historiography" because of the "censorship, suppression, and destruction of many of the important historical source materials."[3] Archivist Andrea D. Lentz, also of the Ohio Historical Society, wrote that to understand the Harding papers one must understand "their various fortunes before final disposition."[4] The professional language of the two archivists serves to downplay the melodramatic story of Harding's papers.

Presidential papers do not just appear in a library or archive after a president leaves office or dies; the papers are deliberately kept—out of necessity, a sense of history, or both. At the time of Harding's death, there was no established precedent for the papers to be placed in a presidential library, where they would become part of the national record, although what happened to the Harding papers helped create a systematic process for handing presidential papers. It was George B. Christian Jr., in his role as personal secretary, who began collecting Harding's papers during the Senate years and the 1920 election. Because the election papers clearly had national importance, Christian brought them to Washington. When Harding moved to Washington to assume his responsibilities in the Senate, he left his personal and business papers in the offices of the *Marion Star*, where they remained until after Harding's death. Following Warren Harding's death, Florence Harding gave Christian the responsibility of shipping the files of the executive office to Marion. However, in the confusion those papers never made it to Marion but instead went to the White House basement. Thus, Harding's papers were in several different locations, with Christian being one of the few people who knew where to find the entire collection. Such confusion was the typical fate of presidential papers.

While Christian played an important, and positive, part in collecting the Harding papers, it was Florence Harding's activities that were a more pressing concern in 1923. Beginning while she still occupied quarters in the White House in the days after Harding's funeral, Florence Harding (with the assistance of Laura Harlan, her secretary, and Major Ora M. Baldinger, Harding's military aide) destroyed materials. She then arranged to have some of the papers shipped to Marion and the remainder shipped to the estate of Edward and Evalyn Walsh McLean, longtime supporters and friends of the Hardings. At the McLean estate in Washington, D.C., from August 17 to September 4, in one of the more cryptic moments in American historiography, Florence Harding and Baldinger burnt boxes of William Estabrook Chancellor's biography and an unopened suitcase from the White House. Standing before the bonfire, Florence Harding justified her actions to Baldinger: "Reddy, we must be loyal to Warren and preserve his memory."[5] The contents of the unopened suitcase remain a mystery. On September 5, Florence returned to Marion to oversee the execution of Harding's will, which had turned up in Marion after several weeks of searching. She and Baldinger spent the next six weeks working in the offices of the *Star*, further purging the papers. At first she thrust the papers into the stove one at a time, but then she began burning entire files. According to Baldinger, she rejected the argument that the papers were historically important and, as such, should be saved. According to Baldinger, the number of wooden archival boxes was reduced from six or eight to two (29).

Florence Harding is often depicted as deranged during these weeks of burning. Duckett argues that "the strain weakened her abilities, and finally her common sense." Florence was not methodical in her destruction. Duckett, who was among the first to thoroughly examine the papers after the association released them, explains that some "of the letters she chose not to burn but to censor, ripping off salutations from some and closings from others." He explained that on "some of the carbons of outgoing correspondence she tore [off] a portion of Harding's text, only to leave intact the original incoming letter which had elicited it" (29). Archivist Lentz diplomatically explained that there was a high "probability" that Harding's early papers located at the *Star* also "came under the scrutiny of his wife" (30). These evaluations of what had been destroyed in Harding's papers came later, decades after Florence Harding had gone through the papers. Florence Harding had one more act of censorship left, and this one was more cultural than tangible.

After Florence Harding censored the papers to protect Warren Harding's memory, she began to hide the papers that remained. When Florence returned to Washington in January 1924, she told Charles Moore of the Library of Congress that she had burned all the papers. She told publisher Frank N. Doubleday the same thing, adding that she had destroyed the documentary record because she "feared some of it would be misconstrued and would harm [Harding's] memory" (30). Thus, not only did she censor the papers, but she also created the impression among the public that there were no remaining Harding papers.

It remains puzzling why Florence Harding would take considerable effort to edit the historical record and would then hide the remaining papers. It would seem that once the papers had been purged of the embarrassing materials, the next logical step would be to make the papers available to the public. Florence Harding's admissions that she destroyed the papers to protect her husband's reputation is only that much more damaging. Surely a woman who had spent so much time in the public eye would have realized that such statements would only arouse suspicion. This was a bizarre act from a woman who although criticized for being strong willed and blunt was also a deft politician and businesswoman. Could Florence Harding have known what was to come? Did she spare her husband's reputation after all?

Then there is the issue of what she destroyed. From what we can tell based on Duckett's observations, Florence was most concerned with the Chancellor affair (see chapter 5) and with Harding's drinking. This makes more sense than the explanation that she was not rational. The information that Chancellor dwelled on was both personal and, in all likelihood, painful. The explanation that records relating to the Chancellor affair were the central focus of her efforts to purge the record is particularly likely when we consider that the government had already moved to eliminate Chancellor's work from the body politic. What is hard to believe is that she, or anybody, would believe that the burning of papers would make the rumors go away. Despite Prohibition, Harding's drinking was well known while he was alive and, again, the burning of papers would hardly seem to bring an end to it. Adams, White, and others had dwelled on his drinking. However, Warren Harding had dealt with his vices (particularly tobacco and alcohol) fairly openly. During the election, Florence had not wanted Warren chewing tobacco or smoking in public; her censorship might have been a continuation of that impulse. Still, it is difficult to actually determine what she did or did not destroy because she kept no records and there is no prior inventory with which to compare the existing papers. In addition, Florence Harding was not the last person to burn Harding papers.

The reported destruction of all the papers prompted a discussion of ownership and historical significance that followed the papers for decades. Throughout the twentieth century the fate of presidential records has been at the center of one controversy after another. The discussion over the Harding papers had two threads. First was the issue of their legal ownership; second was the responsibility that goes with having possession of historically significant materials. Florence Harding, as Warren's heir, had a legal right to dispose of his personal papers. While few questioned Florence's legal rights in this matter, others (including Baldinger, her assistant in destruction) did question the propriety of her actions.

More than once, Harding partisans evoked the authority of the presidential office to fend off attacks and to garner respect, but they ignored related arguments of a national claim to the Harding papers. Did the public have a claim on Harding's papers? Harding partisans consistently answered no. Beginning with George Washington, who established the tradition, outgoing presidents took their papers with them. Several presidents had destroyed all or portions of their papers (30). Florence had the right, both legally and traditionally, to take Warren's papers and destroy them. However, in doing so she not only failed to protect his memory but also placed a lingering taint on the papers.

Florence died on November 21, 1924, leaving her own papers and those of her husband to the Harding Memorial Association. Perhaps even more than Florence, the association faced the issue of how best to use the papers to positively shape Harding's image. In 1925 the association approached Judson C. Welliver, a former personal secretary to Harding, with a proposal to write an official biography. John Van Bibber, an editor with Doubleday, Page and Company, traveled to Marion to work on the project. While in Marion he had approximately five thousand typed pages of Harding letters copied. According to Duckett, had "Harding's reputation rested [on Van Bibber's selected papers], Florence Harding's purpose would have been achieved" and Warren's reputation would have been protected. Unfortunately for Harding's reputation, Harry Daugherty and George Christian stopped the project. Daugherty was in the midst of defending himself against criminal charges and did not want the administration's papers made public. Christian believed that he should be the author of the official biography (31). Key figures within the association, including Joseph Frelinghuysen, Herbert Hoover, and Hoke Donithen, favored the official biography, but Christian and Daugherty prevailed. Van Bibber's copies were stored with the originals, but the HMA would not oversee the writing of an authorized biography.

In the meantime, Charles Moore hoped to pressure the association to make the papers public. But Moore publicly declared that Florence Harding had "burned practically all the letters he [Harding] had left concerning political and national affairs" and that only carbon copies remained of many of the papers (102). Rather than generating pressure on the association to turn over the papers, as he had hoped, Moore instead reinforced the myth that all the papers had been destroyed. But the trail of destroyed papers did not end here.

During Daugherty's trial, in 1926, it was revealed that he had destroyed records at the Midland National Bank in Washington Court House, a bank owned by his brother Mal. The destruction of papers by one of Harding's political friends was damning, particularly in light of the proclamation by Daugherty's attorney that he was "not motivated by any desire to protect himself" but "only by loyalty to the memory of the President." Again, evocations of loyalty turned into implications of guilt. Rumors began that Harding kept a secret fund at the bank to finance extramarital affairs and stock market speculation. Following the trial, the *Washington*

Court House Herald, considered to be friendly to Daugherty, editorialized that "the present disposition of the Harding trustees is to keep all the letters sealed. Maybe sometime soon they, too, will be destroyed" (103). Perhaps the ever-practical Daugherty saw no need to risk conviction to preserve the memory of his deceased friend. For whatever reason, it was Harding's inner circle that continued to damage Harding's already poor reputation.

As Harding documents were discovered, the association claimed them, based on the disposition ordered by Florence Harding's will. Some Harding papers that had been misfiled with Coolidge's papers were discovered and turned over to the association. In 1929 the papers stored in the White House basement were discovered and the association claimed those as well. J. Franklin Jameson, director of the manuscripts division of the Library of Congress, attempted to convince the association to leave the papers in Washington in the care of the Library of Congress, where they "would be kept closed to investigators." Archivists worried not only that these papers might be purposely destroyed but also that they would fall victim to neglect. Jameson found allies among association members who lacked ties with Marion. Herbert Hoover, Harry S. New, Hubert Work, and Joseph Frelinghuysen all supported Jameson's proposal. Jameson began shuttling between Washington and Marion in an attempt to secure all the Harding papers that remained. Again, the specter of scandal alarmed some association members, as they feared that investigators would be interested in Teapot Dome. At this point Hoke Donithen was open to the idea of depositing the papers with the Library of Congress. He and Jameson reached an agreement in 1934, but Donithen died before the agreement could be presented to the board of trustees and the effort failed. During the 1940s, Thomas P. Martin took up the cause of securing the papers for the Library of Congress but he also failed.

Largely because no researchers were allowed access to them, the surviving papers did not have any impact on scholarship other than to fuel speculation. Despite recommendations from Harry New, George Christian, and Harry Daugherty, the association denied a request in 1935 from journalist Mark Sullivan to use the papers, which were now secure in the Sawyer family's White Oaks estate, which served as the association's headquarters. Sullivan wrote to Carl Sawyer, son of Charles, that the manuscript had "taken a trend away from the stereotyped pictures of Harding to be found in most histories. I believe my book will be a more accurate and truthful account of Harding's Presidency than any which has yet been published and I am strongly hopeful that it will destroy some of the rumors and myths about Harding which never had any foundation in fact." Sullivan argued that using the papers would be "completely in harmony with the long-time objective of the Harding Memorial Association, which is to see that Harding's memory be given justice."

Justice, of course, was not the same thing as hagiography, and justice could be interpreted in a number of ways. Sullivan's correspondence revealed that he was more interested in the Washington Naval Conference than the president's sexual proclivities and so he might very well have written a history that would have been to the HMA's liking. Still, he was not allowed to make use of the papers. By 1935 the association had no interest in shaping Harding's memory outside Marion.[6] The working assumption seemed to be the less said the better and that the absence of discussion would protect Harding's reputation.

Although the association kept the Harding papers under wraps, people continued to write about Harding, offering interpretations that were not influenced by the contents of his papers. While there was little scholarship on Harding between the 1920s and the 1960s, Harding remained fair game for popular commentary. Praise of Harding often came in back-handed fashion, and those who chose to compliment the twenty-ninth president had to first establish that they believed that his administration had been a bad one. In a 1941 article, for example, Irvin Cobb writes, "Harding will go down in our history as a man to be sorry for; a loyal, honest, trustful weak man; a man befooled, belittled, betrayed by a host of Iscariots; and, at the back of all that, a man most woefully miscast for the role to which ruthless expediency and the complacent selfishness of party nabobs assigned him." That Harding had met his "utter destruction" did not "grieve them." He did attempt to praise Harding, but only in a back-handed way that linked Harding to small-town ways. Harding "would have made an ideal chairman of the entertainment committee at an Elk's [*sic*] reunion," Cobb claims, but "aside from a profile fitted to be steel-engraved on postage stamps, he probably had fewer qualifications for filling the presidential chair than any other man who ever did fill it."[7] In 1946, James Pollard agreed with this assessment, writing that Harding was a man who "had paid heavily for his friendships, who had seemed to mistake conviviality for competence, who had trusted subordinates and associates too far, and who had misread his obligations to his party." His praise of Harding was limited but more genuine. Pollard credits Harding with drawing on his newspaper background to improve relations between the press and the president.[8] In a book on presidential health, physician Rudolph Marx notes that although Harding never denied having a child with Nan Britton, he "was haunted by the specter that the evidence of his philandering might be used to smear him." Picking up on by-now familiar themes, he blames Harding's weak character and sordid private life, which "made him also a misfit as President."[9]

Other historians disapproved of Harding's character and ordinariness. In 1960 historian John D. Hicks wrote that Harding's "experiment with the 'best minds' served only to demonstrate that a man of ordinary abilities had no business in the Presidency; that the office, as it had developed through the years, required exactly the kind of 'superman' that the party leaders had sought to avoid."[10] Hicks brought out a point that dominated the writing on Harding beginning with the 1920s. One of the key criticisms of Wilson was that he had tried to govern alone. Harding and other Republicans had repeatedly called for a return to party rule and constitutional government. Speaking in Marion during the campaign, Harding addressed the issue of needing "supermen" to govern the nation. The Republican candidate said that "the government is not of supermen, but of normal men, very much like you and me, except that those in authority are, or ought to be, broadened and strengthened in measuring up to great responsibility." Having indirectly attacked Wilson's style of government, Harding assured his townspeople that "if I believed the super-man were necessary to appeal to the sober sense of the Republic and ask our people to plant their feet in secure and forward paths once more, I would not be here in the capacity which has inspired your greetings. Normal men and back to normalcy will steady a civilization which has been fevered by the supreme upheaval of all the world."[11] At the dedication of the Lincoln Memorial, Harding proclaimed, "Abraham Lincoln was no superman."[12] Although Harding's discussion of normal men and normalcy resonated with his contemporaries, for historians like Hicks, Harding's lack of superhuman ability damned not only him but also the people who were foolish enough to vote for him.

With the centennial of Harding's birth approaching, the leaders of the Harding Memorial Association hoped that this sort of interpretation would become a thing of the past. However, the work of Florence Harding in burning papers, and the association in hiding papers, had cast the die for Harding's reputation. For historians, the lack of documents meant there was, in fact, little to debate. The lack of debate meant that there was little dispute over the general conclusions that emerged from the 1920s. Still, the release of the papers in the 1960s offered some hope.

Out of the Woodwork

During the 1960s historians and the public rediscovered Warren G. Harding, Marion, and the association that protected his memory. Despite the turbulent history of the papers, the fact remained that Warren G. Harding had been president during a crucial period in U.S. history, and scholars wanted to conduct research in his papers. The leadership of the association, especially the Sawyer family, hoped to finally use the papers to polish Harding's reputation. Furthermore, the association had before it several commemorative events that could showcase these efforts; the most prominent of these were the anniversaries of Harding's birth and death.

The fruit that Sawyer hoped would grow from the well-cultivated papers was already on the vine when the papers were released. At least two historians, independent of each other, had begun to research major Harding biographies. Each hoped to have his work ready for the hundredth anniversary of Harding's birth, in 1965. The centennial represented an opportunity, the first since the dedication of the memorial, to commemorate Harding in a format that is typically celebratory. As we saw with the dedication, however, it was not preordained that convention be followed.

In 1961, Dean Albertson, a professor of history at Brooklyn College, began working on a biography of Harding. Albertson would develop a friendly rivalry with Professor Randolph Downes of Toledo University, who had also begun researching Harding's presidency.[13] By following Albertson's research on Harding, we can see the unfolding commemorative effort to rehabilitate Harding, as well as the scandal that would derail the effort. We can also watch the tension between commemorative and academic history. However, the HMA did not have a monopoly on information. Because the Harding papers were unavailable, Albertson began researching Harding in depositories such as the National Archives and the Library of Congress. Nevertheless, Albertson recognized the value of the Harding papers not only for his own research but also for the publicity that would follow any biographer who made use of these long-elusive documents. Soon, Albertson was meeting and developing a relationship with Carl Sawyer.[14] In their dialogue, Sawyer vacillated on the question of whether to release the papers.[15]

Albertson and Downes, as both were aware, were not the only scholars to recognize the value of the upcoming Harding centennial. Albertson's "competitors in the field" included Professor Gerald Langford from the University of Texas, who had done some work in Ohio but was "quite far behind in his research," according to Albertson. Albertson had known of another researcher, a Mr. Tucker from North or South Carolina, but was not as concerned about competition from Tucker because his "work sounds more like newspaper man's reminiscences than history." The most serious of the competitors was the popular historian and essayist Francis Russell, who in 1963 had an article forthcoming in *American Heritage* and a book contract with McGraw-Hill. Albertson expected the "would-be Harding biographers to swarm out of the woodwork" when the "Marion papers" were opened.[16]

Among those other "would-be" Harding historians was Ray Baker Harris, who in 1962 was in correspondence with Carl Sawyer regarding an edited volume of Harding papers. Harris was seemingly interested in the type of hagiography that the HMA had traditionally embraced but had failed to effectively promote. Sawyer was enthusiastic about Harris's proposal, expressing his long-held belief that such a book, with its omission of references to "things" Harding was accused of doing, would be of value. The removal of references is as close as Sawyer would come to suggesting that Harding had, in fact, been involved in scandals. The question remains, which scandals was he concerned about? Was it the Chancellor affair, Teapot Dome, or Nan Britton? The answer could have been significant for Harding's reputation. Sawyer's correspondence with Albertson included indirect references to the racial politics that divided the country, linking them to Harding's own controversy when he wrote that Harding "was really a fine man, decent, white and honest." Perhaps Sawyer was hinting at what he and the association had been removing, but here also was an indication that Sawyer did not consider Harding's views on race a cornerstone of rehabilitation. Foreshadowing later difficulties, Sawyer frankly admitted in his correspondence with Ray Baker Harris that the association did not have a clear understanding of who owned the intellectual content of the letters.[17]

While Albertson was eager, as he put it, to get his "hot little hands" on the Harding papers, he pursued other avenues in his quest for information on Harding. In 1963 he contacted historian David Stratton, who was then researching Albert Fall. Stratton replied, "I can only sympathize with you in this undertaking. If you can break through the barrier set up by the Harding Memorial Association and gain access to any papers which may be held there, I think that you should be awarded some kind of medal or citation."[18] Albertson also wrote in the *New York Times* of his hope to find information on Harding. He received at least one reply, this from a man who said he could not offer help in locating Harding papers but did offer the encouragement that, for too long, "Harding has been forgotten or brushed aside as unimportant, and a definitive biography is needed."[19] William Culbertson of the Library of Congress informed Albertson that he was interested in a Harding biography, as it was a subject with "tragic undertones."[20] Still, the papers in the care of the HMA were of great value and Albertson was increasingly confident that "old Sawyer in Marion will release to me the Harding Papers."[21] The papers, Albertson correctly foresaw, offered the key to future interpretations of Harding's place in history and the success of a biography.

As Albertson and Russell knew and other scholars discovered, not only was Marion the source of the Harding papers and a place where Harding hagiography could still be found, but it was also the starting place for investigating the scandals. Albertson wanted to interview Nan Britton, and that quest led him to Ellen Stoll, who agreed to help him obtain an interview. Britton, as it turned out, had become cautious over the years.[22] Stoll, who incidentally was active in the local Democratic Party in Marion, wrote to Nan Britton on Albertson's behalf. When Britton later became critical of Albertson's treatment of Harding, Albertson defended himself by noting that he increasingly believed Britton's story.[23]

In his introductory letter to Britton, Albertson expressed a clear understanding of the issues involved with any historical work on Harding and the sensitivity needed to deal with the people who held the various papers. The continuing ill will between Britton and the HMA held the potential to hinder Albertson's research, but in order to rise above such conflict he stressed that he was a "trained historian, not a writer of sensational material." Evoking academic objectivity, he assured Britton that he sought "only to tell the truth about President Harding, not to comment one way or the other about that truth."[24]

Like so many others before him, Albertson found himself enmeshed in a drama while trying to determine the accurate facts of Harding's life. Britton's information was increasingly important, not only because she was one of the few living people who, so it would seem, knew Harding intimately but also because there developed a competition among the Harding biographers to gain access to Britton. Albertson enlisted the aid of his friend Ray Billington, a noted historian of the day, in his quest to interview Britton. Billington wrote a letter to Britton testifying to Albertson's personal and professional character. Billington emphasized their mutual connections with Northwestern University, where Billington had been a professor and Britton had worked as a clerk. He described Albertson as sober, hard working, and objective. Billington reinforced Albertson's message that academic objectivity would prevent the sensationalism that had been such a large part of Harding's legacy.[25] Billington thought it was important for Britton to speak with Albertson, especially after he had learned that Downes, who he thought did not represent the profession well because of his "somewhat terrifying appearance," had already spoken with her.[26] Albertson was able to arrange meetings with Britton in Illinois and later in California, where Britton was "quite pointed in her inquiry regarding" people in Marion. Albertson concluded that Britton was "more concerned" with Marion than with Harding.[27]

In his attempt to pry facts from Marion's sons and daughters, Albertson played both sides of the reputational fence. Even as he flattered Britton, he wrote that he was "perplexed about the total lack of evidence in support of Miss Britton's allegations—particularly so when people who were in and about the White House during Harding's administration know nothing about Miss Britton beyond what they have read in her book." Still, he thought it best to "approach her in the spirit of complete belief." Albertson was also concerned that the process of transferring the Harding papers over to the Ohio Historical Society had stalled, writing that although he had "gambled" that the papers would be available, he had also made a backup plan. He had spent a year doing research in other archives and so could claim, "I strongly suspect that I already have the bulk of the matter which the Marion papers contain."[28]

While Albertson worked to gain access to Britton's information, he also strengthened his ties with the Harding Memorial Association. He kept Carl Sawyer updated on the progress of his research, while Sawyer kept Albertson informed about the association's progress in releasing the papers.[29] Albertson was also aware of the importance of good relations with the Marion community. A writer for the *Marion Star* contacted Albertson to do a story on the emerging Harding scholarship, noting that the "folks" of Marion would be interested in him as a "historian and a champion of Harding."[30] After the story, Albertson worried that the "awful interview"—in which he had had the "tactlessness to suggest that Harding probably would not rate in American History quite as highly as Abraham Lincoln"—would damage his credibility in Marion. He continued that he had "not yet received any threatening letters from central Ohio, but imagine I'll be tarred & feathered the next time I enter the Marion city limits."[31] Clearly, Albertson was worried about offending Harding partisans in Marion. He was well aware that Britton, Sawyer, and the HMA did not necessarily want the truth to be revealed but rather sought a scholarly stamp on their versions of Harding's life. As events unfolded, the topic of whether Harding compared favorably to Lincoln would soon seem a silly issue.

The Sawyer family decision to make the papers available to the public was not made overnight. In the late 1950s Sawyer had begun to copy the papers, storing the originals in a vault in the basement of the Harding home. Sawyer maintained that he would open the papers to researchers when he finished. While Sawyer copied the papers, Erwin C. Zepp and Kenneth Duckett of the Ohio Historical Society approached the association in the hope of obtaining the papers. The men hammered out an agreement in quick order, in contrast to the many years that the Library of Congress had been after the papers. On October 8, 1963, the association formalized the donation of the papers to the Ohio Historical Society, but things did not proceed smoothly. According to Duckett, the gift agreement was "so ambiguous that the Association released only the presidential letters; the Society, on the other hand, assumed that it had acquired title to the entire collection."

Moving the papers from Marion to Columbus on October 10, 1963, was a dramatic, or rather a melodramatic, process. To begin with, Dr. Sawyer worried that "those Teapot Dome" people might try to highjack the papers, so state highway patrol cars escorted the moving vans carrying the papers. Even after custody of the papers was transferred to the OHS, one final mystery of the Harding papers remained. Duckett wrote that "historians have speculated as to whether it [the HMA] might have continued in the tradition established by Mrs. Harding" of censoring the papers. Once the papers were secured at the Ohio Historical Society, Duckett discovered that the senatorial and *Marion Star* papers had been moved to the Sawyer sanatorium and were not part of the shipment. Verifying his own suspicions regarding the fate of the papers, based on hearing Sawyer talk of his mission to preserve Harding's reputation, Duckett reported finding "occasional empty file folders." He gave the example of a folder labeled Heart Throb Letters. Further concerns regarding the reliability of the papers were raised when Sawyer told Duckett that the originals from which copies had been made had been destroyed. Duckett was "amazed" at what Sawyer had told him and in turn told Albertson he had "one of the prime biographical topics of all time and wait until you see all the goodies we are amassing for your pleasure."[32] Duckett realized that the sensationalism surrounding the papers would only increase the interest in scholarship on Harding.

Although clearly the association's collection would be the heart of the Harding papers, Duckett set about supplementing those papers by collecting materials from many of Harding's close associates. While Duckett was pleased with progress on this front, he reported more "bad news" about the papers from the HMA. Sawyer was concerned that the Ohio Historical Society was moving too quickly in opening the papers and maintained that "biographers should be forced to spend at least ten years working on the papers before being allowed to write." The bottom line was that Sawyer's organization of the papers had been haphazard; archivists would not be able to properly arrange the papers for some time. Furthermore, it appeared that the HMA was holding back some papers, including materials formerly stored at the *Star:* "early political correspondence, and ten or twelve volumes of typescripts of letters from the Harding Papers, the originals of which no longer exist (these, Sawyer says, are the core of the whole collection)." To make matters even worse, Sawyer confessed to Duckett that he had removed one "letter 'which made Harding look bad'" and in another he mentioned a "'box of Fall correspondence.'" In a move that would no doubt have displeased Sawyer, Duckett met with Britton for several hours, after which he proposed to Albertson that he interview her for the collection.[33] Albertson was hardly surprised at Sawyer's depredations, writing to Duckett that Sawyer had "made it perfectly clear to me the first time I talked with him that he had devoted considerable attention to the weeding out of harmful items." Albertson also questioned Sawyer's honesty, asking Duckett if he really knew whether Sawyer had more papers and telling Duckett, "Sawyer once told me that it was true that Mrs. Harding burned all the pre-presidential papers." As for the typed copies of the Harding letters, "the originals of which no longer exist, I wouldn't, under the circumstances, touch them with a ten-foot pole."[34] In March 1964, much to Duckett's relief, the association released the missing files.

In addition to the physical ownership, a key issue with the Harding papers, as we have seen all along, was the intellectual-property rights. Seemingly, it was not clear that the association had the authority to transfer the literary rights and place the Harding papers in the public domain.[35] Britton, of course, continued to be an important part of the process. Duckett noted, "if her [Britton's] story is true, . . . her daughter certainly figures in any question of literary rights."[36] Britton's story gained renewed significance in the drama surrounding Harding's legacy.

The (Not So) Secret Life of President Harding

While Albertson and Duckett pursued various documents and interviews with Nan Britton, Francis Russell, a popular biographer, had been working on his biography of Harding since 1964. His working title was "The President in the Shadows." Note that this original title speaks to Harding's obscurity, while Russell's later title, *The Shadow of Blooming Grove,* points to the importance of locality and scandal. The original title emphasizes Harding as an obscure president, while the second emphasizes Harding as a man followed by a dark past. As we shall see, much of Harding's obscurity was about to end in the controversy over the Carrie Phillips letters. Not quite understanding the magnitude of what he was about to undertake, Russell contacted attorney Donald Williamson, the lawyer who had settled Phillips's estate in 1960. Carrie Phillips had been living as a recluse and on public welfare before her death in a rest home. In the process of handling her estate, Williamson found a large shoe box containing two hundred fifty love letters Harding had written to Phillips throughout his career as a publisher and senator.[37] Before long Russell was reading the letters in Williamson's home. In his conversation with Russell, Williamson foreshadowed the coming conflict. Williamson said, "I felt—rightly or wrongly— that if I turned them over to the Harding Memorial Association they'd go up in smoke." A sense of the letters' historical significance moved him to preserve them. That Harding had been president, in this instance, meant that the letters should be saved. Williamson explained that "if a President of the United States has written something—no matter what it is—it's part of history and nobody has a right to destroy it." He had contacted Phillips's daughter regarding the letters but when she did not respond he simply kept them.[38] His decision to keep the letters was the beginning of the modern Harding scandal, a scandal involving not only the familiar issues of character and sensationalism but also the integrity and purpose of history and memory.

Williamson agreed to let Russell take extensive—verbatim, he claimed—notes from the letters. Russell took his notes to the Ohio Historical Society, where he brought his discovery to the attention of Duckett. Duckett traveled to Marion and persuaded Williamson to donate the letters to the society. Duckett did not tell his superiors about the letters and later informed Russell that he could not study them without making the discovery public. As he explained to Russell, "if the Memorial Association in Marion should get wind of what was in them and that we had them, they might hold up parts of the main Harding papers they haven't sent yet. I don't dare risk it; for the time being I'll have to keep the letters secret." Duckett did, however, make a microfilm copy of the letters. A few days before the ceremony marking the opening of the Harding papers, Duckett told Zepp, who then informed the president of the society and a Columbus lawyer and society trustee, Fred J. Milligan.[39]

The letters proved to be every bit as explosive as Russell had expected. One source has it that officials at the Ohio Historical Society "panicked" when they read the letters and considered destroying them.[40] This might have been the case, but Duckett had acted to protect the letters. In early August 1964 the *New York Times* revealed that copies had been made. Oliver Jensen, the editor in chief of *American Heritage,* had deposited copies in a New York bank. He explained that "disasters have happened before to many private papers, including a number of Lincoln's. Because we fear a repetition now, we have sequestered a complete set of photographic copies of the Harding-Phillips letters for historic safekeeping." The sealed copies would remain hidden until a probate court decided the fate of the original letters. According to the *Columbus Citizen-Journal,* Duckett had made the copies "while the letters were in his custody without the knowledge of society officials." Duckett provided Jensen with the copies because, as he explained to him, "I have heard the words, 'burn, destroy and suppress,' so many times since I acquired the papers that I have determined that extraordinary precautions must be taken to insure their preservation and their use by historians." The *Citizen-Journal* quoted Jensen as saying that the "significance of the letters goes far beyond mere documentary proof that the president had a close relationship with Mrs. Carrie Phillips." Jensen also asked Allan Nevins, of Columbia University and past president of the American Historical Association, to form a committee of historians to advise the magazine. Nevins said, "I feel strongly respecting the situation which has arisen in the Ohio Historical Society, which will do itself and the State of Ohio irreparable harm if it fails to prevent any disposition of any Harding papers which results in the destruction of a single page." As for Duckett's actions, Nevins said, "I feel certain that the American Historical Association and all other groups in the field will stand unequivocally and unflinchingly behind him and behind those associated with him."[41]

Much would be made of who owned the letters and what responsibility the various parties had to history and to Harding. The underlying assumption was that what was good for Harding's reputation was bad for history. The fight only increased Harding's notoriety while making his reputation worse. While the eventual suppression of the letters hid many of their details, the general content of the letters along with a few choice quotations became public. The letters, many of them written on Senate stationery or on postcards, ranged from very brief notes to letters as long as thirty-five or forty pages. Although Harding more often than not signed his own name, he sometimes adopted code names, referring to himself as Constant and to Carrie Phillips as Sis. In one letter, Harding addressed Phillips as Carrie Darling Sweetheart Adorable. He also wrote her a poem on their seventh anniversary: "I love you more than all the world; / Possession wholly imploring; / Mid passion I am oft times whirled; / Oft times admire–adoring. / Oh God! If fate would only give / us privilege to love and live." The letters also revealed strains in the relationship. Phillips wanted money from Harding to maintain her silence, but Harding wrote to her that he could not "secure you the larger competence you have so frequently mentioned." He also wrote, that to "avoid disgrace I will, if you demand it as the price, return to Marion to reside . . . if you think I can be more helpful by having a public position and influence . . . I will pay you $5000 per year, in March each year, so long as I am in that public service."[42] The sensational snippets that were made public reflected the older interpretations of Harding as a man of poor character and a philanderer. Whatever Russell's motives, these quotations could not have improved his relations with the HMA.

Little of Russell's account of discovering the Phillips letters deals with Harding's presidency or national politics. While Russell does not hesitate to join in the sensationalism surrounding the discovery of the letters, he does offer a more sympathetic commentary on Harding in *American Heritage*. He writes that Phillips was the love of Harding's life and that it was "impossible" to read the letters "without feeling a certain pathos." Harding's style of speaking and writing was widely critiqued and mocked, but Russell says that the letters "do not suffer from the infelicities that led the late H. L. Mencken to write his satiric discourses on 'Gamalielese.'" Russell contrasts Harding's style as an orator with the literary style presented in his letters; he calls the letters "clear and comprehensible." Russell argues that few "men in that still very Victorian and inhibited era would have been capable of expressing such feelings, and fewer still would have committed them to paper." The letters revealed an "entirely new dimension—a different Harding," with an "unsuspected integrity and strength of character."[43] Russell does not elaborate what he means by integrity and character.

Russell's comment is important because few people, aside from early Harding boosters and partisans, had praised Harding's character. Here is evidence that Harding's personal papers offer the potential of changing the standard interpretation of Harding. Ironically, this opportunity came not from the highly groomed papers being released by the HMA but from the raw documentation of Harding's relationship with his mistress. This possibility for reinterpreting Harding, however, would not last. Perhaps embittered by his fight with Marionites or perhaps because he was pandering with stories of mistresses, Russell writes in the preface of *The Shadow of Blooming Grove,* "Harding's eroticism as expressed in his letters is naïve, and even pathetic as the quality of his mind peeps through the boudoir phrases. In his sexuality he was Adolphe rather than Don Juan. The letters, if they can be considered shocking—as some of them can—are more so because they were written by a President of the United States than through the tumescence of their content." Russell had abandoned his earlier position, which had offered the hope for revisionism; his analysis quickly degenerated into a discussion of the quality of the prose of Harding's love letters.

Russell also fixates on the questions of Harding's sexual life, pronouncing that the letters confirm the long-standing rumors that Harding had at least two extramarital affairs. Russell told a reporter from the *Washington Post* that Phillips's letters had convinced him that Nan Britton's story was true: "No one believed he would write letters that long, but if he did to Mrs. Phillips, perhaps he did to Nan Britton, too."[44] Because the letters were sealed to researchers, only Russell and a few others would know if the letters really did prove Britton's story. It did not take long for discussions of interpretation, disposition, and Harding's strength of character to descend into the familiar Harding narrative.

It was not clear if the letters would join the other Harding papers. Russell announced that negotiations were under way to have the letters donated to the Library of Congress or some other suitable institution, where they would be sealed for fifty years. The letters, however, came under the control of the local probate court, where Judge Edward Ruzzo appointed Marion lawyer Paul Michel as executor of the Carrie Phillips estate. Michel was the nephew of Hoke Donithen, a key figure in the early years of the Harding Memorial Association, and Michel himself was then serving as the secretary of the association. Ruzzo also ordered Duckett to turn the papers over to Michel. However, when turning over the papers Duckett neglected to mention the existence of microfilmed copies. In his dealings with Michel, Russell found that Michel was more "detached" than he had expected for a Marion resident. Michel told Russell that if "old Doctor Sawyer had got hold of those letters, he'd have made a bonfire fast enough."[45] Another twist came when Mrs. William H. Mathee, Carrie Phillips's daughter, announced that she planned to sell them to pay debts against Phillips's estate.

Harding's letters to Carrie Phillips quickly brought a renewed interest in Nan Britton. The *New York Times* revealed that Britton was living in seclusion in Evanston, Illinois, where she and a partner, Gertrude Davis, operated an employment agency. Randolph Downes said that he had interviewed Britton two and a half years earlier and had been in contact with her since. Britton, Downes said, ran the business under an assumed name. Downes described Britton as "charming, dignified and articulate" and said that she had promised him proof of her affair with Harding. However, Downes said, "'I'm not at all sure what the 'proofs' are." He added, "A historian does not always accept as proof what other people do. Nevertheless I am convinced, and I think most authorities on the Harding period are convinced, that her story is true."[46]

Downes was not the only one to believe Britton's story or want to talk to her. The *Chicago American* soon ran a story with the headline "Harding's Mistress Ends 30-Yr Silence." Britton was making her first public statement since 1939, when Helen Waterhouse of the *Akron Beacon Journal* had interviewed her. The *Chicago American* interview was hardly substantial; the story reported that Britton refused to come to the door, telling the reporter that she did not trust newspaper reporters. Contradicting what she had written in *The President's Daughter* when she discussed rumors of an affair, she now insisted, "I did not know about Mrs. Phillips or about the letters President Harding wrote to her."[47] Britton's daughter, Elizabeth Ann, living in Glendale, California, also spoke to the public for the first time five days after Russell announced his discovery. She told the *Chicago Tribune* that her mother had told her that Harding was her father. She said, "I'm not ashamed, but I don't like the publicity."[48] However, the publicity had only begun.

The fate of the Phillips letters began a very public debate over history and Harding's place in it. George T. Harding III, a nephew of the president, acted to prevent the letters from becoming public. He brought suit against the American Heritage Publishing Company, McGraw-Hill Publishing, Kenneth M. Duckett, and Francis Russell to stop publication of the letters, asking for $1 million in damages to the Harding family. He charged that without permission from the Harding heirs, Russell and Duckett had copied the letters, revealed their content to the public, and had planned to publish magazine articles and books based on the letters. Common pleas judge Henry L. Holden issued a stay, preventing publication.[49]

While the president's nephew blocked further publishing of the Phillips letters, the growing scandal offered good copy for journalists. Robert C. Ruark, of the *Columbus Citizen-Journal,* spoke up in defense of the president—sort of. He admits that Harding was "no rose geranium" and that he was surrounded by a "stout complement of crooks," but Ruark opines that revealing his love letters was "extremely dirty pool." Love letters should remain a "private business between boy and girl, and exhuming the privacies of a passion, legal or illegal, to me is as ghoulish as digging up a body for public display." Besides, he says, everyone eventually writes love letters, and a "poor goof can't help it. He's in love and he's lonesome, and for all you know he may be married to some babe with a face like an ax and a temper to match." Ruark, like so many others, blames Florence for Warren's infidelities. He also maintains that having a mistress was a common practice among men, especially among the powerful. In conclusion, Ruark admits to being "sore." As for Harding, "anybody who will write 250 letters to a couple of dames must have had something more in his heart than naked lust, and certainly very little in his head." Harding, he concludes, deserves better because of his common failings: "he deserves posthumous protection, in the interest of all us sinners who find the inkwell irresistible."[50]

Journalist Henry Lee devotes a great deal of newspaper space to the story of Harding's letters and in doing so returns to older interpretations of Harding and his hometown. Lee has obviously done a little more background reading than the typical reporter—who simply reports information based on interviews. Lee incorporates details from Harding biographies, particularly William Allen White's *Masks in a Pageant,* and has supplemented this with some research in Marion. Lee contrasts Harding's national and local reputations and the resulting awkwardness when the two came into contact. He notes that the forty-first anniversary of Harding's death would be the following week, but "in Marion, Ohio, where he lies buried and a $750,000 white marble memorial of Tuscan columns honors him, ceremonies, if any, will be strangely muted." What was the reason for the muted ceremonies? The "embarrassing proof" of Harding's cheating with Carrie Phillips, on his "plain, bespectacled, ambitious" wife, Florence. Lee writes that Harding had been "blessed" with the "bearing and features of a noble

Roman and [possessed a] sonorous voice," but that the word *normalcy* was "possibly his only creative contribution to American politics." Although Harding appeared to be "the epitome of small-town respectability," he did not practice what he preached and so had fallen outside the national narrative of the presidency. As the result of "a slow historical striptease, [Harding] emerged as anything but a fine example for the young, even though he had been born, most appropriately, in a log cabin." Having invoked the log cabin myth, in contrast to the realities of Harding's biography, Lee turns to the reactions in Marion.[51]

Only in Marion, Lee says, had Harding escaped the degradation of his reputation; in Marion, "old loyalties stubbornly live on." In the lobby of the Harding Hotel hung an "almost life-size oil portrait of a distinguished gray-haired man . . . the solid citizen beyond reproach—and that's the way Marion intends to remember Harding." Lee asked various Marion citizens for their opinion of Harding. One young Marionite said, "Why should people be shocked and surprised to find that a President is just a man, too?" J. C. Woods, who had managed the *Marion Star* under Harding, remained loyal to his old boss. He remembered Carrie Phillips and the two couples doing things together but "now that the scandal is out, he flatly refused to release any old photos or mementos." Mrs. Rose Ishlaub fondly remembered Phillips, but she "refused to look through her papers and albums for any picture of the Phillipses and Hardings." She "appealed to a reporter to please stop the terrible stories appearing in the newspaper now."

To understand such loyalty, Lee argues, one must understand Marion and small-town America. He recounts a brief biography of Harding, featuring the feud with Amos Kling and the rumors that Warren was black. He quotes White: "If now and then the roister youth comes out of his past and leads Warren Harding on a little detour from the straight and narrow way Florence Kling eased him back into the main road, and the episode seems to be forgotten." Harding's affair with Carrie Phillips was no detour, Lee argues. The Phillipses lived only a short distance from the "old Harding home, now a green-painted memorial where school children pay a quarter to see how a President lived when he was home." After Harding's presidency, the Phillipses had fallen on hard times. Carrie liked to live extravagantly but became a recluse when she ran out of money; Jim Phillips moved into a boarding house. Before he died of tuberculosis, in 1939, he called Harry Elliot to him and "pathetically asked that his obituary give him credit for his civic work and booster efforts long ago in behalf of Marion."[52] Phillips, like Harding, became a symbol of the fallen small-town champion.

The Most Ohio of the Ohio Presidents

On Saturday, April 25, 1964, the Ohio Historical Society, then located on the campus of Ohio State University, made the Harding papers available to the public in a ceremony presided over by Erwin Zepp, the society's secretary and director. Although overshadowed by the controversy over the Phillips letters, the ceremony was not about Warren Harding per se but about the relationship between history, reputation, and truth. During the dedication, speakers evoked the facts and the truth all the while, either directly or indirectly, recognizing that the intersection of history and memory involved more than facts. Allan Bovey of the *Star* noted that researchers who had "long pondered what secrets, what revelations, what musing they might hold" would now find their answers. Bovey's commentary points to the primary difficulty in creating Harding's reputation. It was not just a question of facts leading to truth but also of who controlled the facts.

The problem with Harding's legacy is that it had been turned into a series of mysteries and unanswered questions rather than a celebration of the log cabin myth or academic debates. Duckett, more sophisticated in his understanding of academic history than were the journalists who reported on the release of the Harding papers, declared that with the papers "historians will come to a set of conclusions which they will document as facts." He argues that previous interpretations of Harding were not valid because they were formed in the absence of documentary evidence. Historians doing research in the papers, Duckett explains, "will also form opinions about Harding's character and his motivation." Duckett takes the process one more step, a step that academic historians were often reluctant to take, when he says, "finally, if they are good historians, they will develop a sense of empathy with this particular human being and his fate." As for the importance of the papers, only "the manuscripts hold the key to the so-call[ed] 'mysteries' of Harding's life, speculation about which had made sensational reading for years." Duckett concludes that if the "search for truth is a valid cause, if history does have meaning in the space age, then the opening of the Harding papers, closed for more than 40 years, is a major landmark for the Ohio Historical Society." Warren Sawyer spoke on behalf of his father, Carl, and for the Harding Memorial Association. Why had the association kept the papers from the public for so long? Sawyer answered that it was "partly because of previous orders of the trustees, but mostly because we didn't quite know what to do with them." William H. Vodrey Jr. of East Liverpool, Ohio, and the first vice president of the OHS, summarized the ceremony by focusing on regional identity and not national history: "Warren G. Harding was perhaps the most 'Ohio' of the Ohio presidents."[53]

The long-anticipated opening of the Harding papers was not about Harding's political career or presidency, but rather about the quality of his character and the papers themselves. Speakers did not discuss the way the papers could serve as a means to better understand the politics of the 1920s or such events as the Washington Naval Conference or the 1921 coal strike, but rather discussed the relationship between control of the papers and the writing of history. They spoke of finding the historical truth built on "facts," but did so with an ambiguity that revealed a fear that the handling of the papers had made certain "facts" unrecoverable.

After the ceremonies were concluded, Duckett wrote to Albertson, telling him that he wished that Albertson could have attended and offering him an evaluation of the ceremony and papers. He informed him, "we have acquired 25,000 additional papers from the HMA, none of which were screened by Dr. S. They include personal, family, business and political papers, 1895–1920. Allow[ing that] they are light, very light for the senatorial period, they are excellent materials."[54] As for Britton, Duckett had given up on getting papers from her: "she is entitled to her privacy, and I will do what I can to keep her from being badgered."[55] Even after the papers were made available, the HMA continued to release more items and Duckett continued to search for more records that would answer the mysteries in Harding's past. The issue of Harding revisionism hung in the air, as it was uncertain how historians, of whatever stripe, would interpret the papers.

Harding Alley

The excitement over the Phillips letters and the formal opening of the presidential papers brought a great deal of attention to Harding, but serious biographers faced the difficult task of conducting research in the unorganized papers. As a consequence, the number of biographers working in so-called Harding Alley dropped from sixteen to three. Duckett commented wryly on one researcher, "Gross has been here and gone and poses no problem to anyone except perhaps Harding." Edwin K. Gross was the founder of the American Society for the Faithful Recording of History. Gross proved to be dangerous to Harding only in the way that Harding partisans tended to be. After Gross completed his short book *Vindication for*

Mr. Normalcy he gave copies away as a prize in a high school history essay contest, held in Marion and Morrow counties, on the theme Harding Was a Good President.[56] Of those interested in writing more substantial biographies, Albertson saw no reason why he, Downes, and Russell could not "work together happily."[57] They became regulars in Harding Alley, occasionally joined by other historians, such as David Stratton, who was working on Albert Fall, "sometimes eyeball to eyeball."[58]

Apparently, Albertson feared that the society would not receive the intellectual rights for the Harding papers and thus approached George T. Harding for permission to publish from the papers. Albertson stressed his intention to write "the same kind of book which you wish to see published." Having said that, he vacillated: "I would have no hesitation in allowing you to read the manuscript before publication on the following terms: that in all matters of fact, your opinion is to be binding; that in all matters of interpretation, my opinion is to be binding, recognizing, in any case that the line of tact and consideration may not be crossed even in pursuit of truth. That is to say, should a question of my interpretation, or even use of materials, arise between us, I would be happy to discuss the matter with you and come to mutual agreement. I do not want this to be an 'authorized' biography and I doubt that 'authorization' would serve your purposes."[59] Albertson stumbled over the issue that had proved troublesome at the opening ceremonies, the relationship between truth, fact, and interpretation. Here, Albertson clearly tried to maintain his own professionalism while pleasing the Harding heirs. Writing to a member of the Daugherty family for permission to use materials, Albertson stressed that he sought to "give a fair, balanced, accurate presentation of Harding's life" and deplored the "recent sensational publicity."[60] The tension between academic objectivity and partisan championing continued to vex Albertson.

Britton, like Phillips, proved that the line between popular sensationalism and academic objectivity quickly blurred. Although Albertson distanced himself from the sensationalism surrounding the Phillips letters, he continued to pursue access to Nan Britton and her papers. Albertson emphasized the importance of original documents in dispelling the "considerable body of nonsense written about President Harding."[61] Albertson wrote to Britton that he was "delighted" to have her assistance, adding, "your knowledge of Warren G. Harding is crucial to us both." He specifically asked to see Harding's letters to Britton, his wallet, and the "correct names" of the people in her book. While this evidence would have helped verify Britton's story, Albertson also pushed for Britton to identify eyewitnesses who could verify that she had been in the White House. Albertson was also pleased that Britton had declined to write an article for *Fact* magazine, writing to her, "There has been a surfeit of Sunday supplement material written about you and President Harding—I suppose you have seen the recent selections in the Cleveland *Plain Dealer* and *McCall's*."[62] Albertson called Warren Boroson's article on Harding as a black president "nonsense of the most pernicious sort," adding, "I shall deny every part of it in my biography."[63] Again, the shadow of Chancellor fell over Harding's legacy, intertwining itself with that of Britton.

Most of those who were interested in Harding's legacy professed a dedication to the truth, often equating the truth with whatever facts might be available in the elusive documents. However, issues of truth often boiled down to who asked the questions and who controlled the papers. Albertson continued to reassure Britton that he intended to "write the truth about President Harding and of your relation with him" and again asked her for evidence.[64] Even as Albertson conducted research in the Harding papers in Columbus, he wrote to the Witherill Hotel in Plattsburgh, New York, in an attempt to authenticate Britton's claim that she and Harding had stayed there.[65] The manager of the hotel told Albertson that Harding did register at the hotel on August 17, 1918, but would provide no more information. While Albertson clearly viewed himself as writing an objective and truthful biography, the manager scolded him for pursuing exactly the type of sensationalism he had been denouncing: "I appreciate the fact that you are writing a factual history, but it seems to me that some scandals of the past might better be left buried in obscurity."[66] Albertson was finding it increasingly difficult to separate his "factual history" from the scandals, and rumored scandals, of Harding's private life.

Russell wanted help from Downes and Albertson in "getting" to Britton, which they both refused. However, Albertson was further drawn into sensationalism when Francis Russell gave information to the *New York Times* about how to contact Britton. Albertson apologized to Britton, concluding that "Russell has managed to garner a massive dose of national publicity, but the number of people here and in Marion who got trampled in the undertaking is large."[67] Albertson by now was becoming increasingly convinced of Britton's story and sent newspaper clippings to her for her comments, telling her that because "I trust both your accuracy and memory, your own account of this event would aid me greatly."[68] Amid the publicity and sensationalism that Albertson denounced, Britton had now become one of his main sources of facts, as well as his aid in interpreting them.

Centennial

As Britton and Phillips dominated the discussion of Harding's legacy and stimulated a renewed interest in Marion, the HMA, in 1964, restored the Harding Home and converted it into a more conventional house museum that reflected the way Warren and Florence had lived. Previously the first floor of the house had been used to exhibit presidential memorabilia. While the desire to make the Harding Home more reflective of Warren and Florence was understandable, the transformation also mirrored the current obsession with Harding's private life rather than a concern with his presidency. That year, the first issue of the *Harding Star* appeared. The *Harding Star* was the newsletter of the HMA, which trumpeted itself as "a further step in the rebirth of Warren G. Harding history." The association also announced its completion of markings along the Harding Trail. Now tourists could visit places throughout central Ohio that had been important to Harding's life. All told, the newsletter stated, "We are hoping hundreds more will join this growing group which so far has expressed its interest in the true Harding story through the Home, the Museum, the Memorial, the various publications, the Awards and most recently through buying Association and Benefactor memberships."[69] The leadership of the association continued these commemorative events seemingly without acknowledging, at least publicly, the controversy surrounding Britton and Phillips. Perhaps they were right in their prediction that hundreds would join the association to share their interest in the "true Harding story," whatever that might be.

Albertson failed to complete his biography in time for the hundredth anniversary of Harding's birth.[70] He did, however, prepare a short presentation for the centennial celebration on November 2, 1965, and in doing so he gave the HMA the interpretation that it had wanted for so long but had been unable to achieve. Speaking at an event sponsored by the Harding Memorial Association before a crowd composed mostly of Marion citizens, he began by noting that Harding was "a man described in every American textbook as the worst President we have had." Albertson blended elements of a national and a local reputation in an attempt to compromise between the mythology that the moment called for and the rigor that his academic credentials required. Albertson, the academic historian, proclaimed that after three years of extensive research, "with full heart and good historical conscience," he could "join with you in honoring Warren Gamaliel Harding." In a more fitting commemorative address than Hoover's bitter dedication of the Harding Memorial, Albertson argued that Harding would have enjoyed the ceremony because it celebrated "not his birth" but "the birth of an American president" and because patriotism was one of his strongest character traits. Thus, Albertson restored to Harding, at least for this ceremony, an element of the log cabin myth. Here was a step toward restoring the presidency as a central feature of Harding's biography. Albertson portrayed an imperfect Harding who might not have fully understood the "fundamental changes" of his age, but asserted that if one questions Harding's understanding of his times, "one must likewise question it in William Howard Taft, in Woodrow Wilson, in Calvin Coolidge and in Herbert Hoover." Few referred to any of these men as "the worst President of the United States." Significantly, Albertson had returned Harding to the presidential context by evoking the importance of his humble birth for the national narrative, while at the same time fulfilling his role as an academic historian by providing an analytical context for Harding.

Albertson must have pleased his audience by placing the papers at the center of his reevaluation of Harding, asking for evidence from those who relegated Harding to the status of worst. Downes and Albertson were the first historians to "scour" the country for the "scattered bits and pieces" of evidence. Neither scholar regarded Harding as the worst president, and Albertson inverted the order of presidential rankings by asking a new question: "was Harding the best President of the United States?" He was willing to entertain the idea based on certain assumptions. First, he argued that picking the best and the worst was a "value judgement based, not on presumed 'Olympian Truth,' but on hindsight from some given time and place and point-of-view in history." Second, the criteria for the judgment must be known. Third, the evidence for the judgment must also be known. In establishing the credentials he asked a series of questions: "What is a 'good' President?" Should a president be one "of the people," democratically elected, and did he behave "in the presidency very much as any one of 'the people' would behave?" Harding, in Albertson's opinion, had done this. Did he give an "alternative to public questions of great moment for which he made clear he stood during the election campaign?" Harding also met this test. Did Harding perceive "the direction in which his constituency is moving, and so, anticipating what the people want," move in that direction? "Harding was partly this," Albertson said. He then asked, did he "by his breadth" ascertain changes and move "in advance of public enlightenment" to meet the changes? "Harding was not this." Finally, Albertson asked what presumably would be judged the criterion for true greatness. Was "he an executive who, from processes beyond the grasp of the electorate, can conceive of Augustine's heavenly city on earth, and who can lead his people to the promised land?" While Harding fell short on this count, Albertson added that "neither Harding nor his party conceived of the presidency in these terms."

Albertson then turned to an equally important issue, Harding's character. As we have seen, Harding's character had long been judged inadequate. Albertson was more positive in his judgment of Harding's character. Harding "was a good man" whose reputation had fallen victim to the mythology of the presidency. Those virtues—loyalty and friendship—"which were deemed to be his vices were cast off by every one of them [his friends], and the really good man stood alone—faulted entirely by his faults, because a president was not entitled to them—unredeemed by his virtues, because the popular mythology had it that everyone possessed them." Furthermore, Harding was "honorable in his private and public relationships as honor was defined by the overwhelming mass of his countrymen." In praising Harding's loyalty and honor, Albertson ignored his betrayals of Florence Harding, something that was often done even by those who focused on Harding's adultery. So Albertson, who had spent so much time and effort in seeking to secure the truth concerning Nan Britton and Carrie Phillips, in the end decided to ignore the two women. Perhaps, standing before the HMA and Marion citizens on the anniversary of Harding's birth, this was the polite and diplomatic thing to do, but one has to wonder how it served the cause of finding the truth.

Albertson's address continued, asking why Harding had been treated with "unrelenting contempt." Here was a question that could have brought Albertson back to Britton, and even to Phillips, but it did not. Albertson again returned to historical context to reinterpret Harding's legacy and to absolve him of guilt. Albertson acknowledged the scandals in Harding's administration but then pronounced them the result of the "incredible stupidity" of Prohibition. Harding governed during a period of "massive disillusionment," Albertson asserted, and that social climate had caused the scandals. The importance of the disillusionment and the scandals was magnified by the failure of Wilsonianism. Albertson struck another familiar theme in arguing that the writers of the 1920s were progressives and followers of Wilson. Furthermore, the documents on Harding were not available. Albertson did not discuss why they were unavailable. With the documents now available, he concluded by predicting that "the time is swiftly coming when the people of Marion will lift their heads and say, 'Warren G. Harding was born here!'"[71]

Warren Sawyer was delighted with Albertson's talk. He wrote him a note of thanks, adding that "the Harding Memorial Association can never thank you enough for helping make the 100th celebration such a success." Sawyer was so pleased with the talk that he wanted to publish it as part of the "100th Anniversary pamphlet," viewing it as a "good start on the 'reevaluation.'"[72] Indeed, Albertson's conclusions could have restored the old booster faith that had inspired the HMA in 1923.

Albertson reported to Nan Britton that the "Harding Memorial Centennial was interesting. Warren Sawyer did a brilliant job of re-doing the Harding Home." Albertson continued, "I was aghast to find myself quoted in some obscure Ohio publication as having said that Harding was the worst President. What I really said was to the effect that some of my colleagues have said this of him, but that I wanted to know where they got their evidence for such a statement since the four current biographers are the only ones who have ever gone through the Harding papers." Sometimes, as Albertson saw, the media found it easier to report that Harding was the worst than to summarize a discussion on presidential rankings. He continued with praise: "the whole celebration was nicely and tastefully done—there wasn't a wrong note in the whole proceedings. I wish you had been there, as you should have been. I thought of you often and missed you on this fine occasion."[73] Albertson seemed unaware of the bizarreness of wishing that Nan Britton could have attended the ceremony at which he had failed to discuss her contribution to Harding's reputation. He ignored the obvious reality: it was guaranteed that she would not have been welcome at the ceremony.

Despite his disavowals of Russell's conduct and his emphasis on context, Albertson proved unable to resist the lure of the Phillips letters. He wrote to Dennis Brogan, a professor in England, hoping to obtain a microfilm copy of the Phillips letters that Andrew Sinclair had apparently made. Albertson knew he was treading on forbidden ground and assured Brogan that he would assume full responsibility and that "under no circumstances" would he "reveal from whence it came." He reassured Brogan that he was on good terms with the Harding family and told Brogan that Charles Harding had recently tried through the Marion County probate court (without success) for Albertson to be allowed access to the Phillips letters.[74]

Despite his Herculean research, Albertson never produced his biography of Harding, and Downes produced only the first volume of a planned multivolume work on Harding, as he became distracted with the

Vietnam War and his own illness. As it turned out, none of the three scholars who remained in Harding Alley released the first of the new Harding biographies, which was written by Andrew Sinclair. Albertson wrote to Charles Harding that Sinclair's book, *The Available Man,* might have been the first to appear, "but he has fallen far short of having the 'mostest.'"[75] Downes later wrote to him that "Sinclair did a sorry job. Macmillan should be boycotted."[76] The association, however, presented an award to Sinclair for *The Available Man.*[77] The old interpretations of Harding's presidency were not going away soon, as was evident with Sinclair's book. The HMA also observed another passing of the guard with the 1966 death of Carl Sawyer.[78]

Despite his argument before the HMA, Albertson struggled with the idea of Harding being the worst of American presidents. He wrote to Walter Lippman, asking to speak with him regarding his memories of Harding, adding,

> but I would be equally interested to discuss with you the reasons why Harding has been rated in American historical literature as our "worst" President. In your own writings of the period you certainly viewed him as such, and I doubt that you have changed your mind, nor am I suggesting that you should have, but I would be most grateful for the reasoning behind your judgement. Of course my research over the past three years has given me ample reason to suspect you may have been correct; on the other hand it must be recognized that a handful of superbly able writers have contributed those best-remembered phrases which damn Harding to this day, and that nearly all of those writers deeply admired Woodrow Wilson and the ideals for which he died. Was it because Harding was so bad, or because Wilson was so good?[79]

Lippman remembered Albertson from when he had worked with Nevins on the Oral History Project. He was glad to cooperate but warned him that he had little else to say regarding Harding.[80]

The historians of Harding Alley continued to work under increasing pressure, particularly from each other. The competition between them revealed not only their interpretive difficulties but also the outside pressures that shaped their analyses. Andrew Sinclair had won the first slot but none wanted to be last. Tensions arose when Randolph Downes believed that

Albertson's book was due to be published shortly and so only cautiously accepted an invitation to present his work at the American Historical Association (AHA).[81] Albertson graciously reassured Downes of the appropriateness of accepting this invitation: "If you have read John Garraty's review of Sinclair's book, you know that the 'first' is yet to come."[82] Albertson also attempted, unsuccessfully, to get Russell to join the AHA's panel of Harding biographers, prompting yet another exchange on the difficulty of writing about Harding. In Russell's evaluation of Sinclair's book, he wrote, "I was astonished at the amount of information he has, based on so little research. Of course it will remain to be seen how accurate it is."[83] Making indirect reference to the legal fight, he added, "there is always the possibility that by December I may be in the Ohio Penitentiary."[84]

Albertson wrote that he was eager to read the forthcoming article by Russell and "what's-his-name from the OHS" in *American Heritage*.[85] Russell replied that he and Duckett (a.k.a. what's-his-name) had not written a joint piece and added, "My own piece has been so manicured by lawyers that I barely recognize it myself." For example, he added that the observation that "Harding was 'surprisingly well read' never came from my pen," and asked, "Ever get tired of Warren G?"[86] As it turned out, Paul Michel, the attorney handling the Phillips estate, had given the letters to Isabel Mathee's attorney, John Bartram, who then agreed with George T. Harding III's request to hold the letters "in escrow until litigation concerning their publication is settled." Russell continued, "My only concern about the letters has been to see that they are preserved. It is not for me or for any member of the Historical Society to decide as to their value. Anything written by a president of the United States becomes automatically of historical interest, and it is a crime against history to destroy it. Although this may at times prove of embarrassment to the descendants of a political figure, a man who has sought public life cannot expect the privacy of a man who has not."[87] Unlike Albertson, Russell had not managed to diplomatically appease most sides in the Harding feud. Russell found another route to the historical truth in his fight to preserve the Phillips letters, justifying his sensationalism by declaring that presidents do not have a zone of privacy.

The New Regime

The HMA celebrated the new regime, as the members called the renewed effort to positively link Harding's legacy and Marion's reputation, by holding Marion Day on June 5, 1966. The new regime had the flavor of the old booster ethos. The celebration also kicked off the new summer tourist season, which brought with it the hope of new interest in Harding.[88]

As often happens in the writing of history, changing national events influenced how Albertson interpreted and commemorated Harding. The information included in the newly released papers held the potential to put Harding's reputation, to use Gary Fine's phrase, in play. The release of the papers meant several things, including the potential for Harding's reputation to become part of a national dialogue rather than simply an example of failure or the punch line of a joke. Albertson continued his relationship with the HMA and participated in its commemorative events, even as he accepted a position on the faculty of the University of Massachusetts at Amherst.

As the Vietnam War became increasingly controversial, Albertson became involved in antiwar activities and was attracted to Harding's foreign policy. Suddenly Harding's pursuit of international peace and isolationism seemed wiser. In 1967, for the 102nd anniversary of Harding's birth, Albertson wrote that "in the realm of Politics, fairy tales become lies, using the phrase of another President, Abraham Lincoln, as he would quote the Holy Writ, 'He who is without guilt cast the first stone.'" In a twist of interpretation, Albertson revealed a cynicism toward contemporary politics and turned to Harding as an example to hold up to the present. Now Harding's character stood in sharp contrast to events that were unfolding 1967: "His warm personality and his public messages inspired cheer, encouragement, and competence." Albertson admired Harding's calmness and added that Harding "hated strife and discord." Albertson concluded with some speculations about what Harding's character might have meant for modern times: "And to think that since his death we have had World War II, the Korean conflict, and Viet Nam. Little did he or any of our Presidents preceding him believe this would have happened to this country."[89] Clearly, the 1960s were moving Albertson to reconsider his interpretation of the 1920s.

For the HMA, commemoration once again became closely tied to publishing and, to a lesser extent, to academic scholarship. The association's leader felt compelled to cancel the Harding Birthday Banquet, in part, because three books about Harding that had been scheduled for release would not be released on time. According to the HMA's newsletter, the release of Russell's book, which was of "very questionable status both from an ethical and also a legal point of view," had created a great deal of confusion that had contributed to the failure of the other books.[90] That September, 1968, Charles W. Harding asked Albertson about the status of his book, to which Albertson testily replied, "Yes, I'm still alive, and yes I am still writing the biography of Harding, and yes, Harcourt, Brace & World still want it."[91]

Albertson maintained a friendly correspondence with Britton, now living in Glendale, California. They discussed their friends and family, in addition to Harding.[92] Albertson, despite having his publisher "breathing down" his neck, continued to do research, which included speaking with Roxie Stinson.[93] Albertson's thoughts on Britton went to the heart of his work about Harding and Harding's legacy. Again, contemporary events prompted Albertson to rethink aspects of Harding's life. He had moved beyond asking if Harding was the best or the worst. This, in turn, led him to consider issues of morality, both of the 1920s and the 1960s. These were "the same problems which have plagued me from the beginning in writing" his biography. He wrote that "the value systems of the era 1910–1930 were as rapidly changing as the value systems are changing in the present period. No one knew exactly where he or she was. No one today KNOWS either, though many surmise, in their experiments with communal living, with 'swinging' and with experimental marriages." Albertson and Britton were approaching the same topic, only she did so autobiographically. He wrote to Britton, "I think you are on tremendously strong ground when you write autobiographically, for when you write in this vein, you are telling a story which actually happened, you are speaking to the value systems which prevailed then, and you are making a plea for something." He predicted, "Unwed mothers, too, will soon be not a thing of the past, but rather an occurrence which simply did not have to happen because of the advent of the pill." Because the birth control pill made women "absolute masters of their bodies," he wrote, it will no longer be said that "a man *got* a woman pregnant." Albertson noted that Britton wrote from a Christian perspective and then went into some detail on the decline of religion, which he attributed in part to the growing acceptance of premarital sex. Albertson observed that the "sexual value systems of the twenties" would help people of the seventies "understand where we once were." Finally, Albertson addressed the issue of Harding's morality: "If The PRESIDENT'S DAUGHTER had never appeared, if the Carrie Phillips letters had been destroyed, if Albert Fall had never taken a bribe, the remaining scandals of the Harding administration would have been no greater or less than other administrations, and his place in history would be undisturbed." He continued that "the curse upon Harding's head is one of 'morality' whatever that may mean. If it means anything, he was revealed in the Carrie Phillips letters as a wholly moral man, and he is further revealed as wholly moral in his relationship to you. He had nothing to do with Fall's bribe."

Albertson missed the irony of arguing that Harding's letters to his mistress proved that he was "wholly moral" (an irony that was all the greater because he was making this argument to a woman who he also believed had been Harding's mistress). Albertson connected Harding's legacy to current events, noting that at the moment "history" seemed content to let Ted Kennedy have his private life, but such was not the case with Harding. He condemned William Allen White as a keeper of the standards "without knowing a blessed thing about his [Harding's] standards." Britton's story would reveal a "great deal more about 'them,' the mass of confused Americans for whom sex was dirty business, for whom a President was mysteriously expected to behave in ways which few of them could live up to." Albertson urged Britton to write a full autobiography: "Your book could be a great one!" [94]

As late as 1970, Albertson continued to research Harding and to be contacted by people who had an interest in Harding, but at some point he abandoned the topic. [95] When Albertson died of lung cancer, in 1989, there was no mention of his quest to write the Harding biography. His department chair, Roland Sarti, noted that Albertson was a challenging and popular teacher who was known on campus for his "major role" in the protests against the Vietnam War. Sarti summed up Albertson: "When all is said and done, although people thought of him as a radical, a leftist, and a Marxist, he was a very gentle and kind person, and he was upset when he saw that we were less than gentle and kind." [96] One has to wonder how much Albertson's disillusionment with national affairs, particularly growing out of Vietnam, was similar to the disillusionment and desire for stability that led voters to embrace Harding in 1920.

Albertson, in what ultimately became a private quest, proved the potential for revising Harding, perhaps more so than the people who did publish Harding biographies but did not consider Harding's relevance for the late twentieth century. Albertson recognized that Harding's concern with war and peace and his struggles with private morality in changing times were all too common. Albertson, however, did not make these views public and so Harding's reputation remained unchanged. Albertson, however, could not as an academic historian separate Harding's legacy from either Nan Britton or Carrie Phillips. Among Harding scholarship were some serious, and mildly sympathetic, works, but none of them placed the issues that had drawn Albertson's attention at the center. Robert Murray's *Harding Era* dodged the issue of private morality, while Russell reveled in Harding's tawdry side. Albertson alone made the connection between Harding's two sides, the private and the public, by looking at the social and cultural context. Albertson participated in the HMA's commemorative efforts and sympathized with Nan Britton. His work, however, did not contribute to a new meaning for the Harding Memorial. Contrary to the hopes of Duckett, Albertson and the other historians of Harding Alley would not solve the "mysteries" of Warren Harding's life. Indeed, these mysteries would continue to serve as a theme for biographers such as Francis Russell, who pushed aside the log cabin myth and reinforced the idea, first established in the 1920s, that Harding's life was a tragedy.

Dead Last

Warren G. Harding wasn't particularly interested in the presidency. He only enjoyed the office because it allowed him to pursue his true loves in life: gambling, drinking, and women.

—*Martin H. Levinson,* Queens Gazette, *2007*

I think Jimmy Carter would be very close to Warren G. Harding. I feel very strongly that Jimmy Carter was a disaster, particularly domestically and economically. I have said more than once that he was certainly the poorest president in my lifetime.

—*former president Gerald Ford, 1981*

What can we make of Harding's legacy, as bad as it is? The scholarship that emerged after the opening of the Harding papers, and the closing of the Phillips letters, did not alter Harding's place in history. While little of the writing on Harding depicted him as a good president, some of it did move beyond viewing him as a caricature of small-town decadence. However, for the most part Harding remained a historical example of a flawed Babbitt and a self-indulgent philanderer. It was the interpretation of Harding as incompetent and common that established his place in our national memory, the exception that proved the rule of the log cabin myth. Harding established the low-water mark for presidents and became the measure for presidential failure; comparisons to Warren Harding were at best unflattering and usually an insult. This tradition has carried into the twenty-first century. For example, in 2005 *New York Times* columnist Frank Rich criticized the administration of George W. Bush. Beginning with his title, "Bring Back Warren Harding," Rich develops direct comparisons between Bush and Harding. He writes of one indicted lobbyist that his "greasy K Street influence-peddling network makes the Warren Harding gang, which operated out of its own infamous 'little green house on K Street,' look like selfless stewards of the public good."[1] Rich was not the first, nor would he be the last, to hold up Harding as a self-evident unflattering comparison.

Just as the haggard and worn Lincoln is our everyman-as-presidential-hero, the philandering and naive Harding is cited as proof that not everyone is capable of being president. More so than any other president, those who failed (or had failings) in the office risked being compared to Harding. The molding of Harding's reputation to fit contemporary politics has been made easier by the blurry picture of him created by novelists and scholars. Harding has offered journalists, pundits, and other commentators a wide range of topics. However, while many have professed an interest in broader truths, accuracy was often not the concern of those who used Harding's legacy to comment on the national character or the state of democracy.

Facts and Fictions

One of the few ways in which Harding's legacy seemed presidential was in the fictionalization of his life. As we have seen, a good deal of fiction, some of it presented as fact, was written about Harding in the decade following his death. The fictionalization of Harding has continued in subsequent decades; indeed, Harding has received almost as much fictional attention as more prominent presidents. Unlike the fictional treatments typical of more highly regarded presidents, however, there has been little effort to transform Harding into a positive myth. There is no equivalent of Parson Weems's story of Washington and the cherry tree. Samuel Hopkins Adams, with his novel *Revelry*, provides the often unacknowledged template for future authors, from his depictions of poker games and presidential antics to a cynicism regarding the role of the people in selecting a president. Many fictional accounts have incorporated Adams's scene depicting Harding's near confession before his death but have followed by noting that Harding had only "dimly" perceived his betrayal and the corruption of his administration. In many of the novels written about Harding, we see a man struggling with his shortcomings and betrayal only because the office of the presidency exerted a positive influence on his otherwise common intellect and weak character. These near-confessions redeemed the office but not its occupant. In the post–World War II era, this story of the failure of the common man as president became not just a political lesson but a historical one as well. For many, Harding remains proof of the failure of the log cabin myth and a way to gain insight into the darker side of American character. While not all the authors gained commercial success, and fewer achieved critical success, they were part of a persistent and ongoing commentary on Harding and the national character.

In 1959, *The Gang's All Here,* a play by Jerome Lawrence and Robert E. Lee, opened in New York. In it Lawrence and Lee follow the path pioneered by earlier writers like Adams and Fitzgerald. In an article in the *New York Herald Tribune,* which was reprinted as the foreword of the book version, Lawrence and Lee maintain that their play is not about a specific president but rather represents a composite of all the presidents. They are examining the "great American legend" that every boy could grow up to be president, but they focus on the period after the election, answering the question, "what happens to the manboy?" They further ask, "What happens, in particular, if he never should have been elected in the first place; if he sweeps in on his good looks, his 'Hail! Hail! The Gang's All Here' personality?'" The burdens that the American people place on our presidents, they argue, make it reasonable that a president would want to be surrounded by friends. But, they ask, was "government by crony" an inevitable outgrowth of the people's burden? Finally, they remind readers that they are not journalists and ask to be liberated from *"mere* facts."[2] Lawrence and Lee faced a familiar dilemma with Harding. On one hand, they condemn cronyism and manipulation as undermining democracy but, on the other hand, they condemn the democracy that allowed these evils.

So, shedding the mere facts, we delve into their play to learn what broader truths came from presidential failures. The playwrights' composite President Griffith P. Hastings looks and acts like President Warren G. Harding. *The Gang's All Here* is not original if one is familiar with Warren Harding's reputation. As with many treatments of Harding, Hastings is a one-dimensional character who provides the moral of the story. Indeed, it is hard to find other presidents in this "composite." Although there are passing references to Ulysses Grant, James Buchanan, Millard Fillmore, and others who might have contributed to Lawrence and Lee's endeavor, Harding alone serves as our example of democracy gone awry.

The Gang's All Here starts with a deadlocked convention in a mysterious smoke-filled room littered with cigar butts and a bottle of "Prohibition whiskey." Walter Rafferty (a.k.a. Harry Daugherty) is promoting Senator Hastings. He promises Senator Joshua Loomis, from the West, control of

Interior in exchange for his support of Hastings. Here we see how Albert Fall came to the cabinet. This episode foreshadows the corruption of Teapot Dome but misses the more dramatic real story of Fall's nomination and betrayal. Lawrence and Lee comment on the undemocratic nature of party politics, having Charles Webster worry that the deadlocked convention will allow "some grass roots amateur with nobody behind him but the people" to take the nomination. One of the conspirators asks, "Can we consider the possibility of nominating the best man?" This, however, is out of the question. The nomination offers Lawrence and Lee the opportunity to discuss scandal and qualifications. When Hastings initially turns down the offer for fear that he lacks the special quality that presidents need, Rafferty assures him, in words very similar to what Daugherty wrote in his memoir, "Do you think any backwoods lawyer, or country storekeeper, or half-drunk Civil War General knew any more about it than you do?" The log cabin myth is a ruse to deceive the people. Rafferty explains Hastings's qualifications, allowing that when he first saw Hastings, he knew by the "power of his walk, the silver majesty of his head" that Hastings had "what the people vote for." Hastings looks presidential and that alone will satisfy the electorate (15, 19, 21, 23, 32). Of course, Hastings goes on to win the election with ease. By ignoring the campaign, however, Lawrence and Lee miss the debate over party rule.

Hastings quickly finds the intellectual demands of the job overwhelming. Confused, he delegates important foreign policy decisions to a young White House aide before joining his cronies for a drink. While with the gang, Hastings laments his campaign pledge to have the best minds in the cabinet. "I want," he declares to Rafferty, "the Cabinet I want. Not what somebody thinks would look good in a history book" (43, 57). Again, we see the prevalent theme of Harding (as Hastings) turning his back on the best minds in favor of his cronies; we also see the force of history pushing the fictional president toward the greater good. As is so often the case, Harding and his cronies seem to be the real representatives of the people, in contrast to the abstract will of an abstraction called the people. The former dictate politics while the latter create a positive legacy.

Act two begins with the familiar poker game in a house on L Street. Here was the direct connection between Hastings's personal life and the scandals that will ruin his administration. A member of the gang offers his opinion as to what is wrong with Hastings: "I'll tell you what's wrong with Griff: he's got a severe case of Frances Greeley Hastings. With half the country female—and some of 'em even pretty—he had to marry the Duchess!"

Although the authors made up fictive names for most of the characters, they use Florence Harding's nickname. The president's real problem, we learn, is his wife and, in particular, her lack of physical attractiveness. The gang, however, has something in mind other than poker or the state of Hastings's marriage. Rafferty has prepared an executive order transferring oil reserves for the president to sign. Hastings joins the poker game after giving his Secret Service agents the slip. A distraught and drunk Hastings, like Adams's President Willis Markham in *Revelry*, declares that during "the campaign, I had the cockeyed idea that Cabinet meetings could be like this: a box of cigars in the middle of the table; we'd read over the mail together; then we'd deal out who-does-what, have a drink or two, and call it a day." The poker game becomes a farce after the intoxicated Hastings signs the papers. Hastings, angered at the suggestion that he has a responsibility to behave a certain way, defiantly jumps up on the poker table with a dancing girl, a scene not far removed from Gaston Means's account of activities in the K Street house (67, 75).

As the presidency begins to transform Hastings, the authors throw in comparisons to other failed presidents. Hastings turns to history to help find his way, but his selection of *A Boy's Lives of the Presidents* reveals his reliance on childish myths and his intellectual shortcomings. Hastings concludes that Martin Van Buren would have been better off if he had stayed in Albany. An aide responds, "I suppose that if a President has five minutes of greatness in four years he's doing fine." Hastings continues, "That Franklin Pierce—he had about thirty seconds!" (113, 114). What remains to be seen is how many seconds of greatness Hastings will achieve.

Hastings, like Harding, has a confessional moment that is linked to his death. His death is a moment of greatness and deception, much like the story from his earlier reading that any boy can grow up to be president. In a scene reminiscent of Harding's discussion with Hoover, Hastings calls on a cabinet member for advice. The secretary of the treasury advises that he should "call on the deepest resources of his greatness," but Hastings responds that he does not understand all this talk of greatness. After a fight with Rafferty in which Hastings threatens to come clean, Hastings, true to form, poisons himself. Hastings then calls a press conference, but only one reporter, new to the job, arrives. Hastings reveals the scandals to him, even showing him how to take notes. This suggests that Hastings should have remained with his first true calling—newspaper publishing. When left alone with Frances, he says, "For the first time, I felt like a President of the United States. For about forty-five seconds. Well, that's fifteen seconds better than Franklin Pierce." Hastings urges his wife to get rid of the bottle of poison to conceal how he died: "Don't spoil my chance to be on a two-cent stamp!" (126, 129). Following on the heels of Adams's *Revelry,* in *The Gang's All Here* the president hopes to gain a place in the civic religion through suicide disguised as a noble death in office. It takes his death and a lie to achieve forty-five seconds of greatness.

The Gang's All Here faithfully follows the standard treatment of Harding. The authors' exploration of presidential failure deals overwhelmingly with Harding, suggesting that only Pierce was a worse president. They rely heavily on themes found in the works of Adams, Means, and Britton, and their discussion of the seemingly narrow gap between greatness and failure is all about character, not policy. True to their promise, Lawrence and Lee do not confine themselves to mere facts, but in straying from the facts they tell a story that had been told many times before and would be told again.

These themes—the basic story of Harding's failure because of his poor character—also appear in Martin Blinder's *Fluke* (1999). *Fluke* is a novel with a narrative familiar to anyone familiar with Harding's legacy, but it is also clearly influenced by the scandals that emerged from the administration of William Jefferson Clinton. The title and cover of the book reveal a great deal about the content. In the foreground we see the back of a naked blonde woman whose only covering is an American flag draped over her shoulder. In the background, in black and white, is Warren G. Harding standing tall and holding a flag, an image taken from his America First campaign poster. In the acknowledgments, Blinder explains that he has "created" the dialogue but that "significant historical and biographical events" are factual. He concludes, "Sad to say, this is a true story." So, like Lawrence and Lee, Blinder has produced fiction but has wrapped it in the idea that facts are not important when pursuing truth.

Blinder begins his "true story" with Harding's presidential funeral procession in San Francisco. We quickly learn how far the author has gone in creating the dialogue. The narration begins with the deceased Harding commenting on his own demise: "Being dead has its good points. The pain ends. No more insoluble problems. No more betrayals. You're well out of the turmoil, the futile struggle. Now it's all in someone else's hands. Well good riddance. To the whole damn lot. 'Cept for my sweet Nan—I sure wasn't ready to give *her* up. Not in this lifetime."[3] The dead Harding observes Nan Britton who, five months pregnant, stands weeping on a street corner as his body passes. Blinder does not bother to explain why Britton is pregnant in 1923 or why she is in San Francisco when, by her own account, she was in Europe when Harding died. Blinder does not acknowledge that there was controversy regarding Harding's paternity, but rather has Harding confess, "Yeah, that's my bun in the oven" (8). Most of the remainder of the book switches back and forth from the perspective of Nan Britton to that of the deceased Harding. Blinder's Britton is from Marion and falls in love with Harding, but the author has her doing such things as pretending to be the president's nurse so that she can regularly sneak into the White House (the cover of the book depicts one such visit) (14).

Blinder revisits most of the familiar Harding scandal and gossip. He writes of the alleged homosexual relationship between Daugherty and Smith, "Harry Daugherty and Jess Smith arranged themselves together on the old loveseat, the only visible hint of their long standing, clandestine coupling" (37). Blinder gets most of the details about Harding's life in Marion wrong, perhaps for dramatic convenience. He notes the rumors of Harding's black ancestry, having Harding utter his famous response to the rumors (adding a vulgarity for effect), "Maybe a hundred years ago one of my people jumped the fence. Who the hell's to say?" (48). Blinder's Daugherty arranges for Harding's nomination without Harding's participation. Harding learns of his nomination while drinking in a Chicago bar and then goes to Britton, where he confesses his doubts: "I'm an ordinary man dearie. Just an ordinary man. But how can I say no?" (96). Harding and Britton then consummate his nomination, linking Harding's political and private inability to say no. Harding overcomes his doubts when he realizes, "America was 'merely Marion, Ohio, writ large'" (101).

During the election, in Blinder's account, the FBI burns William Chancellor's home (where, in the book, Chancellor runs a white-supremacist publishing house, Purity Press) with the professor inside (104). Blinder combines several sensational elements (the corruption of William Burns, the attempted lynching of Chancellor, and the burning of Chancellor's book) into a single event that is substantially less interesting than the originals, and he adds a fictional murder.

Blinder's next step is having Harding begin to develop as a president and a servant of the people. Harding makes time to meet with the people because, in the narrative of Britton, it "was *their* White House, after all, and he was *their* President" (114–15, emphasis in original). Here, Blinder takes Florence Harding's declaration that the White House is the people's house, and gives it to Britton. Thus he falls into the pattern of treating Britton as a more appropriate partner than Florence for Harding. Britton next observes that in "his second year as President, I saw a definite change in Mr. Harding. He was studying all manner of incredibly difficult books and journals." Weirdly, in Blinder's version, Harding's growth as a president is linked to regular visits by Britton, who during her clandestine visits to the White House gives Harding "vitamin" shots. A "rejuvenated" Harding then pitches his idea for the Washington Naval Conference (128).

Blinder, however, strays from the typical path in stories about Harding, having Harding's politics change as he grows into the office. The Washington Naval Conference proves to be a turning point for Harding. The president is soon engaged in a public fight with the Senate, with Harding seeking to guide the nation into the world court, internationalism, and disarmament. The Senate seeks to stop Harding by investigating Teapot Dome. Rather than have the scandals discovered in the way they actually unfolded, Blinder has H. L. Mencken break the story. Somewhat more accurately, in Blinder's account Sawyer is the one who discovers Forbes's activities at the Veterans' Bureau. Sawyer and Harding, incognito, slip into the Bethesda Veterans' Hospital to discover the poor conditions created by the graft. This sets up Harding's confrontation with Forbes, who in this account has been his childhood friend from Marion. Harding yells, "Those men put their lives on the line for this country, you crooked son of a bitch!" (153, 154).

Finally, Harding storms the country to build support for his new, progressive agenda, sounding like Wilson campaigning for the League of Nations. While his new agenda points to the possibility of a great activist presidency, Harding's personal flaws stand in his way. Nan Britton does not accompany Harding because Hoover urges her to stay at home: "I believe Warren Harding can be recorded by history as a great president. Or he can continue to be with you. But not both" (168). Here, Blinder contradicts his earlier plot line of having their liaisons rejuvenate Harding.

As Harding campaigns for an increasingly progressive agenda, his popularity increases. Harding, however, sounds not so much like Wilson now but rather like Bill Clinton as he comes out against segregation, nativism, and poverty. Indeed, the popularity of Clinton's policies amid the sexual scandal that led to his impeachment seems to have colored Blinder's novel. As congressional investigations continue in an effort to end Harding's new agenda, Blinder creates a confessional moment for Harding. Just before his death, an ailing Harding tells a large, enthusiastic audience that he is distressed by the scandals, vowing, "We'll kick any rotten apples right onto the street" (200). However, this is not to be. The ailing president is taken to the Palace Hotel, where he passes protesters carrying signs that read Equal Pay for Equal Work, All Men Are Created Equal, and Colored People Have Rights Too. Harding asks where they have gotten those ideas. His chauffer answers, "I believe from you, Mr. President" (204–5). Rather than explore the racial politics of the 1920s, Blinder substitutes modern protest politics.

The book concludes with an epilogue featuring Hoover's dedication of the Harding Memorial with, of course, Harding narrating the event. Hoover's fictional dedication is more complimentary than the real-life one, with Blinder's Hoover saying that Harding was on the verge of greatness. In a final note Blinder comments on *The President's Daughter:* "Nan did her best to salvage his reputation from posterity's disrepute" (213). Blinder, however, leaves us with a mixed message about Harding, his politics, and his death.

In Blinder's account, Harding becomes a modern liberal, embracing social justice and an activist government. It is possible to argue that Harding was more liberal (to use the word in its post–civil rights movement sense) on race than was Wilson and that he was more internationalist than the president who followed, Coolidge. However, Harding was a conservative in the booster tradition. In *Fluke,* Harding becomes an advocate for the downtrodden. Both in *The Gang's All Here* and in *Fluke* we see a continued ambivalence toward Harding's common background. In Lawrence and Lee's play, President Hastings finds his forty-five seconds of greatness by sacrificing his own life to expose corruption and to elevate the office he has tainted. Blinder, in his supposedly true account, has the transformed Harding turn his back on his damn friends in the moment of death, but this Harding sounds like an imaginary and unmentioned Wilson or, even more improbably, John Kennedy or Lyndon Johnson. In an argument that resonated during Bill Clinton's second term that featured scandal and impeachment, we are left to assume that the scandals that destroyed Harding's reputation were politically motivated by those who opposed Harding's liberal agenda. Blinder dismisses the morality of Harding's affair with Britton (even asserting that Britton attempted to salvage his reputation). These accounts confer respect on Harding only by transforming him into something he was not.

In 2007, John W. Ravage's *Slick and the Duchess: The Teapot Dome Scandal and the Death of Warren Harding* appeared. The title suggests that the author will link Harding with Clinton (by evoking Clinton's unflattering nickname Slick Willie), but that does not happen. In *Slick and the Duchess,* Ravage combines the stories of a Denver reporter and a prostitute with a heart of gold who stumbles on the Teapot Dome scandal with an "insider's" account of the Harding administration. While Ravage relies heavily on older and familiar Harding scenes, he also focuses on the corruption of cronies and oil money. Rather than recounting the story of Nan Britton and sexual escapades, the novel contains references to "other women" throughout. Ravage focuses on political scandal. A flamboyantly homosexual Jess Smith leads the Ohio Gang until he is murdered by Gaston Means, a main character in the novel. Florence Harding, with connections to Hollywood, stage-manages Warren Harding's image. While Ravage does emphasize Florence's belief in the supernatural, he does not portray her as the shrill and nagging wife that justified Warren's infidelities. Ravage's fictional Harding is a tragic figure who demands that Harry Daugherty resign when he learns of the scandals shortly before his death. Like Blinder, Ravage picks up on themes present in the Clinton administration. In Ravage's book, the common theme is the link between Washington and Hollywood.

Ravage attributes Harding's death to the incompetence of Charles Sawyer. In the novel Sawyer's jealousy motivates him to push aside more competent physicians. As a result the president dies of heart failure. Following Harding's death, Ravage has Gen. John Pershing issue a statement in which he creates the story of Florence reading to Harding during his final moments. Pershing reflects that Harding "had just created an indelible version of reality that would stand forever in the history texts, politics, newspapers and magazines."[4]

While Ravage does entertain the idea of the creation of myth around the presidency, he offers a more substantial conclusion in the epilogue, writing that Harding's legacy "was his country's nearly two-decade loss of interest in world affairs." He continues, "Ominously, his administration was the start of a new, powerful, convergence of money and influence in national politics, as well as a parochialism that stressed local, grassroots issues above all others. Building upon Florence Harding's keen awareness of the public's interest in movies and popular culture, national parties began to apply modern 'mass marketing' techniques to American politics on a scale that would grow beyond anything she dreamed of" (457–58). Although Ravage, influenced by the Harding revisionism of the 1990s, changes his account to emphasize a more positive interpretation of Florence Harding and the rise of popular culture, he still concludes that the Harding administration was a failure that would influence the future.

No Respect

While novelists have used Harding as the measure of failure in comparison to other presidents, journalists and politicians have also used Harding's legacy to offer commentary on contemporary politics. Harding has been compared to John Kennedy, another man who looked presidential and whose private life did not measure up to his public image. In this context, Harding's legacy provided conservatives with an opportunity to criticize both the media and the academy. Conservatives have pointed out that both presidents had similar records but that Kennedy remains a respected president. Harding and Kennedy both served approximately one thousand days, pursued tax cuts, and had foreign policy successes. However, the less-flattering comparison of Harding to Kennedy comes from the personal lives of the two men. As stories appeared discussing Kennedy's sexual appetite, the comparisons with Harding grew, particularly after the appearance of Seymour Hersh's *Dark Side of Camelot*.[5] Here, the question arises as to why Harding's affairs have ruined his reputation while Kennedy's affairs have not. The answer provided by conservatives is that the liberal bias of academics and journalists has led them to overlook the moral shortcomings of Kennedy while condemning those of Harding.

Ronald Reagan was also vulnerable to comparisons with Harding; many of these comparisons came primarily from liberals wanting to discredit Reagan and his policies. This made partisan sense, as we see liberals linking two conservative Republican presidents. The comparisons were based primarily on Reagan's role as an actor and a man who delegated authority. According to Adams, Harding was not a puppet but rather "an actor, cheerfully responsive to the direction of the playwrights."[6] Reagan, an actor by profession, admired the politics of the 1920s. It has been widely noted that both men looked the part of president. In a psychological study that assigned each president a personality type, both Harding and Reagan were classified as actors, innocents, and extroverts.[7]

Historian Douglas Brinkley compares Reagan to Harding, noting that Reagan, like Harding, cut taxes and was a pro-business conservative. The substantial difference, for Brinkley, lies in their attitudes toward defense. Harding cut the size of the military while Reagan accelerated the arms race with the Soviet Union.[8] Harding had his Ohio Gang; Reagan had his cronies from California. Reagan's attorney general, Edwin Meese, like Harding's attorney general Harry Daugherty, was a controversial figure who served as political advisor. Ultimately, the comparisons between Harding and Reagan hinged on management style and intelligence. Both men relied heavily on their cabinets, delegating authority to men who were supposed to be experts. For both presidents, the hands-off approach created an atmosphere from which scandal emerged: Reagan's disengagement led to the Iran-contra scandal; Harding's good nature was exploited by his friends in the cabinet. Both Harding and Reagan have been portrayed as goodnatured men who lacked the intellectual depth to understand the workings of the government. Likewise, both Florence Harding and Nancy Reagan were strong-willed women who dabbled in the occult.[9]

Conservatives who noticed Harding generally portrayed him as a victim. For example, conservative commentator Patrick Buchanan argues that Harding was a victim of the liberal establishment. Following the lead of Alfred E. Eckes, a professor at Ohio University and a former Reagan administration official, Buchanan wholeheartedly endorses a conservative presidential ranking that placed William McKinley first and Warren G. Harding second. Buchanan describes Harding as the president who "was first at cutting the misery index." While Buchanan's argument is essentially anachronistic, in crediting a president from the 1920s with tackling a problem distinctive to the 1970s, he does have a point. Although many conservatives either ignore it or have forgotten it, Warren G. Harding did usher in a period of Republican dominance. Buchanan credits Harding with other accomplishments: he "destroyed the Democratic Party in the greatest popular landslide ever"; he "slashed" the income tax from high wartime rates, helping the country to the "best economic time of the century"; and he convened the Washington Naval Conference, "where the United States convinced Japan to maintain a fleet of virtually no ships." Harding also "ruptured" a potential alliance between Great Britain and Japan. Buchanan, aware of Harding's low ranking in Arthur M. Schlesinger's poll, asks, why is Harding's reputation so bad? For Buchanan the answer is that the popular Harding had been smeared by Nan Britton and others. However, as Buchanan points out, Robert Ferrell's work brings Britton's story into question. The second part of Buchanan's answer involves Woodrow Wilson, whom Buchanan considers a failure. Liberal historians, Buchanan writes, praised Wilson because he stood for "big government, globalism and world government."[10] Thus, in the end, Harding stood as the victim of historians and liberal journalists who ruined his reputation in their eagerness to prop up Wilson's legacy. While there is some truth to the assertion that Harding's reputation suffered at the hands of Wilson's admirers, it was Calvin Coolidge's portrait, not Harding's, that

Ronald Reagan hung in the cabinet room after moving into the White House in 1981.[11]

Despite Buchanan's protest, the fact remains that most people took notice of Harding when his scandals resonated. Because of the nature and the variety of the Harding scandals, this occurred frequently. As we saw in the previous chapter, Harding's reputation held the potential for change but it went unrealized. Scholars often note the similarities between the 1920s and the 1980s, as Americans wrestled with a wide variety of similar social and cultural issues. While not recognized as such while he was alive, Harding's life and reputation reflected the issues of sexual mores, race, and public morality that make the twentieth century so interesting.

Culture Wars

Because of the nature of his scandals, Warren G. Harding was a presence in the culture wars that permeated American politics during the last decades of the twentieth century. While Harding's role was not as prominent as the *Enola Gay* exhibit at the Smithsonian Institute or the national history standards debates of the mid-1990s, he was a figure in the culture wars. The 1990s brought a revival of interest in Harding, especially among pundits, journalists, and ideologues looking for a historical perspective on the Clinton scandals. The comparisons between Harding and Clinton were part of a discussion of the role of personal character in the formation of a presidential legacy. Beyond the interest of journalists seeking a historical angle on a current scandal, Harding's reputation also proved a useful weapon for conservatives in attacking Clinton's personal life. The similarities between the personal lives of the two men became a de facto argument that Clinton should be considered among the worst presidents.

In 1992 Clinton won the White House with conflicting images. Clinton was a new Democrat who was part of a power couple, but he also had a reputation as a rogue and womanizer. Having been elected to restore the American economy, he was rewarded with reelection in 1996 for the ensuing prosperity. Long suspected of lax morals by his enemies, Clinton headed an administration plagued by a series of investigations and scandals. Gary Alan Fine argues that "the fragility of Warren Harding's reputation speaks to the dilemmas of William Jefferson Clinton. The parallels between the two are, if imperfect, nevertheless striking. Harding belonged to a regional political machine outside the national orbit; Clinton, too, was an outsider. Harding was bedeviled by his home-state cronies, facing suicides, scandals, and a general sense of sleaze; that is the Clinton admin-istration in a nutshell."[12]

As Clinton's personal life became enmeshed in contemporary cul-tural politics, the debate over Harding's place in history took a new turn. Buchanan defends Harding much along the lines that some liberals defend Clinton, as a good president but a flawed man under attack by people with questionable or partisan motives. Now conservatives use Harding's reputa-tion to attack Clinton. Much of this has to do with the hot-button issues of morality and family values that define the culture wars and are also prevalent in Harding's legacy.

Commentators have found it easy to select from a variety of com-mentaries on Harding to meet their needs. In *Revelry*, Adams reveals a cynical view of politics, a view that holds politicians and the public that elect them as engaged in a deceptive game, a view similar to the political cynicism of the 1990s. Take, for example, Adams's description of President Markham greeting tourists visiting the White House:

> Reach. Grasp. Draw across. On. Next.—Reach. Grasp. Draw across. On. Next.—Reach. Grasp. Draw across. On. Next. And timed to each motion the accompaniment of the rich, hearty voice, like the sea-chanting of a deep-lunged sailor man. "How do you do?" (*Haul* the line on!) "*How* do you do?" (*Haul* the line on!) "Pleased to see you." (*This* is the way—).[13]

When a character visiting the White House comments, "One would think he liked those people," an aide answers, "He loves 'em." "Queer, isn't it?" (96). Adams directly links the shortcomings of his fictional Harding, President Markham, to his pedestrian background and to his popularity (273–74).

As with Harding, Clinton's ability to campaign and his popularity were sources of puzzlement and cynicism for journalists and pundits. In *Primary Colors*, his best-selling fictionalized account of Clinton's 1992 cam-paign, journalist Joe Klein (writing as Anonymous) explores the nature of modern politics. He opens the book with this description:

> He was a big fellow, looking seriously pale on the streets of Harlem in deep summer. . . . We shook hands. My inability to recall that particular moment more precisely is disappointing: the handshake is the threshold act, the beginning of politics.

I've seen him do it two million times now, but I couldn't tell you *how* he does it, the right-handed part of it—the strength, quality, duration of it, the rudiments of pressing the flesh. I can, however, tell you a whole lot about what he does with his other hand. He is a genius with it. He might put it on your elbow, or up by your bicep: these are basic, reflexive moves. He is interested in you. He is honored to meet you. If he gets any higher up your shoulder—if he, say, drapes his left arm over your back, it is somehow less intimate, more casual. He'll share a laugh or a secret then—a light secret, not a real one—flattering you with the illusion of conspiracy. If he doesn't know you all that well and you've just told him something "important," something earnest or emotional, he will lock in and honor you with a two-hander, his left hand overwhelming your wrist and forearm. He'll flash the famous misty look of his. And he will mean it.[14]

Primary Colors was interpreted as an attack on Clinton, although Klein later wrote that his book was a "defense of larger-than-life politicians—who, inevitably, have mythic weaknesses entangled with their obvious strengths."[15] Both *Revelry* and *Primary Colors* were commercially successful and influential. *Primary Colors* became a movie and *Revelry* a play. In both the 1920s and the 1990s, journalists displayed cynicism about the political process that helped link Harding and Clinton. They interpreted a politician's love of the people and campaigning as a weakness or an act of manipulation.

Almost any discussion of Harding's and Clinton's legacies involved the state of their marriages and the politics of sex. Both Hillary Rodham Clinton and Florence Kling Harding were polarizing figures that, in these fictional alternate realities, authors could eliminate to simplify the sexual politics of both presidencies. President Markham's wife has been confined to a sanatorium because the stress of national politics has overwhelmed her. In a scene that resonates with the appearance of the Clinton-era movie, *The American President* (1995), which features a widowed president, Adams writes, "What enemy could be so brutal, what subordinate so callous as to add persecution or complications to his grief at such a time."[16] As we saw earlier in *Fluke,* Blinder also downplays the First Lady in favor of Nan Britton.

Clinton and Harding underwent a process of degradation that marked their reputations. The discussion of sexual scandal by Harding's biographers continued and increased with comparisons to Clinton's private life.

Many of these comparisons, obviously, deal with Nan Britton, but Gaston Means's wildly inaccurate *Strange Death of President Harding* became an important link. Similarly sensational claims would become part of the Clinton debate. Gary Aldrich, in *Unlimited Access: An FBI Agent inside the Clinton White House* (1996), uses his insider status to accuse the Clintons of various criminal and immoral acts in a manner reminiscent of Means's earlier claims. Aldrich links the Clinton administration with the culture of the 1960s, rather than with traditional American values.[17] Jeffrey Toobin, in his influential book *A Vast Conspiracy: The Real Story of the Sex Scandal That Nearly Brought Down a President,* dismisses the importance of presidents' private lives, concluding that with Harding, FDR, and Kennedy, "their sex lives revealed little about their presidencies."[18]

Race was another of the social divides that played a role in how the public perceived, and remembered, Harding and Clinton. Both men were proclaimed to be black presidents. This issue did not become part of the regular comparisons, perhaps because Americans currently deal with race in a considerably different way than they did during the 1920s. The story that Warren Harding was black went back to his childhood and was used to attack him. While controversial, Toni Morrison's proclamation that Clinton was a black president was not meant to destroy his career, nor was it a claim of actual black ancestry.[19]

The parallels between the Clinton-Lewinsky scandal and Harding-Britton story were striking and brought to the public's attention by the appearance of Carl S. Anthony's book *Florence Harding: The First Lady, the Jazz Age, and the Death of America's Most Scandalous President.* Florence King, writing for the *National Review,* confesses that she had intended to read Anthony's book "purely for pleasure" and skip the "underlining and note-taking of reviewing." However, she "found so many parallels between the Hardings and the Clintons that my four-color pencil ran out of lead." King focuses on the state of Warren and Florence's marriage, goes into detail regarding Florence Harding's "physical shortcomings" and Warren Harding's philandering, and makes unstated but clearly intentional comparisons with Hillary and Bill Clinton.[20]

Mackubin Thomas Owens makes connections between Warren G. Harding and Bill Clinton in the cutely titled article "Warren Gamaliel Clinton." Owens builds on Carl Anthony's "President of the Peephole," in which Anthony draws direct comparisons between the two first couples.[21] Given Harding's consistent ranking "at or near the bottom," Owens goes on to note that the similarities between Harding and Clinton "should keep

President Clinton and his loyalists awake at night." Intentionally or not, Owens draws the first parallel when he introduces the idea of friends keeping one awake at night.[22] According to Owens, the ghost of Harding haunted the Clinton administration and doomed "any hope for a positive Clinton 'legacy.'" Chief among the lessons to be drawn from Harding is that a president's private life is important and will have an impact on his legacy. Describing Harding as a "serial philanderer and a heavy drinker" who had his administration pay off or rough up those who pried into his private life, Owens carefully separates Harding and his cronies from the "decent, honorable, and competent men selected for the cabinet by the party bosses." Owens concludes his comparison between the "scandal-plagued administrations" with the observation that the Harding precedent served to "concentrate the minds wonderfully of such Clinton loyalists as Paul Begala, Rahm Emmanuel, and the odious James Carville." The report of independent counsel Kenneth Starr, he predicts, will expose Clinton as a "carbon copy" of Harding.[23]

Howard Phillips of the Conservative Caucus also uses information from Anthony's biography to attack the Clintons. He lists parallels: Florence and Hillary were both "into the occult"; Clinton played the saxophone, while Harding played the cornet; both Clinton and Harding lost their first bid for elected office; both men had a "gap" in their public careers when they were not in office; both administrations had "homosexuals in high places" (Phillips names Harry Daugherty and Jess Smith as representing the Harding administration in this category). Also, both administrations experienced suicides that, he suggests, were actually part of a cover-up.[24] Both Clinton and Harding retained a "team of assistants," whose job was to "quell 'bimbo eruptions.'" Both Virginia Kelly, Clinton's mother and a nurse, and Phoebe Harding, Harding's mother and a midwife, were suspected of "criminal negligence" in the death of a patient. Charles Sawyer was given the rank of brigadier general as a reward for helping clear Phoebe Harding's name, and Jocelyn Elders was made surgeon general for her earlier help in clearing Virginia Kelly's name. Furthermore, both the Clintons and the Hardings were closely connected with Hollywood's A-list and used those connections to "buff" their images. Florence Harding and Hillary Clinton each had only one child. (Florence's son was the "result of an extramarital liaison before she wed Warren.") Both Florence and Hillary influenced administration appointments; both marriages were "business relationships"; both men would blame unpopular decisions on their wives to avoid antagonizing supporters; and both couples enjoyed foreign travel.

While the above list of comparisons is in many ways superficial, it serves as examples of the focus on the personal, and mundane, aspects of the lives of both the Hardings and the Clintons. In Harding's case, Phillips takes issues without clear answers and simplifies them for partisan reasons. For example, Anthony argues that Florence did not actually marry the father of her child, but that argument is based on the absence of an existing marriage certificate and not on positive evidence; Phillips presents Anthony's speculative argument as established fact.[25] Phillips's list, however, does touch on most of the hot issues of the culture wars and in particular focuses on the controversial elements of the Harding and Clinton families, especially as they contrasted with our other First Families of the nation. According to Phillips, who relies heavily on Anthony for information on Harding, both men fathered illegitimate children and arranged abortions for the women. Of course, the ultimate parallel was to be found in the affairs with younger women, Nan Britton and Monica Lewinsky. The "one big difference" that Phillips sees between the two men is that "Harding was genuinely ashamed of his inappropriate behavior."[26] While the accuracy of Britton's story remains unclear, Harding died before the story became public and thus was hardly in a position to feel shame; in fact, he left no record indicating how he felt one way or the other (other than what might or might not exist in his letters to Carrie Phillips). Howard Phillips accepts Britton's story—one that Buchanan had dismissed as part of a smear campaign—because it was politically useful.

The debate over the values, morals, and influence of the entertainment industry touched both presidents. Therefore, it seems fitting that one of the more modern controversial movie screenwriters, Joe Eszterhas, should comment on Clinton's place in history in his book *American Rhapsody*. This commentary leads him to discuss American history and other presidents, including Harding. Eszterhas does not approach his ruminations on Clinton as a scholar but as a screenwriter. For Eszterhas, the Clinton presidency was about coming of age during the 1960s, about Hollywood, and about America. *American Rhapsody* was partly autobiographical and in part a commentary on Hollywood (emphasizing Clinton's political connections to that town and a shared morality between the Clinton White House and Hollywood).[27] According to Eszterhas, the book is also about "a cultural shadow war that resulted in the figurative assassination of a president (Bill Clinton)." Or, to put it in more scholarly terms, Eszterhas is writing about a period of public degradation in the establishment of a negative reputation.[28]

Eszterhas brings us back to the question of the validity of historical facts. He admits that he is telling two stories, one factual and one fictional. He breaks down the distinction between history as fact and history as construction, but unlike many people involved in legacy debates, he clearly delineates between the two. Eszterhas explains this process of using both fact and fiction by introducing an alter ego whom he calls the Twisted Little Man, who dwells on the seamier side of life (and who wrote such movies as *Showgirls*): "Are all the things the little lowlife wrote about true? Well, as a matter of fact no. But that's also not so simple. Because in the little scuzzball's cockeyed fun-house view, they are. He uses facts wickedly to shape his outrageous fictional perspective. He is a contortionist and a juggler of the historical record."[29]

Eszterhas describes Clinton partisans searching for a way to reframe the "historical context" to "make a case that there was nothing that was really unseemly or un-American or unpresidential or *unique* about Bill Clinton's actions." This brings him to write about Harding, in addition to several other presidents. Eszterhas understands, and argues that the Clinton team did as well, the importance of history for validating or invalidating contemporary arguments. What did they find in the history books? Past presidents and other prominent figures had had affairs, revealing a pattern of behavior that might aid in the defense of Clinton. Eszterhas holds back little in his graphic descriptions of these famous men's alleged sex lives. He writes that George Washington's being "probably bisexual" is "irrelevant." Thomas Jefferson is "very relevant" because he "fathered a black child." Warren Harding scores a "full-scale relevance alert" because he "made love to a young mistress in the White House closet," but "Harding was such a corrupt sleazeball—*Whitewater was not, was not Teapot Dome!*—that any attempt to craft a Harding shield would only hurt." Franklin Roosevelt also merits a "full-scale relevance alert" because of his relationship with Lucy Mercer. He cites Lyndon Johnson's bragging about his sexual prowess, but says, "LBJ was such a barnyard hick that drawing parallels between LBJ and Bill Clinton could boomerang." John Kennedy was a "sex fiend (directly relevant, but, unfortunately, old news, gorged and gobbled by the Beast way too often to distract it from what was on the table now)." According to Eszterhas, the Clinton team abandoned the idea of shaping a historical defense because the "history of American politics was an unswept minefield and rusted shrapnel posed the danger of tearing Bill Clinton's head off."[30] Eszterhas cannot reflect on history without bringing up Richard Nixon, whom he calls the Night Creature, as the nemesis of those involved in the social movements of the sixties. *American Rhapsody* is as much about Nixon as it is about Clinton, but as usual, any discussion of flawed presidents comes back to Harding.

Scholars have also indulged in the impulse to compare Clinton and Harding. They are sometimes not bound to the facts any more than are writers of fiction. Charles W. Dunn, in *The Scarlet Thread of Scandal: Morality and the American Presidency*, denies that he was prompted to write his history of scandal because of Clinton, but then he proceeds to make numerous references to Clinton. Comparisons between Clinton and other scandalous presidents, especially Nixon, dominate the early chapters. Dunn then follows by creating chronological periods of political history based on the theme of the scandals that prevailed. Harding falls under the "Moral Roller Coaster in the Roaring Twenties." Dunn's treatment of Harding offers nothing new. He begins with a familiar quote from Harding (that he was not fit for the office) and adds that his "life and administration littered history with sin and deception."[31]

Dunn's scarlet thread, it could be argued, represents not only the consistency of scandal in our history but also the willingness to continue using scandalous assertions without investigating to determine if they are, indeed, accurate facts. In his section on Harding, Dunn discusses Teapot Dome, Charlie Forbes, and Daugherty, and asserts, "Sexual immorality also hovered over Harding." Dunn then discusses Carrie Phillips, Susie Holder, Grace Cross, Nan Britton, Rosa Hoyde (including the rumor that Harding fathered a child with her), and the first Miss America as Harding mistresses. He also denounces Harding for serving alcohol while president during Prohibition. Dunn cites the treatment of Chancellor as proof of "illegal restrictions on freedom of the press," but he makes no mention of Chancellor's accusations regarding Harding's race. Dunn asks why the press failed to report the scandals, failing to note that the scandals did not make headlines until years after Harding's death. He answers that there was little interest or, adding a new element to conspiracy theories about Harding, suggests that "perhaps Harding's big business supporters, who owned most of the major newspapers, did not want to damage him." Dunn concludes by discussing the suspicious nature of Harding's death and the destruction of his papers. While Dunn does not make a conclusive statement that Warren Harding was murdered, he writes that Florence Harding "had a plausible motive for killing her husband" (72–75). Thus Dunn presents as factual the very stories that Adams had introduced in an act of fiction and that Means had introduced in an act of fraud.

Despite his academic credentials, Dunn's account presents a typical litany of Harding scandals derived from many of the implausible sources we have seen used for decades. Most telling is that in his account Dunn repeatedly refers to the *Washington Post* to add validity to his claims, yet a check of the endnotes reveals that the *Post* piece referred to is Anthony's "A President of the Peephole," which Dunn incorrectly cites as "President of the People." As we have seen, Anthony's article, and the book from which it was derived, compares Clinton and Harding and has become a standard citation in conservative attacks on Clinton. The article is also part of Anthony's effort to promote his biography of Florence Harding, which Dunn does not cite but from which the list of possible Harding mistresses comes. Dunn's other source, not surprisingly, is Francis Russell's *Shadow of Blooming Grove* (193). Nowhere can more substantial scholarship be found. While it is common to see Robert Murray's *Harding Era* cited as the best scholarly work on the Harding administration, it is the work of Russell (and those with similar themes) that continues to have an impact on the public discourse.

Wiki-History

At the beginning of the twenty-first century, Harding's reputation is an amalgam of historic facts, myths, and projections that fit the needs of reputational entrepreneurs. This mix is perfect for the Internet era, and it is not surprising that the Internet plays host to a lively debate over Harding's legacy. The Internet is often described as either the savior or the doom of democracy as it transforms journalism and politics, and, as such, it is a fitting place to debate pubic memory and civic religion. Harding might have appreciated the transformations brought by the Internet. As a newspaper publisher, he embraced new trends in the business. As a politician, he merged serious politics with show business. As a president, Harding has been held up as an example of the potential and the shortcomings of democracy. The public debate over the Harding legacy that has appeared on the Internet has often served the prosaic but useful service of providing access to materials that originally appeared in traditional print form, extending the availability of editorials and punditry where presidential legacies are debated. The advent of blogs and wikis have changed this, allowing for a greater sense of immediacy and ownership of history and memory and eliminating the gatekeepers and peer review that limit access in the world of publishing. Although it seems unlikely that the Internet will produce a new interpretation of Harding that will have the same lasting impact on Harding's legacy that the works of Samuel Hopkins Adams, Nan Britton, or William Estabrook Chancellor have had, the Internet provides a place were old controversies and rumors regarding Harding have found an extended life and continue to be debated in the marketplace of ideas. The Wikipedia format, with its focus on achieving factual objectivity through open access and debate, seems the perfect place to debate the vagaries of Warren G. Harding's legacy.[32] The wiki emphasis on open access for collaborative authoring mirrors the role of reputational entrepreneurs in the creation of Harding's reputation since his death, in 1923.[33]

The Wikipedia article on Warren G. Harding (consulted in June 2007) is, to a large extent, what one might expect and not dramatically different from what appeared on C-Span's *American Presidents* series or what we would find in a typical textbook. We get a variation of Harding's frequently used confession that he was not "not fit for this office" and a sentence about a major sex scandal during his Senate term. Normalcy, a cornerstone of Harding's public identity, is defined as a "renewed isolationism in reaction to World War I, a resurgence of nativism, and a turning away from the government activism of the reform era." There is a flattering discussion of Florence Harding that echoes themes from Carl Anthony's biography of her and represents a change from the negative uses of Anthony's book during the Clinton years. The Wikipedia article lacks the typical treatment of Harding's looks (nowhere is he described as looking like a president or a Roman senator). Instead, readers learn that Harding's appearance, combined with his support for the Nineteenth Amendment in the Senate, "brought huge crowds of women to Marion, Ohio to hear Harding." (In fact, Harding waffled on the Nineteenth Amendment. Suffragists appeared in Marion to pressure Harding to support it.) A paragraph is devoted to the rumor that "Harding's great-great-grandfather was a West Indian black and that other blacks might be found in the family tree," a rumor described as based on "local gossip." Under the heading Personal Scandals and Allegations, we find Extramarital Affairs, which, not surprisingly, contains approximately 630 words, as compared with the 440 words on his death, the 270 words on the administrative scandals, and the 350-word discussion of the administration (although it is not as substantial as the word count suggests because it includes a list of events). Extramarital Affairs begins, "The extent to which Harding engaged in extramarital affairs is somewhat controversial." That statement is followed by a discussion of Carrie Phillips and Nan Britton.[34]

The category Administrative Scandals begins with a discussion of the Ohio Gang. A detour to the Teapot Dome Scandal entry finds an attempt to clarify the scandal and Harding's role in it. The authors write, "Contrary to popular belief, [Fall's] manner of leasing was legal under the Mineral Leasing Act of 1920." The illegality came when Fall received gifts: "it was this money changing hands that was illegal—not the lease itself." Although Harding did not know of Fall's activities, Teapot Dome so ruined his reputation that his memorial was not dedicated until "enough of the scandal had faded from the American consciousness."[35] Finally, following the link to the Harding Memorial, we learn that "it is important in American History because it is the last of the elaborate presidential tombs, a trend that began with the burial of President James A. Garfield in 1881 in Lake View Cemetery."[36] There is no mention of the memorial being important for its commemoration of Harding.

The Wikipedia accounts demonstrate the continuing importance of reputational entrepreneurs in the creation of public memory. While the article on Harding reaches a consensus that is not far removed from the national consensus, the discussion tab reveals the debates behind that consensus. It is here that Harding's reputation is in play. The debate demonstrates that, despite the passing of a generation, Francis Russell's "four mysteries of Harding" remain compelling, these mysteries being created by decisions made in the 1920s. The contributor discussion revolved around long-standing controversies such as Harding's alleged Ku Klux Klan membership, supposed black ancestry, reputed extramarital affairs, and the availability and validity of the Harding papers. Clearly, as Russell wrote in the 1960s, the Harding scandals live on. The liveliest scandals remain the personal scandals, not the political ones. Despite the relative newness of the medium, the Wikipedia debate is driven by the printed word and the passions that still surround Harding in Marion.

A self-proclaimed Harding expert (a.k.a. Skoblentz), an Ohio resident with ties to Marion and the author of "articles and books" on Marion and Marion County, declares that it is offensive to see "rumours reported as fact."[37] He notes that the claims that "Harding was of African American blood have never been proven because the proof doesn't exist." He continues, "While many of the 'vandals' that I have seen attack this page 'think' that they are right, They [*sic*] are not." He argues that none of the vandals had been to Marion or to the Ohio Historical Center to conduct research in the Harding papers. An anonymous discussant finds that "the article could be improved by including the stands Harding took (if any) on the great issues of the day. Golf and poker are probably not the most important ideas he had!" Derek Ross's reply—"Somehow I get the feeling that they were"—proves prophetic. Neither the article nor the debate focuses on important issues of the day.

Conducting research in the Harding papers and in Marion was a key source of credentialing. One contributor, Markalexander, argues that a paragraph stating that historians have plagiarized "unflattering biographies" rather than "do their own research" needs "NPOVing" (NPOV stands for Neutral Point Of View). The disputed paragraph states that "the erroneous conclusion that Warren G. Harding is one of the worst presidents endures because the actual record of his presidency has been largely overlooked." It also explains that, because of the belief that Florence Harding destroyed the papers, Harding's "history was largely written before it was learned that his papers were intact." In defending the position that history was unfair to Harding, Skoblentz points to four items that people think are fact but are not: that Harding had a nervous breakdown, that Harding was of "African American descent," that Harding knew of Teapot Dome (he could not have because the "scandal broke six months AFTER his death," emphasis in original), and that Mrs. Harding killed her husband.

Skoblentz is essentially correct in his assessment of the impact that the lack of availability of primary documents had on Harding's reputation. The irony is not only that Florence Harding first destroyed a portion of the papers but that it was the Harding Memorial Association, based in Marion, that kept the remaining papers out of the public domain for so many years. Much of the damage done to Harding's legacy has been self-inflicted. Skoblentz correctly notes that a generation has passed since the papers were made available, but that generation saw the solidifying of his reputation. Furthermore, the opening of the papers was mired in the controversy over the Carrie Phillips letters. Because of the gap in time and the handling of the papers during that time, the Harding papers did not answer all the mysteries, particularly not the issues that Skoblentz identifies. The restoration of a presidential legacy will not come through debating his race, or determining if Florence Harding had murdered Warren in retaliation for his affairs, but through an appreciation of his policies. As the debate over Harding's supposed Klan membership and African American ancestry has demonstrated, some issues will continue to "cast a shadow" over Harding's legacy, but these issue hold little relevance for those who wish for a more positive Harding legacy.

Regarding Chancellor and his claims, Skoblentz writes, "Those who hold the theory of mixed race do so without proof." Skoblentz continues that if Harding is going to be linked to the "mix[ed] race card using inuendo [*sic*], then Harding should be afforded a defense."[38] The controversy leads to a discussion of the reliability of Internet sources and the responsibility that comes with the easy dissemination of information on the Internet. Two Web pages feature the mixed-ancestry story; both rely on Marsha Stewart's book *Warren G. Harding: Death by Blackness.*[39] On the Warren G. Harding site one finds a traditional blend of conspiracy theory and assertions of a mixed ancestry: "Was he poisoned by his wife? Did he die of a heart attack or stroke? Was he wiped out by the Mob? We believe the US Government did a '1–2 elimination.' The question remains: Did he die at his own hand, a heart attack (on record), the hand of his wife or from a mysterious government conspiracy because of his BLACKNESS?"[40]

Both the Stewart book and the related Web site (which is primarily about the book and offers the opportunity to purchase it) are rambling affairs in which the author claims to be related to Warren Harding and to have genealogical proof that Harding was African American: "While growing up in the 1950's and 1960's we were told of our relationship to one of the US presidents. My niece wrote an essay for her senior English class explaining the Black lineage of Warren G. Harding. She explained. . . . 'He could only find work as a teacher in a "Colored School" in Ohio in 1884— until he crossed the color line.' We were much older when we realized the magnitude of government investigations relating to his candidacy and office. We always knew he was Black—We were cousins."[41] The Web sites contain the type of suspect photographs and genealogical information that have long been part of this controversy.

The Wikipedia discussion includes an attempt to evaluate Web sites about Harding. One comment notes the "interesting details" that are "muddled at times" and the photographs that purportedly depict relatives of Warren Harding. Harding's defender in the Wikipedia discussion argues, "Simply because 'information' appears on the web doesn't make it factual." Citing records from Ohio Central College (currently housed at Muskingum College), Skoblentz notes that the school system in which Harding taught was never segregated, so the claims that Harding could not find work in a white school do not hold up. After a detailed discussion of Harding genealogy and the inaccuracies found on the Wikipedia Web page, he draws a conclusion important for Harding and the formation of public memory: "The bottom line is that both of these web sites are based on a desire to make a connection where none exists. Their own operators evidently feel the need to have a person of Black descent in the White

House so badly that they make all sorts of claims; they can't get the facts for their logical argument straight. Their theories are faulty. Their claims, unverifiable. Their facts don't exist. That isn't good enough for Wikipedia or another source that claims to be truthful and factual." The debate has become one of determining fact and, closely related, of what facts should be presented.

Would the Web site's authors include controversial topics as controversies? On the issue of race, the answer is yes. However, there remains the issue of Harding's alleged membership in the Ku Klux Klan. Skoblentz removed the section on Harding and the Klan, defending his deletion because the story is "utter hogwash." Bcrowell has added a new section on the topic, with a subsection by Skoblentz, arguing against Harding's membership, allowing readers to decide "for themselves which evidence they find more plausible." Skoblentz finds this solution "fairer." Skoblentz writes, "Sweeping previous critisms [*sic*] under the rug . . . cheat[s] people out of factual information."[42] In some ways, the Wikipedia debate represents the inversion of what we saw with the fictional treatments of Harding. For Lawrence, Lee, Blinder, and others it was more important to arrive at the truth than to get the facts right. On Wikipedia, the facts are seen as a way of achieving accuracy.

Debating the authenticity of facts has led Wikipedia's contributors to academic sources as people cite scholarship, demonstrating the interaction between academic and popular history. The detailed discussion between Skoblentz and other contributors, but primarily with Homey, has led to a marshalling of experts. Homey writes that he came to the Harding page after reading that Harding was a Klan member in Steven D. Levitt and Stephen J. Dubner's *Freakonomics: A Rogue Economist Explores the Hidden Side of Everything*. He also relies on Wyn Craig Wade's *The Fiery Cross: The Ku Klux Klan in America*, to support his claim that Harding being a Klan member. Skoblentz counters with the work of Robert Ferrell, Carl Anthony, and John Dean. Homey writes, "We should make mention to the debate on whether or not he was a member [of the Klan] since it is a debate in academia and, as far as I know, Wade is not regarded as a crank or conspiracy theorist and his assertion has been repeated by other academics." Harding's defender counters that, because the story is not true, it should not be included: "I have found dozens of web sites that have taken text from Wikipedia that state[s] that Harding was a member of the Klan (these are sites that take Wikipedia entries and reprint them under their own web page banners)." Homey contends that NPOV means that "our purpose is neither to attack Harding nor to protect his reputation but to make sure the article is objective and covers all sides of various arguments."[43] Therefore, although he does not believe Harding joined the Klan, Skoblentz agrees to include the controversy in the article as a controversy.

There is little debate in the Wikipedia article regarding stories of Harding's mistresses. Nan Britton is not debated. Carrie Phillips is discussed, but only in the context of the controversy surrounding the discovery and sealing of Harding's letters to her, the ownership of the letters, and whether or not Phillips extorted money after her trip. It would seem that in public memory, Nan Britton has carried the day. None of the wiki-historians has disputed the existence of extramarital affairs for Harding.

Skoblentz summarizes his interest in Harding:

> I think the reason why Harding is such a powerful topic for
> me is that the wealth of misinformation about him is so great.
> This was a man who, by his own admission, was in way over his
> head, and he was not a faithful husband. But this was also an
> affiable [*sic*] man who was the target of charecter assissination
> [*sic*] by William Estebrook Chancellor who made up facts about
> Harding's lineage as a means of grinding a personal axe. . . .
> So if I defend Harding, I do so because there is a clear differ-
> ence between what people claim to know about him and who
> he was.

In many ways, this defense of Harding echoes those of the past, but it also points to the limited ambitions of those who would revise Harding. Skoblentz does not go so far as to argue that Harding deserves defending because of the offices he held or that he should be respected as a former president. There is no attempt to place Harding in the pantheon of American civic religion.

Finally, one lone posting asks, given that historians characterize Harding as the worst president because of corruption, what "will future historians make of George W. Bush?" The author argues that he is "not trying to get people up in a tizzy, but if that's the sole reason for considering a person a bad president, modern presidents have some things to worry about." No tizzy follows on the Harding discussion, but had he looked elsewhere, the author would have found that people were debating George W. Bush's legacy and whether or not he should be considered our worst president.

The Ghosts of Warren Harding

As the presidency of George W. Bush headed into its final two years, the inevitable debate as to history's judgment began. Like his predecessors in 1920, Republican strategist Karl Rove had hoped to imitate the success of William McKinley and Mark Hanna in achieving political dominance for a generation. Particularly in the wake of the attacks of September 11, 2001, Bush and Rove were successful in weaving the administration and the Republican Party into the fabric of the civic religion. Indeed, going into the 2004 election the Republicans had successfully claimed saints (those who worked and died on 9/11), sacred places (the World Trade Center sites), sacred objects (military regalia and 9/11 artifacts), and ritual practices (the denouncing of terrorists). However, George W. Bush won re-election in 2004 only to watch his party lose control of Congress in 2006 as the war in Iraq went poorly and the government's response to Hurricane Katrina became not only a disaster but a metaphor for incompetence. Bush's praise of Federal Emergency Management Agency director Mike Brown, "Brownie, you're doing a heck of a job," became a shorthand reference for presidential detachment and administrative incompetence on par with Harding's widely used quotations.[44] Bush's second-term setbacks may or may not relegate him to the bottom tier of presidents. Not surprisingly, his shortcomings have fed the immediate partisan debate; more surprisingly, they have accelerated the academic debate about Bush's legacy. Historians have debated Bush's place in history before he leaves office rather than waiting for the passage of time and the availability of documents.

In a poll of historians conducted in May 2004 by the History News Network and reported by historian Robert S. McElvaine, Bush was overwhelmingly considered a failure. Controversy ensued, with charges of liberal bias and a debate over definitions of success and failure. In the search for a definition of failure, Harding was included in a short list of failed presidencies with which Bush was being compared. McElvaine writes, "Oil, money and politics again combine in ways not flattering to the integrity of the office. Both men also have a tendency to mangle the English language yet get their points across to ordinary Americans." McElvaine hints that Bush might replace Harding in the role of worst president, and that the "comparison does Harding something of a disservice."[45]

In a *Rolling Stone* essay, historian Sean Wilentz argues that Bush deserves the ranking of worst president: "From time to time, after hours, I kick back with my colleagues at Princeton to argue idly about which president really was the worst of them all. For years, these perennial debates have largely focused on the same handful of chief executives whom national polls of historians, from across the ideological and political spectrum, routinely cite as the bottom of the presidential barrel." These have included James Buchanan, Andrew Johnson, Herbert Hoover, and Richard Nixon. And, Wilentz asks, "What about the amiably incompetent Warren G. Harding, whose administration was fabulously corrupt?"[46] Wilentz argues that Bush will be joining the ranks of these failed presidents.

Eric Foner, another prominent historian, joins in the debate over George W. Bush's legacy: "[Andrew] Johnson, Franklin Pierce, James Buchanan, Warren G. Harding, Calvin Coolidge and Richard M. Nixon occupy the bottom rung, and now President Bush is a leading contender to join them." Foner's comparisons between Bush and Harding are more extensive than Wilentz's, with Foner lumping Harding and Coolidge together to argue that they "are best remembered for the corruption of their years in office (1921–23 and 1923–29, respectively) and for channeling money and favors to big business." Central to Foner's comparison are the similarities in the economic policies and corruption of the two administrations. He quotes from an article published in the *Wall Street Journal:* "Never before, here or anywhere else, has a government been so completely fused with business." Foner concludes, "The *Journal* could hardly have anticipated the even worse cronyism, corruption and pro-business bias of the Bush administration."[47] While academics were making pronouncements in newspapers and magazines, journalists were also speculating as to the Bush legacy.

Likewise, a *Boston Globe* editorial drew direct comparisons between Harding and Bush based not only on policies and scandals but also on character. The editorial explains that the "characteristic that links" Bush and Harding is the question of personal strength in the job—a continuing suspicion that subordinates are making many of the key decisions." To the credit of the editorialist, he or she makes use of the scholarly work of Murray rather than relying on the usual sources on Harding in an attempt to explain policies. Many have seen similarities between the scandals of the Harding and Bush administrations, particularly in the Justice Department, but the issues of war and peace have overshadowed the comparisons into Bush's second term. Few who have commented on the men's character have noted the differences in background between the small-town Harding and the patrician Bush.

Writing for the *Cincinnati Post*, Nick Clooney asks, "How will historians judge the Bush presidency?" He explains, "Historians keep a short grim list of failed presidencies," and the names James Buchanan and "William [*sic*] Gamaliel Harding" appear on "virtually every list." While partisanship explains part of the debate over how to rank presidents, "a lack of competence is the deal-breaker for experts." Clooney predicts two possible Bush legacies: it could resemble that of Jimmy Carter, who was overwhelmed by the job, or of Harry Truman, who took the right course despite low poll numbers. Finally, however, the specter of Harding enters the comparisons. Bush's legacy will be shaped by Iraq and New Orleans as well as "the bobbles in the Justice Department, warrantless wire-tapping and corruption which raised ghosts of Warren Harding."[48]

Entering the discussion on how to judge a president, *Nation* essayist Nicholas von Hoffman argues that "lasting damage" is the criteria by which a president should be judged. Using this standard, he writes that Harding was "a slob" and a "not-so-great role model." "But worst President? Not so much." By Hoffman's account, because of the Iraq War and Middle East policy, "With Bush II the reckoning is yet to be made."[49] Hoffman's comparison to Harding was not made out of a lack of familiarity; he has also authored a play on Harding with the title *Wurr'n*.[50] Bush's legacy debate included input not only from academics and journalists but also from the public. In "The 10 Worst Presidents," Jay Tolson notes that in a 2007 *USA Today*/Gallup Poll, 54 percent of respondents said that "history would judge Bush a below-average or poor president." Tolson writes that most scholars prefer to defer judgment on an outgoing president, but not so with Bush. He ranks Harding as the second-worst president, behind James Buchanan: "Warren G. Harding's claim to infamy rests on spectacular ineptitude captured in his own pathetic words: 'I am not fit for this office and should never have been here.'"[51]

Writing for the *Huffington Post*, Frank Dwyer attempts to answer conservative pundits who used the Clinton-Lewinsky scandal to counter the revelations that Republican Congressman Mark Foley made advances toward male interns. He finds a perfect foil in Warren G. Harding: "We are apparently condemned to repeat our history (Viet Nam; Watergate), as well as spin and distort it in a desperate attempt to obfuscate present culpability and to keep the less bright voters (somebody's base) safely confused and frightened, but there's another juicy historical episode back a little further than Clinton, [Dan] Crane, and [Gerry] Studds [also known for scandals] that is worth pausing to remember and, depending on what kind of person you are, to feel nauseated by, or savor (or both)." The history that evoked such visceral reactions was the Harding legacy.[52]

As we have seen, the public debate over political rankings has several components, including partisanship, comparison, and policy justification. The debate takes place in four interlocking arenas: academia, popular history, historical fiction, and punditry. In the early twenty-first century, Arthur M. Schlesinger Jr. discusses failed presidents: "Most polls inevitably end up with Grant and Harding as the two conspicuous failures among American presidents. I wonder whether Grant and Harding really deserve this. They're stigmatized because of the scandal and corruption that disgraced their administrations, but they were careless and negligent rather than villainous; their sin was excessive loyalty to crooked friends."[53] Schlesinger's point is that the "feckless Harding" and the "hapless Grant" did less to damage the public welfare than other presidents who pursued "misconceived or errant public politics." Despite some revisionism and Schlesinger's comments, however, Warren G. Harding's reputation has sunk so low that it transcends partisan and ideological boundaries. In *Blink: The Power of Thinking without Thinking*, Malcolm Gladwell explores the role of the "adaptive unconscious" in making decisions. According to Gladwell, people can make good decisions rapidly through the use of this unconscious process of accessing data. But the process is not infallible. What does he call it when the unconscious misfires? The Warren Harding error. He continues, "the Warren Harding error is the dark side of rapid cognition." Relying on Francis Russell and Mark Sullivan, Gladwell recounts how Harry Daugherty and others promoted Harding's career because he looked the part of president. Ignoring the substance behind the veneer, the people elected Harding, whom Gladwell describes as "one of the worst presidents in American history."[54]

While one might fault Gladwell for not digging a little deeper into history, it is likely that more reading would not have changed his conclusion. Liberals and conservatives, both the left and the right as Russell notes, all agree that Harding was bad. Republicans and conservatives, with a few exceptions, abandoned Harding long ago. With the Clinton scandals, conservatives abandoned their efforts to justify or explain Harding's personal behavior in favor of an opportunity to attack Clinton because they found it easy to link Harding's lax morality with their perceptions of liberals. The legacy debate of the 1990s brought to a climax the long process of Harding's legacy being disowned by his own party. Here, conservatives were following the lead of historians and journalists who showed little interest in what the similarities between Harding or Clinton might mean for the office of the presidency or for the history of the American family. As a partisan tool, the historical Harding has been stripped of his ideology and party and left as the standard by which to measure bad presidents.

By the end of the twentieth century Harding's legacy stood as a warning that the log cabin myth could deceive the nation and the people. The harmonious image of civic boosterism and the log cabin myth had helped elect Harding in 1920. Harding was Babbitt before being Babbitt was really all that bad. However, by the time of the dedication of his memorial, this traditional narrative of triumph had become a story of tragic betrayal. As a place of tragedy, the magnificent Harding Memorial placed the pageantry of national political power within the commonness of small-town Ohio. Power in American politics is supposed to flow from the people, but in many treatments of Harding the people competed with party bosses as the source of corruption. In the spirit of the booster ethos, Harding's reputation served to shame the public into doing better next time. With the passing of time, the story of Harding as a common man, the farm boy who became president, has come to represent the age-old fears that democracy might not work because the ordinary people lacked the ability to properly exercise power. Perhaps this is the meaning of the Harding Memorial. It is a tribute to the idea that in our republic leaders can rise from the people. But this is also an idea that many scholars, politicians, and journalists have viewed with cynicism and as folly. Yes, they might say, a leader did rise from a humble childhood, but see what happened. Corruption was lowbrow, not highbrow.

There will be no Age of Harding in the conventional sense, but in another way most of the twentieth century has proven to be Harding's age. While other presidents have lost their relevance, Harding continues to hover at the edge of our national memory, where he is rediscovered when one of our leaders fails. Ironically, the compromising and peace-loving Harding now emerges when Americans discuss scandal and turmoil. Harding, in this way, has remained one of the most relevant, if not respected, of presidents.

NOTES

HMAP   Harding Memorial Association Papers, Warren G. Harding Home, Ohio Historical Society, Marion.

WGHP   Warren G. Harding Papers (microfilm ed.), Ohio Historical Society, Columbus, Ohio.

Chapter 1: Questions Asked

1. Benjamin Hufbauer writes that since the "beginning of the Republic, national identity and the presidency have been linked, and it is not surprising that, as one textbook puts it, 'for most Americans the president is the focal point of public life.'" Hufbauer, *Presidential Temples: How Memorials and Libraries Shape Public Memory* (Lawrence: University Press of Kansas, 2005), 5.

2. Edward Pessen, *The Log Cabin Myth: The Social Backgrounds of the Presidents* (New Haven, CT: Yale University Press, 1984); Evan Cornog, *The Power and the Story: How the Crafted Presidential Narrative Has Determined Political Success from George Washington to George W. Bush* (New York: Penguin, 2004), 35.

3. Pessen, *Log Cabin Myth*, 1.

4. John A. Morello, *Selling the President, 1920: Albert D. Lasker, Advertising, and the Election of Warren G. Harding* (Westport, CT: Praeger, 2001).

5. Robert K. Murray and Tim H. Blessing, *Greatness in the White House: Rating the Presidents from George Washington through Ronald Reagan* (University Park: Pennsylvania State University Press, 1994), 4.

6. Steven E. Schier, ed., *The Postmodern Presidency: Bill Clinton's Legacy in U.S. Politics* (Pittsburgh, PA: University of Pittsburgh Press, 2000), 15.

7. Murray and Blessing, *Greatness*, 6. For an extensive discussion of the ranking of presidents, including the influence of partisanship, see Meena Bose and Mark Landis, eds., *The Uses and Abuses of Presidential Ratings* (New York: Nova Science, 2003).

8. Tim H. Blessing, "Presidents and Significance: Partisanship as a Source of Perceived Greatness," in Bose and Landis, *Presidential Ratings*, 61.

9. Alan Brinkley, *American History: A Survey*, 10th ed., vol. 2, *Since 1865* (Boston: McGraw-Hill, 1998), 670.

10. Eric Foner, *Give Me Liberty! An American History*, 2 vols. (New York: Norton, 2005), 2:783.

11. John Dean, *Warren G. Harding* (New York: Time Books, 2004), 1.

12. C-Span, "American Presidents: Life Portraits," http://www.americanpresidents.org/presidents/yearschedule.asp (accessed May 26, 2005). Quotes in subsequent paragraphs are taken from the video.

13. Robert Ferrell, *The Strange Deaths of President Harding* (Columbia: University of Missouri Press, 1996); Eugene Trani and David L. Wilson, *The Presidency of Warren G. Harding* (Lawrence: University Press of Kansas, 1977).

14. Francis Russell, *The Shadow of Blooming Grove: Warren G. Harding and His Times* (New York: McGraw-Hill, 1968), xiv–xvi.

15. Jon C. Teaford, *Cities of the Heartland: The Rise and Fall of the Industrial Midwest* (Bloomington: Indiana University Press, 1993).

16. Ferrell, *Strange Deaths*, vii.

17. Russell, *Shadow*, xiii–xiv.

18. Gary Alan Fine, *Difficult Reputations: Collective Memories of the Evil, Inept, and Controversial* (Chicago: University of Chicago Press, 2001). An earlier version of the chapter on Harding appeared as "Reputational Entrepreneurs and the Memory of Incompetence: Melting Supporters, Partisan Warriors, and Images of President Harding," *American Journal of Sociology* 101, no. 5 (1996): 1159–93. According to Alvin S. Felzenberg, "Harding and Coolidge, like Grant before them, received little reward for their enlightened racial policies and attitudes. All three favored federal laws that outlawed lynching. None received much credit from most historians surveyed." Felzenberg, "Partisan Biases in Presidential Ratings: Ulysses, Woodrow and Calvin . . . 'We Hardly Knew Ye,'" in Bose and Landis, *Presidential Ratings*, 77.

19. According to Fred Greenstein, "Presidential greatness is sort of nonsensical. . . . Because greatness is a value judgment." Quoted in James P. Pfiffner, "Ranking the Presidents: Continuity and Volatility," in Bose and Landis, *Presidential Ratings*, 27.

20. David W. Blight, *Beyond the Battlefield: Race, Memory, and the American Civil War* (Amherst: University of Massachusetts Press, 2002), 1.

21. Hufbauer, *Presidential Temples*, 1.

22. C-Span, "American Presidents."

23. Willis Fletcher Johnson, *The Life of Warren G. Harding: From the Simple Life of the Farm to the Glamour and Power of the White House* (Philadelphia, PA: John C. Winston, 1923), 7.

24. On the importance of childhoods in presidential biographies, see Cornog, *Power and Story*, 78.

25. Fine, *Difficult Reputations*, 76–77.

26. For more on the relationship between place and history, see David Glassberg, *Sense of History: The Place of the Past in America Life* (Amherst: University of Massachusetts Press, 2001); Robert R. Archibald, *A Place to Remember: Using History to Build Community* (Walnut Creek, CA: AltaMira, 1999).

27. C-Span, "American Presidents."

28. Russell, *Shadow*, xiii–xiv.

29. For example, see John Ehrman, *The Eighties: America in the Age of Reagan* (New Haven, CT: Yale University Press, 2005); David Greenberg, *Nixon's Shadow: The History of an Image* (New York: Norton, 2003); John Hellman, *The Kennedy Obsession* (New York: Columbia University Press, 1997).

30. Meena Bose, "Presidential Ratings: Lessons and Liabilities," in Bose and Landis, *Presidential Ratings*, 11.

31. Stephen Skowronek, *The Politics Presidents Make: Leadership from John Adams to Bill Clinton* (Cambridge, MA: Belknap Press, 1997), 39.

32. Herbert Hoover, *The Cabinet and the Presidency, 1920–1933*, vol. 2 of *The Memoirs of Herbert Hoover* (New York: Macmillan, 1952), 52.

33. Pessen, *Log Cabin Myth*, ix.

34. Blessing, "Presidents and Significance," 53.

35. Cornog, *Power and Story*, 65.

36. C-Span, "American Presidents."

37. Annette Gordon-Reed, *Thomas Jefferson and Sally Hemings: An American Controversy* (Charlottesville: University of Virginia Press, 1997), 158–59.

Chapter 2: The President's Hometown

1. For example, Lewis L. Gould writes, "Handsome and a pleasing orator, Harding reassured voters that he would not press for reform in office. In his most famous statement of his placid philosophy, he avowed: 'America's present need is not heroics, but healing; not nostrums, but normalcy." Gould, *Grand Old Party: A History of the Republicans* (New York: Random House, 2003), 221.

2. Historian David Glassberg has written on the connection between community, region, and nation. Glassberg, *Sense of History*, 7.

3. Historian Sally Foreman Griffith writes that for boosters, "Harmony within the community was therefore a means to both economic growth and social cohesion." *Home Town News: William Allen White and the* Emporia Gazette (New York: Oxford University Press, 1989), 7.

4. Ibid., 1, for quotes see 6.

5. Douglas Flamming, *Creating the Modern South: Millhands and Managers in Dalton, Georgia, 1884–1984* (Chapel Hill: University of North Carolina Press, 1992), 47.

6. Barry Schwartz, *George Washington: The Making of an American Symbol* (New York: Free Press, 1987), 31; Michael Kammen, *Mystic Chords of Memory: The Transformation of Tradition in American Culture* (New York: Knopf, 1991), 4.

7. William Allen White, *Masks in a Pageant* (New York: Macmillan, 1928), 409. Harding delivered this speech to the Home Market Club in Boston in May 1920. "Back to Normalcy" was also a Harding campaign slogan. See Robert K. Murray, *The Harding Era: Warren G. Harding and His Administration* (Minneapolis: University of Minnesota Press 1969), 70, for a fine discussion of this speech and its context. The complete text, with audio, is available from the Library of Congress at http://memory.loc.gov/cgi-bin/query/r?ammem/nfor:@field (DOCID+@range (90000076+90000077)).

8. Ibid., 422.

9. Samuel Hopkins Adams, *Incredible Era: The Life and Times of Warren Gamaliel Harding* (Boston: Houghton Mifflin, 1939), 175.

10. Henry L. Stoddard, *As I Knew Them: Presidents and Politics from Grant to Coolidge* (New York: Harper and Brothers, 1927), 474.

11. Joe Mitchell Chapple, *Life and Times of Warren G. Harding: Our After-War President* (Boston: Chapple, 1924), 9.

12. John Bodnar, *Remaking America: Public Memory, Commemoration, and Patriotism in the Twentieth Century* (Princeton, NJ: Princeton University Press, 1992), 79.

13. Chapple, *Life and Times*, 115.

14. "Old Town Steps High," *Marion Star*, June 14, 1920, 5. Chapple offers a brief biography of Crissinger in *Life and Times*, 114–15.

15. "Old Town Steps High," *Marion Star*, 5.

16. For a description of a similar and typical booster campaign, see Flamming, *Modern South*, 42–43.

17. "Old Town Steps High," *Marion Star*, 5.

18. Chapple, *Life and Times*, 113.

19. On themes of boosterism, see Griffith, *Home Town News*, 40.

20. "Hardings Expected Home Early in July," *Marion Star*, June 14, 1920, 1; "Council Orders Old City Hall Torn Down," *Marion Star*, June 16, 1920, 8; "The Old City Hall," *Marion Star*, June 23, 1920, 11; "The Building of the Old Days," *Marion Star*, July 1, 1920, 6.

21. "Names Harding Club Executive Committee," *Marion Star*, June 15, 1920, 2; for quote see "Harding for President Club for Entire County," *Marion Star*, June 15, 1920, 14; "Sees Vindication for Homeopathy," *Marion Star*, June 23, 1920, 4; Jack Warwick, "Harding in the Band," *Marion Star*, June 23, 1920, 11 (repr. from *Toledo Blade*).

22. "A Morrow County Man for President," *Marion Star*, June 29, 1920, 6 (repr. from *Morrow County Sentinel*). Chapple recalls that Harding had saved this editorial in his scrapbook. See Chapple, *Life and Times*, 125

23. "Election Has Deep Meaning," *Marion Star*, June 14, 1920, 1.

24. Glassberg, *Sense of History*, 62.

25. Murray, *Harding Era*, 52.

26. "Front Porch Campaign," *Marion Star,* June 16, 1920, 1; "Chairman Hays Well Pleased," *Marion Star,* June 22, 1920, 1.

27. David M. Kennedy, *Over Here: The First World War and American Society* (New York: Oxford University Press, 1980), 12.

28. Robert H. Ferrell, *Woodrow Wilson and World War I: 1917–1921* (New York: Harper and Row, 1985), 200.

29. "Warren G. Harding," Hub of Commerce, *Marion Star,* June 16, 1920, 6 (repr. from *Chicago Tribune*).

30. "Harding and Coolidge," Hub of Commerce, *Marion Star,* June 18, 1920, 6 (repr. from *New York Sun*).

31. "Honors Richly Deserved," Hub of Commerce, *Marion Star,* June 17, 1920, 6 (repr. from *Cincinnati Enquirer Democrat*); "A Trained Legislator," *Marion Star,* June 28, 1920, 6 (repr. from *Newark-American Tribune*); "Harding Is a Big Favorite," *Marion Star,* July 1, 1920, 1. On the log cabin myth, see Pessen, *Log Cabin Myth.*

32. "D. R. Crissinger Will Give Welcome Address," *Marion Star,* June 24, 1920, 2.

33. Ibid.

34. For quote see "Stage Set in Order to Hold Big Celebration," *Marion Star,* June 17, 1920, 14; "Carroll B. Huntress Is Back in Marion Again," *Marion Star,* June 19, 1920, 5; "Great Crowd Expected in Marion on July 22," *Marion Star,* June 22, 1920, 2.

35. Griffith, *Home Town News,* 40.

36. "Opportunity Knocks at Our Gates," *Marion Star,* June 24, 1920, 4.

37. "Daugherty Will Come to Marion on Monday," *Marion Star,* June 25, 1920, 2; "Notification to be at Chautauqua Pavilion," *Marion Star,* June 26, 1920, 3; for quote see "Combing this City to Secure Needed Rooms," *Marion Star,* June 28, 1920, 10.

38. "Will March to Harding Home from the Square," *Marion Star,* July 1, 1920, 12; "Final Plans for Big Celebration Monday," *Marion Star,* July 1, 1920, 14; for quote see "President Harding Will Arrive Here Monday," *Marion Star,* July 2, 1920, 1. The *Star* did prematurely refer to Harding as "president."

39. Glassberg, *Sense of History,* 68.

40. For quote see "Combing this City to Secure Needed Rooms," *Marion Star,* June 28, 1920, 10; "Woman's Harding Club Now has 1,826 Members," *Marion Star,* July 1, 1920, 7.

41. "Active Part Taken in Arrangements," *Marion Star,* July 2, 1920, 9; for quote see "Fully 100,000 in City for Notification Day," *Marion Star,* July 2, 1920, 16; "Ohio Senator on Road Home," *Marion Star,* July 3, 1920, 1; "Special Arrangements for Handling Traffic," *Marion Star,* July 3, 1920, 3; "Every Preparation to Care for the Crowds," *Marion Star,* July 3, 1920, 14.

42. "Crissinger Is Heard by Many," *Marion Star,* July 6, 1920, 1.

43. Warren G. Harding, "The Metal of Real Friendship," in Harding, *Speeches of Senator Warren G. Harding of Ohio: Republican Candidate for President, from His Acceptance of the Nomination to October 1, 1920* (New York: Republican National Committee, 1920), 17.

44. "Enthusiastic Welcome Is Given Senator Harding," *Marion Star,* July 6, 1920, 1; "Crissinger Is Heard by Many," *Marion Star,* July 6, 1920, 1, 3; "Some High Lights in Harding's Response," *Marion Star,* July 6, 1920, 1; "Cheers Greet Harding Party," *Marion Star,* July 6, 1920, 1; "Neighbors and Friends," *Marion Star,* July 6, 1920, 6; for quotes see "Harding Talks to Home Folks," *Marion Star,* July 6, 1920, 1, 7.

45. Stoddard, *As I Knew Them,* 470.

46. "School Board Grants Bandstand Privilege," *Marion Star,* July 7, 1920, 5.

47. "Hayes Expected Here This Week," *Marion Star,* July 7, 1920, 14; "Appreciation Is Expressed," *Marion Star,* July 8, 1920, 5; "Planning for Notification," *Marion Star,* July 9, 1920, 2.

48. "Notification Day Program" *Marion Star,* July 10, 1920, 1.

49. "Marion Getting Ready," *Marion Star,* July 9, 1920, 6 (repr. from *Ohio State Journal*).

50. "Now on Sale, the Warren G. Harding Records on the League of Nations at Hoover Rowlands Co.," *Marion Star,* July 9, 1920, 8; "Marion's Shade Trees," *Marion Star,* July 19, 1920, 6.

51. "Funds of the Marion Civic Association," *Marion Star,* July 14, 1920, 14.

52. "Plans Are Made for Entertaining Women," *Marion Star,* July 20, 1920, 16.

53. "Parade Arrangement for Women Tomorrow," *Marion Star,* July 21, 1920, 2.

54. "Entertainment for Out-of-Town Women," *Marion Star,* July 17, 1920, 3.

55. For a discussion of the role of women within the Republican Party, see Melanie Susan Gustafson, *Women and the Republican Party, 1854–1924* (Urbana: University of Illinois Press, 2001).

56. "Arrangements for Handling of Trains," *Marion Star,* July 15, 1920, 5; "Civic Association Ready for Crowds," *Marion Star,* July 19, 1920, 10.

57. "Flag Raising Early Today," *Marion Star,* July 22, 1920, 11.

58. "Suffragists See Senator," *Marion Star,* July 22, 1920, 3; "Delegation of Women Calls on the Nominee," *Marion Star,* July 22, 1920, 11.

59. "Crowds Here for Big Event," *Marion Star,* July 22, 1920, 1; "Ohio Harding Woman Club," *Marion Star,* July 22, 1920, 12.

60. Warren G. Harding, "Speech of Acceptance of the Republican Party's Nomination to the Presidency Delivered at Marion, Ohio, July 22, 1920, by Senator Warren G. Harding," in Harding, *Speeches of Senator,* 20–36, for quote see 20.

61 "Senator Harding Is Formally Notified of His Nomination for the Presidency," *Marion Star,* July 22, 1920, 1; for quote see "Most Notable Is Event Today," *Marion Star,* July 22, 1920, 1.

62. "Notification Parade Sidelights in Marion," *Marion Star,* July 23, 1920, 4. Chapple offers a description of the notification ceremony from the perspective of a visiting journalist. Chapple, *Life and Times,* 119–24.

63. "A Great Day for Marion," *Marion Star,* July 22, 1920, 6.

64. "Mr. Harding's Gratitude," *Marion Star,* July 23, 1920, 6; "A Work Well Done," *Marion Star,* July 23, 1920, 6.

65. Warren G. Harding, "A Speech by Senator Warren G. Harding to Delegation from Wayne County, Ohio, Marion, Ohio, August 4, 1920," in Harding, *Speeches of Senator,* 43–44.

66. Warren G. Harding, "A Speech by Senator Warren G. Harding to Delegation from Wyandotte Co., Ohio, Marion, Ohio, August 25, 1920," in Harding, *Speeches of Senator,* 71.

67. Warren G. Harding, "A Speech by Senator Warren G. Harding, to Richland County, Ohio, Harding and Coolidge Club, Marion, Ohio," in Harding, *Speeches of Senator,* 39, 41, 42.

68. "Harding Meets Friends Today," *Marion Star,* July 31, 1920, 1; "Labor Day Address Is Next Big Event Here," *Marion Star,* September 1, 1920, 4; "Majors Are the Draw[:] Big Crowd Tomorrow," *Marion Star,* September 1, 1920, 14.

69. Warren G. Harding, "A Speech by Senator Warren G. Harding to Representatives of Chicago National League Baseball Club, September 2, 1920," in Harding, *Speeches of Senator,* 107.

70. "Team Play Is What Counts," *Marion Star,* September 2, 1920, 1; "5,000 See Cubs Win from Marion's Team," *Marion Star,* September 2, 1920, 9.

71. Morello, *Selling the President,* 56–57; "Adequate Pay for Teachers," *Marion Star,* September 2, 1920, 2.

72. "Cooperation a Necessity," *Marion Star,* September 5, 1920, 2.

73. "A Speech by Senator Warren G. Harding, to Richland County, Ohio, Harding and Coolidge Club, Marion, Ohio," *Speeches of Senator,* 37–42, for quote see 39.

74. Warren G. Harding, "A Speech by Senator Warren G. Harding Delivered Labor Day, Monday, September 6, at Marion, Ohio," in Harding, *Speeches of Senator,* 114–25.

75. "Marion and Labor Day," Hub of Commerce, *Marion Star,* September 4, 1920, 6 (repr. of 1903 editorial).

76. Warren G. Harding, "A Speech by Senator Warren G. Harding to Citizens of Deerfield, Illinois, while Enroute to Minneapolis, Minn., September 7, 1920," in Harding, *Speeches of Senator,* 126–27.

77. "Spokesman for Negro Baptists," *Marion Star,* September 11, 1920, 16.

78. "Urges Joining of Some Party," *Marion Star,* September 16, 1920, 3.

79. "Harding Heard in Northwest," *Marion Star,* September 8, 1920, 1; "Mr. Harding's Speech," Hub of Commerce, *Marion Star,* September 10, 1920, 6 (repr. from *Minneapolis Tribune*); "Two Addresses Next Saturday," *Marion Star,* September 2, 1920, 2; "Special on Way Back to Marion," *Marion Star,* September 9, 1920, 1; "Pershing with Harding Party," *Marion Star,* September 10, 1920, 12; "Wilson League Dead, Editor M'Neal Says," *Marion Star,* September 10, 1920, 16; "Will Address Rail Workers," *Marion Star,* September 16, 1920, 2; "Constitution or Covenant?" *Marion Star,* September 17, 1920, 1; "Akron GAR Veterans Here," *Marion Star,* September 20, 1920, 14; "Constitution Is His Theme," *Marion Star,* September 23, 1920, 3. Complete speeches can be found in Warren G. Harding, "A Speech by Senator Warren G. Harding to Colored Delegations, Marion, Ohio, September 10, 1920"; "A Speech by Senator Warren G. Harding to Delegation of Business Men, Marion, Ohio, September 11, 1920"; "Statement by Senator Warren G. Harding on the 133rd Anniversary of Constitution Day, When the Constitution was Adopted by the Philadelphia Convention, September 16, 1920," all in Harding, *Speeches of Senator,* 144–55, 172–73.

80. Gustafson, *Women,* 90–143.

81. Griffith, *Home Town News,* 8.

82. "Would Create a Department," *Marion Star,* October 1, 1920, 1, 12.

83. "Loud in their Praise of Marion Hospitality," *Marion Star,* October 2, 1920, 16.

84. "Senator W. G. Harding Guest of Newspapermen," *Marion Star,* October 1, 1920, 7.

85. "Fine Tribute Paid Soldiers," *Marion Star,* October 4, 1920, 1; "Ohio Senator at Louisville," *Marion Star,* October 15, 1920, 1; "Harding in the Hoosier State," *Marion Star,* October 16, 1920, 1; "Harding Back from His Trip," *Marion Star,* October 18, 1920, 3; "Engagements for Harding," *Marion Star,* October 19, 1920, 2.

86. "Local Plants to Close Half Day Election Day," *Marion Star,* October 13, 1920, 8.

87. "Citizenship Obligation," *Marion Star,* October 18, 1920, 1.

88. "Women Urged to Vote in Morning November 2," *Marion Star,* October 25, 1920, 4.

89. "Thirty Six Colleges Represented Monday," *Marion Star,* October 19, 1920, 14; "Big Reception Given Harding," *Marion Star,* October 28, 1920, 1.

90. Chapple, *Life and Times,* 116.

91. "Many Cameras Click When Hardings Vote," *Marion Star,* November 2, 1920, 11; "Harding Wins," *Marion Star,* November 3, 1920, 1; "Hardings Are Deeply Moved," *Marion Star,* November 3, 1920, 2.

92. "Home County for Harding," *Marion Star,* November 3, 1920, 2.

93. Advertisement, *Marion Star,* November 3, 1920, 3.

94. "The *Star's* Acknowledgment," Hub of Commerce, *Marion Star,* November 3, 1920, 6.

95. "Marion Opens Throttle Wide," *Marion Star,* November 3, 1920, 16.

96. Chapple, *Life and Times,* 131.

97. Warren G. Harding, "Address of President Harding at the Centennial Celebration, Marion, Ohio, July 4, 1922," in Harding, *Speeches of the Late President Harding, 1920–1923* (Washington, DC: GPO, 1920–23).

Chapter 3: Commemorating the Tragedy of Warren Harding

1. Kammen, *Mystic Chords,* 626.

2. William G. Clotworthy, *Homes and Libraries of the Presidents: An Interpretive Guide* (Blacksburg, VA: McDonald and Woodward, 1995), 210.

3. Kirk Savage, *Standing Soldiers, Kneeling Slaves: Race, War, and Monument in Nineteenth-Century America* (Princeton, NJ: Princeton University Press, 1997), 7.

4. Sanford Levinson, *Written in Stone: Public Monuments in Changing Societies* (Durham, NC: Duke University Press, 1998), 4, 7, 10.

5. *Harding Star* 1, no. 5 (October 1966), News Releases and Newsletters, file 6, box 1, Harding Memorial Association, Ohio Historical Society.

6. Here I am making use of Gary Alan Fine's and Barry Schwartz's concept of reputational entrepreneurs. Fine, *Difficult Reputations,* 12; Schwartz, *Abraham Lincoln and the Forge of National Memory* (Chicago: University of Chicago Press, 2000), 20.

7. David Greenberg has an extensive discussion of the search for the "real Nixon" or Nixon's "true character" that is in many ways similar to the way people sought to understand the true Harding as an explanation for the scandals and paradoxes of the 1920s. Greenberg, *Nixon's Shadow: The History of an Image* (New York: Norton, 2003).

8. Bodnar, *Remaking America,* 14. Bodnar describes vernacular culture as representing "an array of specialized interests that are grounded in parts of the whole." He continues, "Defenders of such cultures are numerous and intent on protecting values and restating views of reality derived from firsthand experience in small-scale communities rather in the 'imagined' communities of a large nation . . . . But normally vernacular expressions convey what social reality feels like rather than what it should be like" (13–14).

9. Fine, "Reputational Entrepreneurs"; Fine, *Difficult Reputations,* ch. 2, "Warren Harding and the Memory of Incompetence"; Ferrell, *Strange Deaths.*

10. Chapple, *Life and Times,* 73.

11. Herbert Hoover, *The Memoirs of Herbert Hoover: The Cabinet and the Presidency, 1920–1933* (New York: Macmillan, 1952), 52.

12. Schwartz, *George Washington,* 49–51.

13. Schwartz, *Abraham Lincoln,* 59–60.

14. Burl Noggle, *Teapot Dome: Oil and Politics in the 1920s* (Baton Rouge: Louisiana State University Press, 1962).

15. Adams, *Incredible Era,* 195.

16. Chapple, *Life and Times,* 9.

17. For Lincoln and Hoover quotes, see Murray, *Harding Era,* 457–58.

18. The original members of the HMA executive committee were Calvin Coolidge (honorary president), Charles E. Hughes, Andrew Mellon, John W. Weeks, Harry M. Daugherty, Harry S. New, Edwin Denby, Hubert Work, Henry C. Wallace, Herbert Hoover, James J. Davis, Joseph S. Frelinghuysen (acting president), Charles E. Sawyer (chairman), D. R. Crissinger, Charles G. Dawes, Edward B. McLean, John Barton Payne, Fred Upham, John Hays Hammond, George B. Christian Jr., Hoke Donithen, and James F. Pendergast. For quote see Harding Memorial Association, For Release by all Newspapers on Friday, November 9, Warren G. Harding Papers, Ohio Historical Society (microfilm ed., roll 248), Columbus (hereafter, WGHP).

19. Charles Sawyer, "Personal Characteristics of Warren G. Harding," WGHP, roll 248.

20. http://www.americanpresidents.org/presidents/yearschedule.asp.

21. In *Strange Deaths,* Ferrell argues for heart failure rather than a stroke or other cause of death: "all five physicians present at Harding's last illness mistook the cause of death. The bulletin that night, August 2, signed by all the physicians, designated the cause as apoplexy, a word popular at the time, meaning a stroke." He continues, "In actual fact, it is now clear that Harding died of a heart attack" (26). Carl S. Anthony argues that Sawyer was almost willfully negligent in his care of Harding: "Hospital care would have allowed Harding's heart damage to be detected by the large, untransportable, ECG machines, but it was Florence's decision to keep him out of a hospital, where Doc [Sawyer] would have even less control." Anthony, *Florence Harding: The First Lady, the Jazz Age, and the Death of America's Most Scandalous President* (New York: Morrow, 1998), 444.

22. Sawyer, "Personal Characteristics"; Sawyer, "Reminiscences of Warren G. Harding," WGHP, roll 248.

23. For a discussion of the advertising of Harding during the 1920 campaign, see Morello, *Selling the President.*

24. General Plan for the Harding Memorial Campaign, Misc. folder; Harding Memorial Association Papers, Warren G. Harding Home, Marion, Ohio Historical Society (hereafter, HMAP); Lyle Abbot to Harding Memorial Association, November 9, 1923, WGHP, roll 248. There are two sets of papers. The Harding Memorial Association Papers, housed in Columbus at the Ohio Historical Association Archives (microfilm roll 248), and part of the Harding Papers. The association papers located in the Harding Home, in Marion, are also part of the Ohio Historical Society. The papers in the Harding Home are more

inclusive and detailed and have escaped much use by scholars. Wesley M. Bagby, *The Road to Normalcy: The Presidential Campaign and Election of 1920* (Baltimore, MD: Johns Hopkins University Press, 1962), 126.

25. Savage, *Standing Soldiers*, 6–7.

26. Frank W. Murphy to International Syndicate, December 7, 1923, Misc. folder, HMAP; John W. Weeks to Dear Mr. Noyes, December 7, 1923; John W. Weeks to Frank B. Noyes (President, Associated Press), December 10, 1923; John W. Weeks to Earl A. Bickel (President, United Press and United News), December 10, 1923; John W. Weeks to George G. Shore (General Manager, International News Service, Universal Service and Cosmopolitan News Service), December 10, 1923, all in Misc. folder, HMAP. Weeks's letter has a notation that a similar letter was sent to all wire services, including the Associated Press, International News Service, United News, United Press, and Universal Service.

27. Mr. Tamblyn to Mr. Lockwood, November 14, 1923, memo, Publicity folder, HMAP.

28. Frank W. Murphy, "Suggestions for Membership Certificates," n.d., Publicity folder, HMAP.

29. "The Children's Tribute," n.d., Publicity folder, HMAP.

30. Frank W. Murphy to John W. Martyn, December 11, 1923; John W. Weeks to Oscar L. Straus, n.d., telegram; E. F. Dierks, President, New York Coffee and Sugar Exchange, Inc., to John W. Weeks, December 11, 1923, telegram; Oscar L. Straus to Secretary Weeks, December 12, 1923, telegram confirming Straus's appearance on radio; John W. Weeks to Dear Mr. Editor, November 2, 1923; Plan for Pictures of Meeting of Trustees of Harding Memorial Association, Thursday, November 25, 1923; Elizabeth P. Schumann to Mr. Frank W. Murphy, memo regarding interview with Mrs. Votaw; Frank W. Murphy to Mr. Walter Newmiller, November 20, 1923; Walter H. Johnson to National Electric Light Association, November 30, 1923; Frank M. Murphy to Mr. Walter Newmiller, November 30, 1923; Frank W. Murphy to Mr. Walter Newmiller, December 1, 1923; Mr. Murphy to General Sawyer, December 1, 1923, memo; Frank W. Murphy to Mr. C. Bascom Slump, December 1, 1923; John W. Weeks to Dear Sirs, December 3, 1923; John W. Weeks to Dear Sirs, December 4, 1923; John W. Weeks to Mr. Walter Newmiller, n.d.; G. A. Betzold to Harding Memorial Association, December 3, 1923; Frank W. Murphy to Editor, *Key West Citizen*, December 4, 1923; Secretary of War to Editor, December 4, 1923; Charles E. Sawyer to Mr. William Randolph Hearst, December 4, 1923; Gen. Charles E. Sawyer to Mr. Arthur Brisbane, December 4, 1923; John G. Williams to Hon. John W. Weeks, December 5, 1923; W. de Sanssure Trenholm to Hon. John W. Weeks, December 5, 1923; Frank W. Murphy to Mr. Tamblyn, December 5, 1923; Gen. Charles E. Sawyer to Gen. Charles G. Dawes, December 5, 1923; Frank W. Murphy to Mr. Tamblyn, December 5, 1923, memo; Gen. Charles E. Sawyer to W. B. Woodbury, December 5, 1923;

Herbert Hoover to All Radio Stations, December 5, 1923; Frank W. Murphy to Miss Ruth Byers, December 7, 1923; Frank W. Murphy, Harding Memorial Association, to Mr. Wm. B. Conover, December 7, 1923, press release, all in Misc. folder, HMAP.

31. Schwartz, *George Washington*, 107.

32. Frank Murphy to Stacy V. Jones, Memorandum, December 15, 1923; Frank Murphy to Roland Kilbon, December 15, 1923; Frank W. Murphy to Mr. L. Hogin, December 19, 1923; Frank W. Murphy to James J. Jones, December 27, 1923; Frank W. Murphy to John W. Martyn, Sec., December 7, 1923; Sidney L. Schwartz to John Weeks, December 11, 1923, telegram; Charles G. Dawes to Gen. Charles E. Sawyer, December 7, 1923, postal telegram, all in Misc. folder, HMAP.

33. Russell, *Shadow*, 256.

34. Adams's footnote states, "Will Irwin and the writer separately heard almost identical accounts of this fracas from widely diverse sources." Adams, *Incredible Era*, 297.

35. Murray, *Harding Era*, 459–61.

36. Ferrell, *Strange Deaths*, 114–21, 130.

37. Charles E. Sawyer to Mr. C. D. Schaffner, April 11, 1924; Charles E. Sawyer to My Dear Mrs. Freeland, November 2, 1923; Charles E. Sawyer to Miss Isabelle V. Freeland, December 5, 1923; Charles E. Sawyer to Mr. E. H. Cowan, November 1, 1923; E. H. Cowan to Charles E. Sawyer, November 3, 1923; Charles H. Conley to Gen. Charles E. Sawyer, December 31, 1932; Charles E. Sawyer to Charles H. Conley, January 11, 1924; Sawyer to Charles C. Fisher, April 9, 1924; Charles E. Sawyer to Charles C. Fisher, April 15, 1924; Charles E. Sawyer to Charles C. Fisher, April 23, 1924; Charles H. Conley to Dr. C. E. Sawyer, January 15, 1924; Charles E. Sawyer to Charles H. Conley, January 21, 1924; Charles H. Conley to Gen. Charles E. Sawyer, June 24, 1924; Mr. Charles H. Conley to Charles Sawyer, June 26, 1924; Charles H. Conley to Dr. C. E. Sawyer, June 2, 1924; E. H. Cowan to Brig. Gen. Charles E. Sawyer, October 29, 1923, all in Property Offered to Memorial Site folder, HMAP.

38. Patricia West, *Domesticating History: The Political Origins of America's House Museums* (Washington, DC: Smithsonian Institution, 1999).

39. Hoke Donithen to Breck Throwbridge, Esq., November 20, 1924; SBP Throwbridge to Honourable J. S. Frelinghuysen, November 6, 1924, both in S. B. P. Throwbridge folder, HMAP.

40. See letters dated March 27, April 8, April 21 (two), May 7, May 8, May 9, May 15, July 22, July 27, July 30, July 30, July 31, July 22, July 1, July 1, July 3, July 27, all in Design of Structure, E. P. Mellon, Advisory Architect folder, HMAP; draft of program of a Competition for the Selection of an Architect for the Tomb to be Erected at Marion, Ohio, in Memory of Warren G. Harding, Architects Program folder, HMAP. For a more detailed account of the building

and architecture of the Memorial, see Phillip G. Payne, "Building the Warren G. Harding Memorial," *Timeline* 15, no. 5 (1998): 18–29.

41. S. B. P. Throwbridge to Hoke Donithen, December 1, 1924; S. B. P. Throwbridge to Hoke Donithen, December 6, 1924; S. B. P. Throwbridge to Hoke Donithen, December 10, 1924; Hoke Donithen to Breck Throwbridge, December 13, 1924; Hoke Donithen to Breck Throwbridge, December 22, 1924; Charles M. Schwab to Hoke Donithen, December 27, 1924; Hoke Donithen to Charles M. Schwab, December 29, 1924; S. B. P. Throwbridge to Hoke Donithen, January 22, 1925; Hoke Donithen to S. B. P. Throwbridge, January 26, 1925; Charles M. Iverson, Secretary, to Mr. Throwbridge, January 28, 1925, all in S. B. P. Throwbridge folder, HMAP. Hoke Donithen to J. S. Frelinghuysen, August 3, 1925; Edward Mellon to Hoke Donithen, August 3, 1925; Hoke Donithen to E. P. Mellon, August 8, 1925; Hoke Donithen to E. P. Mellon, August 10, 1925, all in Design and Structure, E. P. Mellon Advisory Architect folder, HMAP.

42. James N. Giglio, *H. M. Daugherty and the Politics of Expediency* (Kent, OH: Kent State University Press, 1978).

43. Hoover, *Memoirs*, 49.

44. Adams, *Incredible Era*, 45–46.

45. Murray, *Harding Era*, 475.

46. Hoke Donithen to E. P. Mellon, December 1, 1925; E. P. Mellon to Hoke Donithen, December 14, 1925; Hoke Donithen to E. P. Mellon, December 9, 1925; Hoke Donithen to Charles M. Schwab, September 12, 1925; HMA minutes, October 5, 1925, all in Prospective Bidders folder, HMAP.

47. Hoke Donithen to E. P. Mellon, November 17, 1925, Design and Structure folder, E. P. Mellon Advisory Architect folder, HMAP; E. P. Mellon to Hoke Donithen, November 19, 1925; Hoke Donithen to E. P. Mellon, November 21, 1925; E. P. Mellon to Hoke Donithen, November 24, 1925; Hoke Donithen to E. P. Mellon, December 2, 1925; B. Kayser to Hoke Donithen, March 10, 1925; H. Van Buren Magonigle to Harry M. Daugherty, April 6, 1925; Hoke Donithen to Harry M. Daugherty, April 11, 1925; Edward W. Jones to Mr. John Martyn (Secretary to Weeks), July 22, 1925; Hoke Donithen to Seward W. Jones, March 3, 1925; Clyde A. Tolson to Mr. Donithen, July 24, 1925; Hoke Donithen to Clyde A. Tolson, March 3, 1925; Major O. M. Baldinger to Mr. Arthur H. Guntrum, March 29, 1926; O. M. Baldinger to Mr. Arthur H. Guntrum, May 11, 1926; Hoke Donithen to John Gill and Sons, August 2, 1926; G. Hoagland to Hoke Donithen, August 11, 1926; Hoke Donithen to Henry Hornbostel, August 10, 1926; Henry Hornbostel and Eric Fisher Wood to Hoke Donithen, August 16, 1926, all in Prospective Bidders folder, HMAP.

48. Hoke Donithen to E. P. Mellon, January 27, 1926; Hoke Donithen to E. P. Mellon, February 13, 1923; Hoke Donithen to E. P. Mellon, March 13, 1923; E. P. Mellon to Hoke Donithen, July 15, 1926; Hoke Donithen to E. P.

Mellon, July 3, 1926; E. P. Mellon to Hoke Donithen, July 13, 1926, telegram; Hoke Donithen to E. P. Mellon, n.d., Design and Structure, E. P. Mellon Advisory Architect folder, HMAP.

49. Barry Schwartz makes a similar point in *Abraham Lincoln,* 51–54.

50. E. P. Mellon to Hoke Donithen, October 4, 1927; Hoke Donithen to E. P. Mellon, October 6, 1927; Edward P. Mellon to Hoke Donithen, October 7, 1927; Edward P. Mellon to Hoke Donithen, September 14, 1926; Edward Mellon to Hoke Donithen, November 17, 1926; Edward Mellon to Hoke Donithen, December 27, 1926; Edward Mellon to Hoke Donithen, December 7, 1926; Edward Mellon to Hoke Donithen, December 7, 1926 (second letter); Hoke Donithen to E. P. Mellon, December 1, 1926; for quote see Hoke Donithen to E. P. Mellon, December 16, 1927; Edward Mellon to Hoke Donithen, September 12, 1928; Edward Mellon to Hoke Donithen, December 9, 1927; Edward P. Mellon to Hoke Donithen, March 7, 1927; Henry Hornbostel and Eric Fisher Wood to Presbry-Leland Company, January 18, 1927; Henry C. Brockman to Hoke Donithen, January 26, 1927; E. P. Mellon to Hoke Donithen, January 24, 1927; E. P. Mellon to Hoke Donithen, January 3, 1927; E. P. Mellon to Hoke Donithen, January 21, 1927; Hoke Donithen to E. P. Mellon, October 29, 1927; Edward Mellon to Hoke Donithen, October 27, 1927; E. P. Mellon to Hoke Donithen, January 20, 1927; Hoke Donithen to E. P. Mellon, January 28, 1927, all in Design and Structure, E. P. Mellon Advisory Architect folder, HMAP.

51. Hoover, *Memoirs,* 52.

52. Harry S. New to Hoke Donithen, December 28, 1930; Hoke Donithen to Harry S. New, January 6, 1931, Correspondence Related to Dedication folder, HMAP.

53. "Harding Memorial Dedication," *Akron Beacon Journal,* January 23, 1931; "The Harding Memorial," *Evanston News-Index,* January 27, 1931; Ann Cohen to Chairman of the President Harding Memorial, December 1930; Richard Harvey to Hoke Donithen, January 21, 1931, all in Correspondence Related to Dedication folder, HMAP.

54. Peter Gouled to Secretary, Harding Memorial Association, January 19, 1931; Hoke Donithen to Major O. M. Baldinger, January 27, 1931, both in Correspondence Related to Dedication folder, HMAP.

55. Hoover, *Memoirs,* 52–54.

56. Harry M. Daugherty, in collaboration with Thomas Dixon, *The Inside Story of the Harding Tragedy* (1932; repr., Boston: Western Islands, 1975), 2–3.

Chapter 4: My Damned Biographers

1. White, *Masks,* 432.

2. Paul S. Boyer et al., *The Enduring Vision: A History of the American People,* vol. 2, *From 1865* (Boston: Houghton Mifflin, 2000), 685.

3. Fine, *Difficult Reputations,* 33. Fine has described this creation of negative reputations as an "extended degradation ceremony." Because of their importance, two of the other works that contributed to the degradation of Harding's reputation and memory, Nan Britton's *President's Daughter* and William E. Chancellor's biography of Harding, will be treated in separate chapters.

4. F. Scott Fitzgerald, *The Vegetable, or, From President to Postman* (New York: Charles Scribner's Sons, 1923).

5. Jeffrey Meyers, *Scott Fitzgerald: A Biography* (New York: Harper Collins, 1994), 83, 105–07.

6. Ibid., 105.

7. Kammen, *Mystic Chords,* 22–24.

8. Niall Palmer, *The Twenties in America: Politics and History* (Edinburgh: Edinburgh University Press, 2006), 29.

9. Quoted in Fitzgerald, *Vegetable,* 54.

10. Samuel Hopkins Adams, *Revelry* (New York: Boni and Liveright, 1926), 15–16.

11. Lewis, *Babbitt,* 146.

12. Adams, *Revelry,* 38–39.

13. Also see Lewis, *Babbitt,* 61. Lewis wrote that Babbitt "liked to like the people about him; he was dismayed when they did not like him."

14. "Daugherty Calls Harding 'A Great President,' Victim of Underhand Whisperings," clipping in Nan Britton Collection (467), box 8, file 8, Nan Britton Papers, University of California, Los Angeles.

15. Griffith, *Home Town News,* 1, for quotes see 6, on breakdown, see 95.

16. Murray, *Harding Era,* 533.

17. William Allen White, *The Autobiography of William Allen White,* ed. Sally Foreman Griffith, 2nd ed. (1946; University Press of Kansas, 1990), 325.

18. White, *Masks,* 388. There are multiple versions of this quotation. Some variations appear to be somewhat sanitized for public consumption.

19. Adams, *Incredible Era,* 39.

20. Murray, *Harding Era,* for quote see 479.

21. Giglio, *Daugherty,* 130–31.

22. Daugherty, *Harding Tragedy,* 1.

23. Giglio, *Daugherty,* 142.

24. Daugherty, *Harding Tragedy,* 112.

25. Harding pardoned Debs after a public campaign for Debs's release and over the objections of members of his cabinet. Harding was influenced by a visit from Norman Thomas, the socialist leader, who had grown up in Marion and had been a carrier for the *Star.* The release of Debs was part of a broader communication for opponents. See Murray, *Harding Era,* 166–69.

26. Alice Roosevelt Longworth, *Crowded Hours: Reminiscences of Alice Roosevelt Longworth* (New York: Scribner's, 1933), 323–25.

Chapter 5: The Shadow of William Estabrook Chancellor

1. Gary Gerstle, *American Crucible: Race and Nation in the Twentieth Century* (Princeton, NJ: Princeton University Press, 2001), 83.

2. In all likelihood, I would not have made the connection between the 1919 race riot in Marion and Chancellor had I not lived in Marion and worked at the Harding Home. It was only through my interaction with the good people of Marion who were interested in local history that I learned of the race riot and it was the regular questions by visitors to the Harding Home regarding the president's race that started me thinking about these issues.

3. C-Span, "American Presidents," http://www.americanpresidents.org/presidents/yearschedule.asp.

4. Edwin Abramson, "William Estabrook Chancellor," paper read at a meeting of the Century Club, Wooster, Ohio, October 1985, College of Wooster Libraries (hereafter Wooster Libraries), 6–9. Abramson's and Russell's descriptions of Chancellor at the convention were remarkably similar. Russell describes Chancellor at the convention: "the shadow of Blooming Grove that had darkened every political campaign of Harding's, spread to Chicago as a tall man with gray hair parted in the middle, bushy eyebrows, and rimless spectacles moved unobtrusively from one headquarters to the other distributing flyers." Russell, *Shadow,* 372.

5. Russell, *Shadow,* 372.

6. See "Harding Letters Support Ex-Woosterians' Charges," *Wooster Daily Record,* July 10, 1964, clipping available in the Department of Special Collections, Wooster Libraries.

7. J. A. Rogers, *The Five Negro Presidents, U.S.A.* (St. Petersburg, FL: Helga M. Rogers, 1965), 5.

8. Auset BaKhufu, *The Six Black Presidents: Black Blood, White Masks, USA* (Washington, DC: PIK2 Publications, 1993), 177–215, for quotes see 177, 179. For Harding quote, see Adams, *Incredible Era,* 280.

9. Fine, "Reputational Entrepreneurs"; Carl S. Anthony, "The Most Scandalous President," *American Heritage* 49, no. 4 (1998): 53–58.

10. Anthony, *Florence Harding,* 125.

11. Francis Russell, "The Four Mysteries of Warren Harding," *American Heritage* 14, no. 2 (1963). Russell repeats the four mysteries in the foreword to *Shadow:* "Was Harding a mulatto? Did he have a child by his mistress? Was he murdered? What were the papers his wife so hastily burned after his death?" (xiv).

12. Randolph C. Downes, *The Rise of Warren Gamaliel Harding, 1865–1920* (Columbus: Ohio State University Press, 1970), 3–15, for quote see 3.

13. Adams, *Incredible Era,* 179.

14. Abramson, "William Estabrook Chancellor."

15. Ibid.; for "student mind" quote see 6; for "progressive thinker" quote see James R. Blackwood, *Howard Lowry: A Life in Education* (Wooster, OH: College of Wooster, 1975), 37 (copy available in the Wooster Libraries); see also obituary in *Wooster Alumni Bulletin,* 1962–63, Wooster Libraries). Chancellor's works include *Our Presidents and Their Office: Including Parallel Lives of the Presidents of the People of the United States and of Several Contemporaries, and A History of the Presidency* (New York: Neale, 1912) [Champ Clark, Speaker of the House of Representatives, wrote the introduction.]; with Fletcher Willis Hewes, *The United States: A History of Three Centuries, 1607–1904: Population, Politics, War, Industry, Civilization* (New York: G. P. Putnam's Sons, 1905); *Educational Sociology* (New York: Century, 1919); *Our Schools, Their Administration and Supervision* (Boston: D. C. Heath, 1908); *Our City Schools, Their Direction and Management* (Boston: D. C. Heath, 1908); *Class Teaching and Management* (New York: Harper and Brothers, 1910); *The Health of the Teacher* (Chicago: Forbes, 1919).

16. Daugherty, *Harding Tragedy,* 56–57.

17. Joseph DeBarthe, *The Answer* (Marion, OH: Answer, 1928), 195, 197.

18. Adams, *Incredible Era,* 15, 23, 62, 63.

19. The extant depositions are now located in the Wooster Libraries.

20. Adams, *Incredible Era,* 64.

21. Faculty—Chancellor, William E., Calvin G. Keifer, Affidavits (copy)—1920 October 9, Wooster Libraries.

22. Faculty—Chancellor, William E., Elias Shaffer, Affidavits (copy)—1920 October 9, Wooster Libraries.

23. Faculty—Chancellor, William E., George W. Cook, Affidavits (copy)—1920 October 13, Wooster Libraries.

24. Chancellor, *Harding,* for "very high coloring" quote see 36.

25. Faculty—Chancellor, William E., Montgomery Lindsay, Affidavits (copy)—1920 October 28, Wooster Libraries.

26. Chancellor, "This Is the Lineage of Warren Gamaliel Winnipeg Bancroft Harding," Department of Special Collections, Wooster Libraries, emphasis in original; Warren Boroson, "America's First Negro President," *fact* 1, no. 1 (1964): 55.

27. W. E. Chancellor "Hardings [*sic*] Family Tree," Wooster Libraries.

28. W. E. Chancellor, "Below Is the Genealogy of Warren G. Harding," Wooster Libraries. See *Harding,* 32, 66, 114.

29. W. E. Chancellor to W. Howard Ross, Esq., August 21, 1920, Wooster Libraries. On Hogan and the election see Downes, *Rise,* for quotes see 195, 639. For a more detailed discussion of anti-Catholicism in the election, see Russell, *Shadow,* 250–52. As for the reference to Florence DeWolf Harding,

Chancellor was referring to Florence's first marriage to Pete DeWolf. Accounts vary and some argue that Florence and Pete were never married. See Anthony, *Florence Harding*, ch. 4, "Living in Sin."

30. See Chancellor, *Harding*, 15, ch. 19, "The League of Nations and the Coming Wars," emphasis in original.

31. William E. Chancellor to Dear Sirs, October 28, 1920, Wooster Libraries.

32. W. E. Chancellor to W. Howard Ross, Esq., August 21, 1920, Wooster Libraries.

33. Chancellor, *Harding*, 77.

34. "Woman's Body on Ash Heap," *Marion Star,* January 30, 1919, 2; "Probing into Woman's Death," *Marion Star,* January 31, 1919, 3.

35. "Woman's Body on Ash Heap."

36. "Probing into Woman's Death."

37. "Better Protection Needed," *Marion Star,* January 30, 1919, 6.

38. "Conditions Have Changed," *Marion Star,* February 1, 1919, 4.

39. "Time for Calm Judgement," *Marion Star,* February 1, 1919, 4.

40. "Negro Attacks White Woman," *Marion Star,* February 3, 1919, 3. Includes material in the next paragraphs.

41. "Marion Negroes Flee to Escape Violence of Mob," *Columbus Dispatch,* February 4, 1919, 3.

42. "Negro Attacks White Woman." The Mount Gilead paper's report on the mob, which the *Star* reprinted, did not hesitate to name names. Ten Marion men appeared before the mayor's court in Mount Gilead: E. C. Northup, C. W. Brickley, H. C. Osborne, T. Trail, W. E. Finch, W. V. Towers, E. E. Towers, W. F. Lindsey, O. H. Monts, and Will Christian.

43. "$1,000 Reward for Murderer of Woman," *Marion Star,* February 3, 1919, 3; "Story from Mt. Gilead," *Marion Star,* February 3, 1919, 3.

44. "Quiet Night Follows Trouble of Monday," *Marion Star,* February 4, 1919, 3. Includes material in the following paragraph.

45. "Major Pealer Is Sent Here by Governor Cox," *Marion Star,* February 5, 1919, 2.

46. "Furnish Bond for Payment of Fines," *Marion Star,* February 5, 1919, 2; "He Just Wanted to Put His Arms around Her," *Marion Star,* February 5, 1919, 14.

47. Frank Bohn, "Ku Klux Klan Interpreted," *American Journal of Sociology* 30 (January 1925): 385–87, for quote see 386–87.

48. Adams, *Incredible Era*, 279.

49. Ibid., 181.

50. Blackwood, *Howard Lowry,* for quote see 36; see also Howard F. Lowry, "Wooster." Lowry was one of the students who defended Chancellor's house that night.

51. Chancellor, *Harding.* Page 65 features a map of Crawford, Marion, and Morrow counties with the caption, "Little Africa—Harding Land."

52. Lowry, "Wooster," 7. Lowry was president of the College of Wooster from 1944 to 1967, Wooster Libraries.

53. Adams, *Incredible Era,* 273–76.

54. Ibid., 278.

55. Russell, *Shadow,* 431–32.

56. Adams, *Incredible Era,* 282.

57. Chancellor, *Harding,* 7, 23; Russell, *Shadow,* 645.

58. "William E. Chancellor," obituary, *Wooster Alumni Bulletin,* 1962–63, Wooster Libraries.

59. Fine, "Reputational Entrepreneurs."

60. Buck, *Worked to the Bone: Race, Class, Power, and Privilege in Kentucky* (New York: Monthly Review Press, 2001), 150. Although discounted in scholarship on Harding, the story that Harding joined the Klan can be found in the literature on the Klan, often as a side note and not as a definite fact. When Harding is discussed, his public condemnations of the Klan carry more weight than a rumored secret membership. David Chalmers, in *Hooded Americanism: The History of the Ku Klux Klan,* 3rd ed. (Durham, NC: Duke University Press, 1987 [1965]), notes that rumors existed of a secret meeting between Imperial Wizard Hiram Evans and Harding (200). David Horowitz, in *Inside the Klavern: The Secret History of the Ku Klux Klan of the 1920s* (Carbondale: Southern Illinois University Press, 1999), regarding the prevalence of the Klan during the 1920s, writes, "Rumors even suggested that President Warren G. Harding had been inducted in a White House Ceremony" (4). Nancy MacLean, in *Behind the Mask of Chivalry: The Making of the Second Ku Klux Klan* (New York: Oxford University Press, 1995), notes that Harding belonged to the Junior Order of United American Mechanics, an anti-Catholic nativist organization allied with the Klan (4). Wyn Craig Wade, in *The Fiery Cross: The Ku Klux Klan in America* (New York: Oxford University Press, 1987), gives one of the more definite statements on Harding, writing: "[Imperial Wizard William] Simmon's ultimate vindication came when President Warren G. Harding agreed to be sworn in as a member of the Ku Klux Klan. A five-man 'Imperial induction team,' headed by Simmons conducted the ceremony in the Green Room of the White House. Members of the team were so nervous that they forgot their Bible in the car, so Harding had to send for the White House Bible. In consideration of his status, Harding was permitted to rest his elbow on the desk, as he knelt on the floor during the long oath taking. Afterward, the President appreciatively gave members of the team War Department license tags that allowed them to run red lights all across the nation" (165). In fairness to Wade, this is not a significant point in his overall argument that the Klan sought vindication

and legitimacy. Wade cites original source materials, writing in his citation, "The matter [of Harding's joining the Klan] was a major issue in letters sent to Coolidge during the 1924 election (see Case File 28, Calvin Coolidge Papers, Manuscript Division, Library of Congress). The description here is from the recollections of former Imperial Klokard Alton Young, who had been a member of the Presidential Induction Team. Stetson Kennedy and Elizabeth Gardner tape-recorded Young's recollections in the late 1940s, while Young was on his death bed in a New Jersey hospital (Stetson Kennedy to W. C. W., 5 June 1985)." Stetson Kennedy is an anti-Klan activist who wrote *I Rode with the Ku Klux Klan* (1954) (later reissued as *The Klan Unmasked*). In the book Kennedy recounted his exploits infiltrating the Klan with the purpose of exposing the organization's secrets. Recently, some controversy has arisen over the accuracy of Kennedy's accounts. Stephen J. Dubner and Steven D. Levitt in their book *Freakonomics* discuss the Klan, mentioning Harding's alleged induction (see chapter 8). However, in an article ("Hoodwinked?" *New York Times,* January 8, 2006, http://www.nytimes.com/2006/01/08/magazine/08wwln_freakonomics .html?pagewanted=1&_r=1), the authors discuss Kennedy's reliability. They write: "A close examination of Kennedy's archives seems to reveal a recurrent theme: legitimate interviews that he conducted with Klan leaders and sympathizers would reappear in 'The Klan Unmasked' in different contexts and with different facts. In a similar vein, the archives offer evidence that Kennedy covered public Klan events as a reporter but then recast them in his book as undercover exploits. Kennedy had also amassed a great deal of literature about the Klan and other hate groups that he joined, but his own archives suggest that he joined most of these groups by mail." Dubner and Levitt, citing others, conclude that Kennedy bent the truth. However, they do not directly address the story of Harding joining the Klan. In short, the evidence that Harding was secretly inducted into the Klan is based on the Young confession with no substantiating confirmation.

61. Anthony, *Florence Harding,* 421–23.

62. Trani and Wilson, *Presidency,* 104.

63. Murray, *Harding Era,* 398; Warren G. Harding, "Address of the President of the United States, April 12, 1921" in Harding, *Speeches of Late President;* "A Race Commission—A Constructive Plan," *Nation* (April 27, 1921), 612.

64. Murray, *Harding Era,* 400.

65. Warren G. Harding, "Address at Birmingham, October 26, 1921," in Harding, *Speeches of Late President,* emphasis in original.

66. Warren G. Harding, "President Harding's Address at the Dedication of the Lincoln Memorial," Washington, DC, May 30, 1922, in Harding, *Speeches of Late President.*

67. Murray, *Harding Era,* 401, 402–3.

Chapter 6: He-Harlot

1. Nan Britton did leave behind some papers, deposited in the University of California at Los Angeles archives and sealed until January 2000. Those papers include no smoking gun, no clear proof of the paternity of Elizabeth Ann. The papers validate only part of Britton's story. It seems clear from the papers that people around Britton, especially her family and friends, believed her story and that she had written, or played a major part in the writing of, *The President's Daughter*. Britton's papers included copies of the manuscripts that became her two books, and in both cases it appeared that Britton wrote the books, which were then edited by others. While the papers do not include some of the information that the researcher might hope for, they do offer insight into what it meant to be at the center of the scandal. The papers reveal a Nan Britton that was not as naive as she portrayed herself in the two books. Although she appears more worldly than her public persona, Britton does not appear to be the gold digger that Harding partisans would hope. File 13, draft of *The President's Daughter*, with editorial markings, n.d.; file 14, draft of *Honesty or Politics* (original title, *Stony Limits*), n.d., Mr. Clifton Fadiman (see his letter in Misc. Corres., no. 10).

2. Frederick Lewis Allen, *Only Yesterday: An Informal History of the Nineteen-Twenties* (New York: Blue Ribbon Books, 1931), 128–29.

3. Murray, *Harding Era*, 487, 489.

4. Ferrell, *Strange Deaths*, 65, 68, 69.

5. Anthony, *Florence Harding*, xiii–xiv.

6. White, *Autobiography*, 270.

7. Adams, *Incredible Era*, 7–8.

8. Patricia Raub, *Yesterday's Stories: Popular Women's Novels of the Twenties and Thirties* (Westport, CT: Greenwood Press, 1994), 21. Raub does not comment on Britton but she discusses novels with thematic similarities to the Britton story. She quotes from historian Joan Shelly Rubin, who suggests that a novelist "established her modern credentials by facing sex squarely and refraining from conventional moralism." Rubin, *The Making of Middle Brow Culture* (Chapel Hill: University of North Carolina Press, 1992).

9. Raub, *Yesterday's Stories*, xiii.

10. Ibid., ch. 2, "The Flapper and Her Sisters."

11. For quote see "Sumner and Vice Leaguers Sued by Mother over Book," *New York Daily News*, July 9, 1927, 5; "Guild Opens Fight for Britton Book," *New York World*, July 9, 1927, 1; "Six Burly Men," clipping found attached to the inside cover of *The President's Daughter*.

12. Nan Britton, *The President's Daughter* (New York: Elizabeth Ann Guild, 1927), i, emphasis in original.

13. Warren G. Harding to Nan Britton, May 9, 1917, Documentary file, Letters from Warren G. Harding to Nan Britton, box 1, file 1, Nan Britton Papers (collection 467).

14. Warren G. Harding to Nan Britton, May 17, 1917, file 2, box 1, Nan Britton Papers.

15. Britton, *President's Daughter*, 31; Raub discusses novels in which flappers petted but preserved their virtue. She quotes from a novel of the period: "she would move with him into a darkened corner and permit him to kiss her, to paw her unrestrainedly. The limit? No, she would not go to the limit. She would lie against his shoulder, moist-lipped, panting, but ever alert lest the purely physical barrier that guaranteed her self-respect be taken away from her." Raub, *Yesterday's Stories*, 14.

16. Britton did not use the phrase *companionate marriage*. The term is defined as a marriage "held together not by rigid social pressures or religious conceptions of moral duty but by mutual affection, sexual attraction, and equal rights." This concept had found its way into the popular women's novels of the period and it would not be surprising if Britton was influenced by them. The definition is from Raub, *Yesterday's Stories*, 18. Raub quotes historians Steven Mintz and Susan Kellogg.

17. Britton, *President's Daughter*, 35.

18. Warren G. Harding to Dr. Frank T. Spaulding, Superintendent of Public Schools, May 25 [1918], Documentary file, box 1, file 6, Nan Britton Papers (collection 467).

19. Warren G. Harding to Nan Britton, May 25, 1918, box 1, file 4, Documentary file, Nan Britton Papers (collection 467).

20. Warren G. Harding to Nan Britton, December 5 [1918], Documentary file, box 1, file 5, Nan Britton Papers (collection 467).

21. Britton, *President's Daughter*, 43–44; emphasis in original.

22. Nan Britton, *Honesty or Politics* (New York: Elizabeth Ann Guild, 1932), x–xi.

23. Robert Sklar, *Movie-Made America: A Cultural History of American Movies*, revised and updated (1975; repr., New York: Vintage Books, 1994), 75.

24. Britton, *Honesty*, 336.

25. Ibid., 218–19.

26. Ferrell, *Strange Deaths*, 69.

27. DeBarthe, *Answer*, 5–6.

28. Adams, *Incredible Era*, 106.

29. Ferrell, *Strange Deaths*, 70.

30. Britton, *Honesty*, 319.

31. Daugherty, *Inside Story*, 261.

32. Murray, *Harding Era*, 491.

33. Russell, *Shadow*, 517.

34. Adams, *Revelry*, 107, 253.

35. Means, *Strange Death,* 22.

36. Marcia, as told to Herbert Corey, "The Tragic Love of Mrs. Warren Harding," box 4, file 12, Nan Britton Collection (467), Special Collections, University of California, Los Angeles, for quote see 22.

37. Means, *Strange Death,* 39.

38. Adams, *Incredible Era,* 44. Here Adams comes very close to directly addressing this rumor. Of the relationship between the two men he writes, "no inferences of an abnormal phase to the friendship are to be drawn. Both men were thoroughly masculine."

39. Adams, *Incredible Era,* 107.

40. Murray, *Harding Era,* 489.

41. Daugherty, *Inside Story,* 248.

42. Ferrell, *Strange Deaths,* 71.

Chapter 7: Harding Alley

1. Francis Russell, "The Harding Papers . . . and Some Were Saved," *American Heritage* 16, no. 2 (1965): 26–27.

2. Ibid.

3. Kenneth W. Duckett, "The Harding Papers: How Some Were Burned . . ." *American Heritage* 16, no. 2 (1965): 26.

4. Andrea D. Lentz, "Introduction and Providence," in *The Warren G. Harding Papers: An Inventory to the Microfilm Edition* (Columbus: Archives and Manuscripts Division, Ohio Historical Society, 1970), 3.

5. Duckett, "Harding Papers," 28.

6. Ibid., 24–31; Russell, "Harding Papers," 102–10; Mark Sullivan to Dr. Sawyer, July 19, August 10, 1935, both in Warren G. Harding Papers, Ohio Historical Society (microfilm ed., roll 248), Columbus, Ohio.

7. Irvin S. Cobb, *Exit Laughing* (Indianapolis: Bobbs-Merrill, 1941); "Presidents as They Pass," Article Reprints about Harding file, MSS 402, box 22, Sources of Information A to G, 278–79, Dean Albertson Collection, University of Massachusetts, Amherst (hereafter, Albertson Collection).

8. James E. Pollard, *The Presidents and the Press* (New York: Macmillan, 1947), 712; Article Reprints about Harding file, box 22, Sources of Information A to G, Albertson Collection.

9. Rudolph Marx, MD, *The Health of the Presidents* (New York: G. P. Putnam's Sons, 1960), 323–36, Article Reprints about Harding file, box 22, Sources of Information A to G, Albertson Collection.

10. John D. Hicks, *Republican Ascendancy: 1921–1933* (New York: Harper and Row, 1960), 27.

11. Warren G. Harding, "The Metal of Real Friendship," *Speeches of Warren G. Harding of Ohio, Republican Candidate for President, From His Acceptance of the Nomination to October 1, 1920* (New York: Republican National Committee, 1920), 18–19.

12. Warren G. Harding, "President Harding's Address at the Dedication of the Lincoln Memorial," May 30, 1922, in Harding, *Speeches of Late President.*

13. Dean Albertson to Betty Horn, October 21, 1961, George B. Harris file, MSS 402, box 23, Warren G. Harding Papers, Sources of Information H to L, Harding Family file, Albertson Collection.

14. Dean Albertson to Dr. Carl W. Sawyer, September 11, 1961; Carl Sawyer to Dean Albertson, September 15, 1961; Dean Albertson to C. S., April 6, 1962, all in Marion, Ohio file, MSS 402, box 24, Sources of Information M to Z, Albertson Collection.

15. Carl Sawyer to Dean Albertson, April 10, 1962, Marion, Ohio, file, MSS 402, box 24, Sources of Information M to Z, Albertson Collection.

16. Dean Albertson to Professor Randolph C. Downes, August 24, 1963, Randolph C. Downes file, box 22, Sources of Information A to G, Albertson Collection.

17. Carl W. Sawyer, MD, to Mr. Ray Baker Harris, January 26, 1962; Harris to Sawyer, January 23, 1962, both in Ray Baker Harris Collection OHS, MSS 402, box 23, Warren G. Harding Papers, Sources of Information H to L, Harding Family file, Albertson Collection.

18. David H. Stratton to Dean Albertson, May 7, 1963, Huntington Library file, MSS 402, box 23, Warren G. Harding Papers, Sources of Information H to L, Harding Family file, Albertson Collection.

19. James Ramsey to Dean Albertson, July 10, 1963, Columbia University file, box 22, Sources of Information A to G, Albertson Collection.

20. William S. Culbertson to Dean Albertson, January 7, 1963, William S. Culbertson file, box 22, Sources of Information A to G, Albertson Collection.

21. Dean Albertson to Allan Nevine, May 14, 1963, Huntington Library file, MSS 402, box 23, Warren G. Harding Papers, Sources of Information H to L, Harding Family file, Albertson Collection.

22. Ellen Lucile Stoll to Dean Albertson, August 17, 1963, Marion, Ohio, file, MSS 402, box 24, Sources of Information M to Z, Albertson Collection.

23. Dean Albertson to Mrs. C. B. Stoll, August 28, 1963, Marion, Ohio, file, MSS 402, box 24, Sources of Information M to Z, Albertson Collection.

24. Dean Albertson to Nan Britton, August 28, 1963, Correspondence Dean Albertson with Nan Britton, 1963–70, Albertson/Britton box, MSS 402, Albertson Collection.

25. Ray A. Billington to Nan Britton, September 17, 1963, Huntington Library file, MSS 402, box 23, Warren G. Harding Papers, Sources of Information H to L, Harding Family file, Albertson Collection.

26. Ray Billington to Dean Albertson, September 17, 1963, Huntington Library file, MSS 402, box 23, Warren G. Harding Papers, Sources of Information H to L, Harding Family file, Albertson Collection.

27. Dean Albertson to Ellen L. Stoll, March 2, 1964, Marion, Ohio, file, MSS 402, box 24, Warren G. Harding Papers, Sources of Information M to Z, Albertson Collection.

28. Dean Albertson to Nan Britton, November 14, 1963, Correspondence Dean Albertson with Nan Britton, 1963–70, Albertson/Britton box, MSS 402, Albertson Collection; Dean Albertson to Ray Billington, September 26, 1963, Huntington Library file, MSS 402, box 23, Warren G. Harding Papers, Sources of Information H to L, Harding Family file, Albertson Collection.

29. Dean Albertson to Carl Sawyer, March 29, 1963, Marion, Ohio, file, MSS 402, box 24, Sources of Information M to Z, Albertson Collection; Carl Sawyer to Dean Albertson, April 12, 1963; Carl Sawyer to Dean Albertson, August 30, 1963, Marion, Ohio, file, MSS 402, box 24, Warren G. Harding Papers, Sources of Information M to Z, Albertson Collection.

30. Allan E. Bovey, *Marion Star,* to Dean Albertson, August 16, 1963, Marion, Ohio, file, MSS 402, box 24, Warren G. Harding Papers, Sources of Information M to Z, Albertson Collection.

31. Dean Albertson to Professor H. Wayne Morgan, December 4, 1963, Marion, Ohio, file, MSS 402, box 24, Sources of Information M to Z, Albertson Collection.

32. Ken [Duckett] to Dean [Albertson], January 22, 1964, Ohio Historical Society, Kenneth Duckett file, MSS 402, box 24, Sources of Information M to Z, Albertson Collection.

33. Ken [Duckett] to Dean [Albertson], February 7, 1964, Ohio Historical Society, Kenneth Duckett file, MSS 402, box 24, Sources of Information M to Z, Albertson Collection.

34. Dean Albertson to K. W. Duckett, February 11, 1964, Ohio Historical Society, Kenneth Duckett file, MSS 402, box 24, Sources of Information M to Z, Albertson Collection.

35. Ken [Duckett] to Dean [Albertson], n.d.; D. A. to K. W. D., December 18, 1963, both in Ohio Historical Society, Kenneth Duckett file, MSS 402, box 24, Sources of Information M to Z, Albertson Collection.

36. Ken [Duckett] to Dean, Dec 9, 1963, Ohio Historical Society, Kenneth Duckett file, MSS 402, box 24, Sources of Information M to Z, Albertson Collection.

37. "Harding's Secret Love Notes Found," *San Francisco Chronicle,* July 10, 1964, 26; Susanna McBee, "President Harding's Love Letters to Townman's Wife Uncovered," *Washington Post,* July 11, 1964, p. A3, Albertson Collection.

38. Russell, "Harding Papers," 28.

39. Ibid., 106–7.

40. Henry Lee, "The Secret Life of President Harding," *Sunday News,* July 26, 1964, 68, Albertson Collection.

41. Harry Gilroy, "Copies Are Made of Harding Notes," *New York Times*, August 4, 1964; "Magazine Fights Move to Hide Harding Letters," *Columbus Citizen-Journal*, August 4, 1964, 1, both in Albertson Collection.

42. "Harding's Secret Love Notes"; McBee, "President Harding's Love Letters."

43. Russell, "Harding Papers," 30–31.

44. "Harding's Secret Love Notes"; McBee, "President Harding's Love Letters."

45. Russell, "Harding Papers," 107–8.

46. R. W. Apple, "Nan Britton Lives in Seclusion in Chicago Suburb," *New York Times*, July 15, 1964, Albertson Collection.

47. "Harding's Mistress Ends 30-Yr. Silence," *Chicago American*, July 18, 1963, Albertson Collection.

48. "Harding Love Child Bares Her Identity," *Chicago Tribune*, July 17, 1964, Albertson Collection.

49. "Judge Stays Publication of Harding Love Notes," Associated Press, Columbus, Ohio, clipping, Albertson Collection.

50. Robert C. Ruark, "Let Harding's Old Loves Alone," *Columbus Citizen-Journal*, July 24, 1964, Albertson Collection.

51. Lee, "Secret Life of President Harding."

52. Ibid.

53. Allan Bovey, "Harding's Files to Unlock New Doors for Historians," *Marion Star*, April 27, 1964, Albertson Collection.

54. Ken [Duckett] to Dean [Albertson], April 27, 1964, Ohio Historical Society, Kenneth Duckett file, MSS 402, box 24, Sources of Information M to Z, Albertson Collection.

55. Ken [Duckett] to Dean [Albertson], May 2, 1964, Ohio Historical Society, Kenneth Duckett file, MSS 402, box 24, Sources of Information M to Z, Albertson Collection.

56. The American Society for the Faithful Recording of History News Release (for publication May 11 and after), Ohio Historical Society, Kenneth Duckett file, MSS 402, box 24, Sources of Information M to Z, Albertson Collection.

57. Dean Albertson to K W Duckett, April 19, 1964, Ohio Historical Society, Kenneth Duckett file, MSS 402, box 24, Sources of Information M to Z, Albertson Collection.

58. Dean Albertson to Mrs. Virginia Rust, Assistant in Manuscripts, August 11, 1964, Huntington Library file, MSS 402, box 23, Warren G. Harding Papers, Sources of Information H to L, Harding Family file, Albertson Collection.

59. Dean Albertson to Dr. George T. Harding, July 15, 1964, MSS 402, box 23, Warren G. Harding Papers, Sources of Information H to L, Harding Family file, Albertson Collection.

60. Dean Albertson to Mr. H. Ellis Daugherty, July 26, 1964, Harry Daugherty file, box 22, Sources of Information A to G, Albertson Collection.

61. Dean Albertson to Nan Britton, March 8, 1964, Correspondence Dean Albertson with Nan Britton, 1963–70, Albertson/Britton box, MSS 402, Albertson Collection.

62. Albertson to Miss Nan Britton, Correspondence Dean Albertson with Nan Britton, 1963–70, Albertson/Britton box, MSS 402, Albertson Collection.

63. Dean Albertson to Nan Britton, April 15, 1964, Correspondence Dean Albertson with Nan Britton, 1963–70, Albertson/Britton box, MSS 402, Albertson Collection.

64. Dean Albertson to Nan Britton, May 24, 1964, Correspondence Dean Albertson with Nan Britton, 1963–70, Albertson/Britton box, MSS 402, Albertson Collection.

65. Dean Albertson to Nan Britton, June 16, 1964; Nan Britton to Dean Albertson, June 29, 1964; Dean Albertson to Mr. W. H. Howell Jr., Manager, Witherill Hotel, Plattsburg, New York, July 1, 1964, all in Correspondence Dean Albertson with Nan Britton, 1963–70, Albertson/Britton box, MSS 402, Albertson Collection.

66. W. H. Howell Jr. to Dean Albertson, Correspondence Dean Albertson with Nan Britton, 1963–70, Albertson/Britton box, MSS 402, Albertson Collection.

67. Dean Albertson to Nan Britton, July 14, 1964, Correspondence Dean Albertson with Nan Britton, 1963–70, Albertson/Britton box, MSS 402, Albertson Collection.

68. Dean Albertson to Nan Britton, September 29, 1964, Correspondence Dean Albertson with Nan Britton, 1963–70, Albertson/Britton box, MSS 402, Albertson Collection.

69. *Harding Star* 1, no. 1 (June 5, 1965), News Releases and Newsletters, file 6, box 1, Harding Memorial Association, Ohio Historical Society.

70. Dean Albertson to Dr. Erwin C. Zepp, Ohio Historical Society, Kenneth Duckett file MSS 402, box 24, Sources of Information M to Z, Albertson Collection.

71. Dean Albertson, Address at Marion, Ohio, November 2, 1965, Albertson Collection.

72. Warren C. Sawyer, VP, HMA, to Dean Albertson, November 12, 1965, Marion, Ohio file, MSS 402, box 24, Sources of Information M to Z, Albertson Collection.

73. Dean Albertson to Nan Britton, January 9, 1966, Correspondence Dean Albertson with Nan Britton, 1963–70, Albertson/Britton box, MSS 402, Albertson Collection.

74. Dean Albertson to Professor Dennis Brogan, Corpus Christi College, Cambridge, England, January 3, 1965, Columbia University file, MSS 402, box 22, Sources of Information A to G, Albertson Collection.

75. Dean Albertson to Dr. Charles W. Harding, April 5, 1965, MSS 402, box 23, Warren G. Harding Papers, Sources of Information H to L, Harding Family file, Albertson Collection.

76. Randolph Downes to Dean Albertson, April 22, 1965, Randolph C. Downes file, MSS 402, box 22, Sources of Information A to G, Albertson Collection.

77. Dean Albertson to Warren C. Sawyer, President, HMA, October 25, 1966, Ohio Historical Society, Kenneth Duckett file, MSS 402, box 24, Sources of Information M to Z, Albertson Collection.

78. Daniel R. Porter, director, to Dean Albertson, February 23, 1966, Ohio Historical Society, Kenneth Duckett file, MSS 402, box 24, Sources of Information M to Z, Albertson Collection.

79. Dean Albertson to Walter Lippmann, April 5, 1965, Columbia University file, MSS 402, box 22, Sources of Information A to G, Albertson Collection.

80. Walter Lippmann to Dean Albertson, April 9, 1965, Columbia University file, MSS 402, box 22, Sources of Information A to G, Albertson Collection.

81. Randolph C. Downes to Dean Albertson, March 27, 1965, Randolph C. Downes file, MSS 402, box 22, Sources of Information A to G, Albertson Collection.

82. Dean Albertson to R. C. D., April 7, 1965, Randolph C. Downes file, MSS 402, box 22, Sources of Information A to G, Albertson Collection.

83. Dean Albertson to Francis Russell, February 14, 1965, Randolph C. Downes file, MSS 402, box 22, Sources of Information A to G, Albertson Collection.

84. Francis Russell to Dean Albertson, November 16, 1964; Dean Albertson to Downes, April 1, 1965; Downes to Dean Albertson, February 17, 1965; Dean Albertson to Downes, March 22, 1965, all in Randolph C. Downes file, MSS 402, box 22, Sources of Information A to G, Albertson Collection.

85. Dean Albertson to Francis Russell, February 26, 1965, Randolph C. Downes file, MSS 402, box 22 Sources of Information A to G, Albertson Collection.

86. Russell to Dean Albertson, March 3, 1965, handwritten note, Randolph C. Downes file, MSS 402, box 22, Sources of Information A to G, Albertson Collection.

87. "Carrie's Daughter Gets Love Letters," *Citizen Journal,* February 26, 1965, Randolph C. Downes file, MSS 402, box 22, Sources of Information A to G, Albertson Collection.

88. Warren C. Sawyer to Dean Albertson, May 18, 1966, Ohio Historical Society, Kenneth Duckett file, MSS 402, box 24, Sources of Information M to Z.

89. Virgil D. Hess, address on 102nd Birthday of Warren G. Harding at Memorial, Marion, Ohio, November 2, 1967, News Releases and Newsletters, file 6, box 1, Harding Memorial Association, Ohio Historical Society.

90. "No Birthday Banquet in 1968," *Harding Star* 3, no. 11 (November 1, 1968), News Releases and Newsletters, file 6, box 1, Harding Memorial Association, Ohio Historical Society.

91. Dean Albertson to Dr. Charles W. Harding, September 26, 1968, MSS 402, box 23, Warren G. Harding Papers, Sources of Information H to L, Harding Family file, Albertson Collection.

92. Nan Britton sent Dean Albertson a change of address card dated May 6, 1965, indicating that she had moved to Glendale, California, Correspondence Dean Albertson with Nan Britton, 1963–70, Albertson/Britton box, MSS 402, Albertson Collection.

93. Dean Albertson to Nan Britton, February 13, 1966, Correspondence Dean Albertson with Nan Britton, 1963–70, Albertson/Britton box, MSS 402, Albertson Collection.

94. Dean Albertson to Nan Britton, September 3, 1969, Correspondence Dean Albertson with Nan Britton, 1963–70, Albertson/Britton box, MSS 402, Albertson Collection, emphasis in original.

95. Handwritten note from Jacklyn E. Hendrick to Dean Albertson, September 18, 1970, Columbia University file, MSS 402, box 22, Sources of Information A to G, Albertson Collection.

96. "History Professor Dies at 68," *Amherst Collegian*, April 3, 1989, 1.

Chapter 8: Dead Last

1. Frank Rich, "Bring Back Warren Harding," *New York Times*, September 25, 2005.

2. Jerome Lawrence and Robert E. Lee, *The Gang's All Here: A Play* (Cleveland, OH: World, 1960), 7–9; emphasis in original.

3. Martin Blinder, *Fluke* (Sag Harbor, NY: Permanent Press, 1999), 5, emphasis in original.

4. John W. Ravage, *Slick and the Duchess: The Teapot Dome Scandal and the Death of Warren Harding* (Denver, CO: Outskirts Press, 2007), 442.

5. Seymour Hersh, *The Dark Side of Camelot* (Boston: Little, Brown, 1997).

6. Adams, *Incredible Era*, 169.

7. Steve Rubenzer, "What Makes a Good President?" was a widely circulated story based on Steven Rubenzer, Deniz S. Ones, and Tom Faschingbauer, "Personality Traits of U.S. Presidents" (paper presented at the Annual Convention of the American Psychological Association, Washington, DC, August 5, 2000).

8. Douglas Brinkley, *The Unfinished Presidency: Jimmy Carter's Journey beyond the White House* (New York: Viking, 1998), 4.

9. "Warren Gamaliel Harding: 29th President of the United States, 1921–1923," http://redbud.lbjlib.utexas.edu/eisenhower/28.htm (accessed September 16, 2000).

10. Patrick J. Buchanan, "Now Let Us All Praise Warren G. Harding," July 9, 1997, Internet Brigade: Articles, Letters, and Speeches, http://www.buchanan.org/pa-97-0709.html.

11. Hugh Sidney, "Puritan in the Cabinet," *Time,* November 16, 1981, http://www.time.com/time/magazine/article/0,9171,953170,00.html (accessed October 28, 2008).

12. Gary Alan Fine, "Hail to the Crook: Clinton, Harding, and the Politics of Reputation," *Reason* 28, no. 6 (1996): 55.

13. Adams, *Revelry,* 92–93, emphasis in original.

14. Anonymous [Joe Klein], *Primary Colors: A Novel of Politics* (New York: Warner Books, 1996), 1–2, emphasis added.

15. Joe Klein, *The Natural: The Misunderstood Presidency of Bill Clinton* (New York: Doubleday, 2002), 27–28.

16. Adams, *Revelry,* 266.

17. Gary Aldrich, *Unlimited Access: An FBI Agent inside the Clinton White House* (Washington, DC: Regnery, 1998), ix.

18. Jeffrey Toobin, *A Vast Conspiracy: The Real Story of the Sex Scandal That Nearly Brought Down a President* (New York: Touchstone, 2000), 5, 83.

19. Toni Morrison, "The Talk of the Town," *New Yorker,* October 5, 1998, 32; Micki McElya, "Trashing the Presidency: Race, Class, and the Clinton/Lewinsky Affair," in *Our Monica, Ourselves: The Clinton Affair and the National Interest,* ed. Lauren Berland and Lisa Duggan (New York: New York University Press, 2001), 156.

20. Miss King, "The Misanthrope's Corner," *National Review,* October 26, 1998.

21. Carl Sferrazza Anthony, "A President of the Peephole," *Washington Post,* June 7, 1998.

22. For the famous quote about Harding's friends keeping him up at night, see White, *Masks,* 432.

23. Mackubin Thomas Owens, "Warren Gamaliel Clinton," *Providence Journal,* http://www.ashbrook.org/publicat/oped/owens/98/harding.html (accessed May 22, 2008).

24. With Clinton it was, of course, the Vince Foster suicide; with Harding it was the suicide of the "financial bagman for Harding and Daugherty who carried out many criminal assignments for friends and officials."

25. Anthony, *Florence Harding,* 24–25.

26. Howard Phillips, "A Tale of Presidents and Their Sexual Escapades," *Insight on the News,* October 19, 1998, http://www.findarticles.com/cf_)/m1571/n38_v14/21224321/print.jhtml.

27. Joe Eszterhas, *American Rhapsody* (New York: Knopf, 2000), 65. Eszterhas is also the author of such screenplays as *Music Box, Telling Lies in America, F.I.S.T., Betrayed, Basic Instinct, Showgirls, Sliver,* and *Jade.*

28. Gary Allan Fine, "Warren G. Harding and the Memory of Incompetence," in *Difficult Reputations;* Ferrell, *Strange Deaths.*

29. Eszterhas, *American Rhapsody,* xiii.

30. Ibid., emphasis in original.

31. Charles W. Dunn, *The Scarlet Thread of Scandal: Morality and the American Presidency* (New York: Rowman and Littlefield, 2000), 72.

32. Wikipedia is collaboratively written by volunteers with the ideal that "over time, and in general this results in an upward trend of quality, and a growing consensus over a fair and balanced representation of information." Many articles move from partisan to a "balanced consensus." "Wikipedia: About," http://en.wikipedia.org/wiki/Wikipedia:About.

33. According to Wikipedia, "A wiki (sometimes wiki wiki) is a web application designed to allow multiple authors to add, remove, and edit content. The multiple author capability of wikis makes them effective tools for mass collaborative authoring." http://en.wikipedia.org/wiki/Wiki.

34. "Warren G. Harding," http://en.wikipedia.org/wiki/Warren_G._Harding.

35. The article incorrectly reports that Hoover dedicated the memorial in 1930; actually it was dedicated in 1931. Wikipedia, "Teapot Dome scandal," http://en.wikipedia.org/wiki/Teapot_Dome_Scandal.

36. Wikipedia, "Harding Memorial," http://en.wikipedia.org/wiki/Harding_Memorial.

37. On the contributor's background, see "User: Skoblentz," http://en.wikipedia.org/wiki/User:Skoblentz. Stuart Koblentz is the author of *Marion (OH) (Images of America)* (Mt. Pleasant, SC: Arcadia, 2004) and *Marion County* (Marion, OH: Marion County Historical Society, 2007). Koblentz's biography, as described on Amazon.com, identifies him as a graduate of Marion High School, a member of the Marion County Historical Society, and a resident of Columbus, Ohio.

38. Wikipedia, "Talk: Warren G. Harding," http://en.wikipedia.org/wiki/Talk:Warren_G._Harding.

39. http://www.stewartsynopsis.com/warren_gamaliel_harding.htm; http://warrengharding.net/; Marsha Stewart, *Warren G. Harding U.S. President 29: Death By Blackness* (Charlotte, NC: Conquering Books, 2005).

40. *Stewart Synopsis,* "Warren Gamaliel Harding," http://www.stewartsynopsis.com/warren_gamaliel_harding.htm.

41. "Warren G. Harding," http://warrengharding.net/Look%20Inside%20This%20Book.htm. See also http://stewartsynopsis.com/warren_gamaliel_harding.htm.

42. Wikipedia, "Talk: Warren G. Harding," http://en.wikipedia.org/wiki/Talk:Warren_G._Harding.

43. Wikipedia, "Wikipedia: Neutral Point of View," http://en.wikipedia.org/wiki/Wikipedia:Neutral_point_of_view.

44. The speech that includes the reference to Brownie is available at "President Arrives in Alabama, Briefed on Hurricane Katrina," White House Press Release, September 2, 2005, http://www.whitehouse.gov/news/releases/2005/09/20050902-2.html.

45. Robert S. McElvaine, "Historians vs. George W. Bush," May 17, 2004, http://hnn.us/articles/5019.html.

46. Sean Wilentz, "The Worst President in History? One of America's Leading Historians Assesses George W. Bush," *Rolling Stone,* http://www.rollingstone.com/news/profile/story/9961300/the_worst_president_in_history (posted April 21, 2006).

47. Eric Foner, "He's the Worst Ever," *Washington Post,* December 3, 2006, B01 http://www.washingtonpost.com/wp-dyn/content/article/2006/12/01/AR2006120101509.html.

48. Nick Clooney, "How Will Historians Judge Bush Presidency?" *Cincinnati Post,* June 11, 2007, http://news.cincypost.com/apps/pbcs.dll/article?AID=/20070611/LIFE03/706110340/1008/LIFE.

49. Nicholas von Hoffman, "The Worst President Ever," *Nation,* http://www.thenation.com/doc/20070226/howl (posted February 14, 2007).

50. Frank Dwyer, "Another Historical Analogy for Desperate Republicans," *Huffington Post,* http://www.huffingtonpost.com/frank-dwyer/another-historical-analog_b_31196.html (accessed October 7, 2006).

51. Jay Tolson, "The 10 Worst Presidents," *U.S. News and World Report,* February 26, 2007, http://www.usnews.com/usnews/news/articles/070218/26presidents.htm.

52. Dwyer, "Historical Analogy."

53. James MacGregor Burns, Arthur M. Schlesinger Jr., and Fred I. Greenstein, "Commentary," in Bose and Landis, *Presidential Ratings,* 98.

54. Malcolm Gladwell, *Blink: The Power of Thinking without Thinking* (New York: Little, Brown, 2005), 72–75, 76.

BIBLIOGRAPHY

Manuscript Collections

Albertson, Dean. Papers. University of Massachusetts, Amherst.
Britton, Nan. Papers. University of California, Los Angeles.
Chancellor, William Estabrook. Papers. College of Wooster.
Harding, Florence Kling. Papers. Ohio Historical Society (microfilm).
Harding, Warren G. Papers. Ohio Historical Society (microfilm).
Harding Star. Harding Memorial Association.
Marion Star. Ohio Historical Society (microfilm).
Russell, Francis. Papers. University of Wyoming, Laramie.
Sawyer, Charles E. Papers. Ohio Historical Society (microfilm).
Warren G. Harding Memorial Association Papers. President Warren G. Harding Home. Ohio Historical Society.

Books and Articles

Adams, Samuel Hopkins Adams. *Incredible Era: The Life and Times of Warren Gamaliel Harding.* Boston: Houghton Mifflin, 1939.
———. *Revelry.* New York: Boni and Liveright, 1926.
Allen, Frederick Lewis. *Only Yesterday: An Informal History of the Nineteen-Twenties.* New York: Harper, 1931.
Anthony, Carl S. *Florence Harding: The First Lady, the Jazz Age, and the Death of America's Most Scandalous President.* New York: Morrow, 1998.
Bagby, Wesley M. *The Road to Normalcy: The Presidential Campaign and Election of 1920.* Baltimore, MD: Johns Hopkins University Press, 1962.
BaKhufu, Auset. *The Six Black Presidents: Black Blood, White Masks, USA.* Washington, DC: PIK2 Publications, 1993.
Bates, J. Leonard. *The Origins of Teapot Dome: Progressivism, Parties, and Petroleum, 1909–1921.* Urbana: University of Illinois Press, 1963.

Blight, David W. *Beyond the Battlefield: Race, Memory, and the American Civil War.* Amherst: University of Massachusetts Press, 2002.

Bodnar, John. *Remaking America: Public Memory, Commemoration, and Patriotism in the Twentieth Century.* Princeton, NJ: Princeton University Press, 1992.

Bose, Meena, and Mark Landis, eds. *The Uses and Abuses of Presidential Ratings.* New York: Nova Science Publishers, 2003.

Britton, Nan. *Honesty or Politics.* New York: Elizabeth Ann Guild, 1932.

————. *The President's Daughter.* New York: Elizabeth Ann Guild, 1927.

Chancellor, William Estabrook. *Warren Gamaliel Harding: President of the United States.* Dayton, OH: Sentinal Press, 1922.

Chapple, Joe Mitchell. *Life and Times of Warren G. Harding: Our After-War President.* Boston: Chapple, 1924.

Clotworthy, William G. *Homes and Libraries of the Presidents: An Interpretive Guide.* Blacksburg, VA: McDonald and Woodward, 1995.

Connelly, Thomas L. *The Marble Man: Robert E. Lee and His Image in American Society.* Baton Rouge: Louisiana State University Press, 1977.

Cornog, Evan. *The Power and the Story: How the Crafted Presidential Narrative Has Determined Political Success from George Washington to George W. Bush.* New York: Penguin, 2004.

Daugherty, Harry M., in collaboration with Thomas Dixon. *The Inside Story of the Harding Tragedy.* 1932. Reprint, Boston: Western Islands, 1975.

Dean, John W. *Warren G. Harding.* New York: Times Books, 2004.

DeBarthe, Joseph. *The Answer.* Marion, OH: Answer Publications, 1928.

Downes, Randolph C. *The Rise of Warren Gamaliel Harding: 1865–1920.* Columbus: Ohio State University Press, 1970.

Duckett, Kenneth W. "The Harding Papers: How Some Were Burned . . ." *American Heritage* 16, no. 2 (1965): 25–31, 102–9.

Ferrell, Robert H. *The Strange Deaths of President Harding.* Columbia: University of Missouri Press, 1996.

Fine, Gary Alan. *Difficult Reputations: Collective Memories of the Evil, Inept, and Controversial.* Chicago: University of Chicago Press, 2001.

————. "Reputational Entrepreneurs and the Memory of Incompetence: Melting Supporters, Partisan Warriors, and Images of President Harding." *American Journal of Sociology* 101, no. 5 (1996): 1159–93.

Fitzgerald, F. Scott. *The Vegetable, or, From President to Postman.* New York: Scribner's, 1923.

Frederick, Richard G., comp. *Warren G. Harding: A Bibliography.* Westport, CT: Greenwood, 1992.

Giglio, James N. *H. M. Daugherty and the Politics of Expediency.* Kent, OH: Kent State University Press, 1978.

Glassberg, David. *Sense of History: The Place of the Past in America Life.* Amherst: University of Massachusetts Press, 2001.

Gordon-Reed, Annette. *Thomas Jefferson and Sally Hemings: An American Controversy.* Charlottesville: University of Virginia Press, 1997.

Greenberg, David. *Nixon's Shadow: The History of an Image.* New York: Norton, 2003.

Griffith, Sally Foreman. *Home Town News: William Allen White and the* Emporia Gazette. New York: Oxford University Press, 1989.

Gross, Edwin K. *Vindication for Mr. Normalcy: A 100th-Birthday Memorial.* Buffalo, NY: American Society for the Faithful Recording of History, 1965.

Harding, Warren G. *Speeches of Senator Warren G. Harding of Ohio: Republican Candidate for President, from His Acceptance of the Nomination to October 1, 1920.* New York: Republican National Committee, 1920.

———. *Speeches of the Late President Harding, 1920–1923.* Washington, DC: GPO, 1920–23.

———. *The Warren G. Harding Papers: An Inventory to the Microfilm Edition.* Ed. Andrea D. Lentz. Columbus: Ohio Historical Society, 1970.

Hellman, John. *The Kennedy Obsession.* New York: Columbia University Press, 1997.

Hoover, Herbert. *The Cabinet and the Presidency, 1920–1933.* Vol. 2 of *The Memoirs of Herbert Hoover.* New York: Macmillan, 1952.

Hoyt, Edwin P. *Spectacular Rogue: Gaston B. Means.* Indianapolis, IN: Bobbs-Merrill, 1963.

Hufbauer, Benjamin. *Presidential Temples: How Memorials and Libraries Shape Public Memory.* Lawrence: University Press of Kansas, 2005.

Johnson, Willis Fletcher. *The Life of Warren G. Harding: From the Simple Life of the Farm to the Glamour and Power of the White House.* Philadelphia, PA: John C. Winston Company, 1923.

Kammen, Michael. *In the Past Lane: Historical Perspectives on American Culture.* New York: Oxford University Press, 1997.

———. *Mystic Chords of Memory: The Transformation of Tradition in American Culture.* New York: Knopf, 1991.

Lawrence, Jerome, and Robert E. Lee. *The Gang's All Here: A Play.* Cleveland, OH: World Publishing, 1960.

Levinson, Sanford. *Written in Stone: Public Monuments in Changing Societies.* Durham, NC: Duke University Press, 1998.

Longworth, Alice Roosevelt. *Crowded Hours: Reminiscences of Alice Roosevelt Longworth.* New York: Scribner's, 1933.

Lowry, Edward G. *Washington Close-Ups: Intimate Views of Some Public Figures.* Boston York: Houghton Mifflin, 1921.

McCartney, Laton. *The Teapot Dome Scandal: How Big Oil Bought the White House and Tried to Steal the Country.* New York: Random House, 2008.

Means, Gaston B. *The Strange Death of President Harding: From the Diaries of Gaston B. Means, a Department of Justice Investigator.* New York: Guild Publishing, 1930.

Mee, Charles L. *The Ohio Gang: The World of Warren G. Harding, an Historical Entertainment.* New York: M. Evans, 1981.

Morello, John A. *Selling the President, 1920: Albert D. Lasker, Advertising, and the Election of Warren G. Harding.* Westport, CT: Praeger, 2001.

Murray, Robert K. *The Harding Era: Warren G. Harding and His Administration.* Minneapolis: University of Minnesota Press, 1969.

———. *The Politics of Normalcy: Governmental Theory and Practice in the Harding-Coolidge Era.* New York: Norton, 1973.

———, and Tim H. Blessing. *Greatness in the White House: Rating the Presidents, Washington through Clinton.* University Park: Pennsylvania State University Press, 1988.

Noggle, Burl. *Teapot Dome: Oil and Politics in the 1920s.* Baton Rouge: Louisiana State University Press, 1962.

Payne, Phillip G. "The Accomplishments of Warren G. Harding." *Presidential History* 1, no. 4 (1999): 4–15.

———. "Building the Warren G. Harding Memorial." *Timeline* 15, no. 5 (1998): 18–29.

———. "Instant History and the Legacy of Scandal: The Tangled Memory of Warren G. Harding, Richard Nixon, and William Jefferson Clinton." In *Prospects: An Annual of American Cultural Studies* 28, no. 1 (2004): 597–625.

———. "Mixed Memories: The Warren G. Harding Memorial Association and the President's Home Town Legacy." *Historian* 62, no. 2 (2001): 257–74.

———. "The Shadow of William Estabrook Chancellor: Warren G. Harding, Marion, Ohio, and the Issue of Race." *Mid-America: An Historical Review* 83, no. 1 (2001): 39–62.

Pessen, Edward. *The Log Cabin Myth: The Social Backgrounds of the Presidents.* New Haven, CT: Yale University Press, 1984.

Pitzer, Donald E. "An Introduction to the Harding Papers." *Ohio History* 75, nos. 2–3 (1966): 76–84.

Plunkett, Robert. *My Search for Warren Harding.* New York: Knopf, 1983.

Potts, Louis W. "Who Was Warren G. Harding?" *Historian* 36, no. 4 (1974): 621–45.

Raub, Patricia. *Yesterday's Stories: Popular Women's Novels of the Twenties and Thirties.* Westport, CT: Greenwood, 1994.

Rogers, J. A. *The Five Negro Presidents, U. S. A.* St. Petersburg, FL: Helga M. Rogers, 1965.

Russell, Francis. "The Four Mysteries of Warren Harding." *American Heritage* 14 (April 1963): 4–10, 81–86.

———. "The Harding Papers . . . and Some Were Saved." *American Heritage* 16, no. 2 (February 1965): 25–31, 102–10.

———. *The Shadow of Blooming Grove: Warren G. Harding and His Times.* New York: McGraw-Hill, 1968.

Savage, Kirk. *Standing Soldiers, Kneeling Slaves: Race, War, and Monument in Nineteenth-Century America.* Princeton, NJ: Princeton University Press, 1997.

Schwartz, Barry. *Abraham Lincoln and the Forge of National Memory.* Chicago: University of Chicago Press, 2000.

———. *George Washington: The Making of an American Symbol.* New York: Free Press, 1987.

Sinclair, Andrew. *The Available Man: The Life behind the Masks of Warren Gamaliel Harding.* New York: Macmillan, 1965.

Skowronek, Stephen. *The Politics Presidents Make: Leadership from John Adams to Bill Clinton.* Cambridge, MA: Belknap Press, 1997.

Stewart, Marsha. *Warren G. Harding, U.S. President 29: Death by Blackness.* Charlotte, NC: Conquering Books, 2005.

Stoddard, Henry L. *As I Knew Them: Presidents and Politics from Grant to Coolidge.* New York: Harper and Brothers, 1927.

Stratton, David H. *Tempest over Teapot Dome: The Story of Albert B. Fall.* Norman: University of Oklahoma Press, 1998.

Sullivan, Mark. *The Twenties.* Vol. 6 of *Our Times: The United States, 1900–1925.* New York: Scribner's, 1933.

Thacker, May Dixon. "Debunking 'The Strange Death of President Harding': A Complete Repudiation of a Sensational Book by Its Author." *Liberty* 8 (November 7, 1931): 8–12.

Trani, Eugene P., and David L. Wilson. *The Presidency of Warren G. Harding.* Lawrence: University Press of Kansas, 1977.

White, William Allen. *The Autobiography of William Allen White.* Ed. Sally Foreman Griffith. 2nd ed. 1946. Reprint, Lawrence: University Press of Kansas, 1990.

———. *Masks in a Pageant.* New York: Macmillan, 1928.

INDEX

1920, role in, 31, 44, 45; fictional representations of, 74, 76, 195–96, 200–201; health of, 55, 92, 94; marriage with Warren Harding, state of, 129–30, 133–35; Means on, 146, 147–54; presidential papers, destruction of, 14, 155, 158–59, 160–61, 215; Reagan, Nancy, comparison to, 203; reputation of, 7, 89, 99–100, 170, 176, 177; rumors about, 18, 67, 85, 211–13

Harding, George, 24, 100, 102–6, 108, 115, 129

Harding, George, III, 128, 138, 140, 143, 145, 175, 180

Harding, Warren: accomplishments of, 16–17; as Babbitt, 3, 12, 71, 192, 223; Birmingham, Alabama, speech on race relations, 120–24; as black president, 98, 114, 117–25, 216; as booster, 9, 12–13, 32, 42, 46, 61, 71, 76, 83, 84, 120, 122–23; Bush, George W., comparison to, 192–93, 219–22.; Carter, Jimmy, comparison to, 192; Clinton, William Jefferson, comparison to, 196, 199, 200–201, 204–12; death of, 48, 51–52, 65, 151; health of, 55; humble origins of, 32, 83 (*see also* log cabin myth); Johnson, Lyndon, comparison to, 200; Kennedy, John, comparison to, 200, 202; Ku Klux Klan, rumors of membership in, 114, 117, 118–19, 215, 217; Lincoln, Abraham, comparison to, 80, 85, 88, 145, 168–69; papers of, 49, 100, 156, 215; Reagan, Ronald, comparison to, 202–3; Washington, George, comparison to, 80; Wikipedia entries on, 212–18

Harding Memorial: Britton on, 139–40, 142; dedication of, 68–69, 94; design of, 49, 62; historical narrative, role in, 13, 69; Marion, Ohio, relationship to, 60, 70; mausoleum, 65; reputation of Harding, role in, 191, 200, 214, 223; Russell on, 155–56

Harding Memorial Association: boosterism, role in, 143, 156; formation and

planning of, 49–50; and Harding centennial, 185; and Harding Memorial, 62, 67; and Harding Memorial Week, 56, 57, 58, 59, 60, 61; presidential papers, handling of, 100, 161, 163, 164, 168, 171, 174, 178–79, 215; and revisionism, 182, 186, 187–88; scandals, difficulties created by, 59, 65, 66

Hays, Will, 33, 141

Hersh, Seymour, 202

Hollywood, 63, 131, 141, 201, 209

Hoover, Herbert: cabinet, service in, 17, 63, 90; commemoration of, 5, 49; and commemoration of Harding, 161, 162; fictional representations of, 199, 200; on Harding, 16, 52, 53, 156; Harding Memorial, dedication of, 65–69; reputation of, 15, 183, 220

Hughes, Charles Evans, 5, 17, 53, 67

Incredible Era (Adams), 74, 103, 147

Inside Story of the Harding Tragedy, The (Daugherty), 71, 86–93

Kling, Amos, 102, 104

Kling, Florence. *See* Harding, Florence (Kling)

Klunk, Charles A., 153

Ku Klux Klan: Chancellor affair, involvement in, 116; denouncement by Harding, 124, 125; Marion, Ohio, activity in, 114; membership of Harding, rumor of, 18, 117, 118–19, 147, 214, 215, 217, 218

Lasker, Albert, 39

Lawrence, Jerome, 194–97, 200

League of Nations, 34, 40, 42, 101, 108, 199

Lee, Robert E., 194–97, 200

Lewis, Sinclair, 12, 20, 70–71, 73, 75–78

Library of Congress, 159, 162, 165, 167, 169, 174

Lincoln Memorial, 11, 124, 164

Little Green House on K Street, 63, 77, 92, 193, 196